Whatever happened to Tory Liverpool?

Success, decline, and irrelevance since 1945

Whatever happened to Tory Liverpool?

Success, decline, and irrelevance since 1945

David Jeffery

LIVERPOOL UNIVERSITY PRESS

First published 2023 by
Liverpool University Press
4 Cambridge Street
Liverpool
L69 7ZU

This paperback edition published 2023

British Library Cataloguing-in-Publication data
A British Library CIP record is available

ISBN 978-1-80207-848-0 (hardback)
ISBN 978-1-83764-145-1 (paperback)

Typeset by Carnegie Book Production, Lancaster
Printed and bound by CPI Group (UK) Ltd, Croydon CR0 4YY

Contents

Acknowledgements

This book is the culmination of over eight years of work. Although all mistakes are my own, it has benefited immensely from the involvement of people much smarter than I.

First and foremost, I would like to thank my doctoral supervisor, Professor Tim Bale, for his advice and mentoring throughout my doctoral journey and afterwards. Ever since I emailed a draft PhD proposal to him back in October 2013, Tim has been generous with his time and supportive when things have not gone quite to plan. This book, and the thesis it was based on, is all the stronger for his involvement. His advice not to make the perfect the enemy of the good will stick with me, and I am sorry that I still do not properly understand the semicolon.

I am grateful to the Economic and Social Research Council and Queen Mary University of London for awarding me the QMUL Principal's Studentship to fund my doctoral studies. I hope the contribution this book makes to our understanding of Liverpool's rich history, and the history of the Conservative Party, is worth it.

I would also like to thank all the people who have offered their comments, thoughts, and insights over the course of my journey in producing this book. These include my doctoral examiners, Dr Nicholas Allen and Professor Jonathan Tonge, and my friends Dr Antony Mullen and Dr Sam Blaxland, who provided detailed feedback on the final draft (Sam even read it twice — a true glutton for punishment). Your advice has been invaluable. Liverpool University Press, especially Alison Welsby, deserve a special thanks for their patience with this (very delayed) book, and I would like to thank the anonymous reviewers for their kind and thoughtful comments.

On a personal level, I would like to thank my friends and family for putting up with me for so long. My parents Lynne and Dave, for always encouraging me to do my best; my sister Laura, for reminding me that academia is a relatively easy gig, all things considered; my partner Ben, for making life fun; and, of course, Dublin, Bella, Jess, and Hugo, for their unconditional love.

I would especially like to thank Gareth Anderson for the advice, support, and encouragement he has given me over the years. I am a much better person for knowing you. Thank you.

There is one final acknowledgement that I should make. Like many doctoral students, I chose my topic because it was of immense interest to me. I was born in Liverpool and, apart from some years in Sheffield and London for university, I have lived in Liverpool all my life. I also joined the Conservative Party in Liverpool in early 2010 and have been a member ever since. I have even stood as a Conservative candidate in a number of Liverpool's local elections and as a result I am a data point in my own data set, which is a strange feeling.

Often academics will seek to hide their political views, emerging only after a few drinks at the end-of-year social, but for better or worse that has never been the path I have taken and it has not been unknown for people to discount my work because of my publicly held views. However, I have written this book as an academic, not a partisan, because I believe the story of Conservative decline in Liverpool is one that deserves to be told to a wider audience. I hope you agree.

And please, if you have any comments about this book, my overall argument, or an interesting fact about some long-forgotten Liverpudlian Conservative politician, the best place to find me is on Twitter: @DrDavidJeffery.

Note on figures

Colour versions of the book's figures can be accessed online at: https://liverpooluniversitypress.manifoldapp.org/.

1 Introduction

In the municipal election of 1968, the Liverpool Conservatives won 62 per cent of the vote and 78 per cent of the seats on Liverpool City Council. Moreover, they had run Liverpool's municipal government for 86 of the previous 100 years. In 1972 they lost control of the council. In 1983 they lost their last two MPs, and in 1998 they lost their final councillor. They have not won an electoral contest in the city since.

Today, Liverpool is a by-word for anti-Tory sentiment. So implausible is the idea that the Conservatives could be electorally successful in Liverpool that, following the city's 2012 mayoral election, BBC Radio 5 Live reported that the Conservative candidate had been defeated by a rival dressed as a polar bear (Morse 2012). Whilst incorrect — there was no candidate dressed as a polar bear — the Conservative candidate still finished a humiliating seventh on 4.5 per cent of the vote to Labour's 59.3 per cent (*ITV News* 2012). The Conservatives have not topped that performance in the city's two subsequent mayoral elections.

1.1 Why is this important?

Conservative decline in Liverpool is chronically understudied. As will be shown below, explanations for Conservative decline in Liverpool tend to take one of two paths. The first is that the decline of religious sectarianism eroded the Conservatives' electoral base, leading to their decline. The second is that Conservative prime minister Margaret Thatcher is solely to blame. Both explanations have elements of truth to them, but are by no means the whole story.

If sectarianism was the only reason for Conservative support in Liverpool, then why did the party do so well in general elections until 1964 (in terms of seat share) or 1970 (vote share), and still manage to win over 30 per cent of the vote in local elections until 1980? The beneficial effects of sectarianism should have been dulled before this, especially as class began to eclipse religion as a key determinant of voting behaviour in the early twentieth century.

The second argument, that Thatcher is the cause of decline, is intuitively appealing. It passes for common knowledge that there is strong anti-Thatcherite feeling within Liverpool's body politic. However, to attribute Tory decline to Thatcher ignores the fact that, on a constituency level, Conservative decline had already been occurring between 1964 and 1979 and, on a municipal level, the Conservatives faced their first period of decline in the 1970s, before the Thatcher government came into office and well before the conflict with the Militant-led Labour council began. Both arguments, then, fail to explain why the Conservatives declined when they did. This presents a gap in the literature, filled by this book.

The argument put forward here sees Conservative decline in Liverpool through the prism of a tripartite framework of success (1945–1972), decline (1973–1986), and a continued irrelevance (1987 onwards). Each of these eras can — and should — be explained via different phenomena.

Conservative success in Liverpool is primarily explained by the socialisation effect of Protestantism, boosted in years when the Conservatives were doing well nationally. Conservative decline is chiefly a result of the perfect storm of unresponsive local parties, an energetic, nascent Liberal Party, dissatisfaction with the Heath (national) government, and an all-out local government election in 1973, triggered by local government reform. Finally, Conservative irrelevance is attributable to a change in Scouse identity, which took on an element of anti-Thatcherism and anti-Conservatism that has persisted to this day.

1.2 Contextualising decline

There are two ways of exploring Conservative decline in Liverpool. The first is to compare Conservative support in Liverpool with that in other major northern cities — Manchester, Sheffield, Leeds, Newcastle — and Birmingham, in the Midlands. The results clearly show that the Conservatives went from outperforming in Liverpool to underperforming. The second approach to contextualising decline looks within Liverpool, and compares Conservative support with support for other parties within the city.

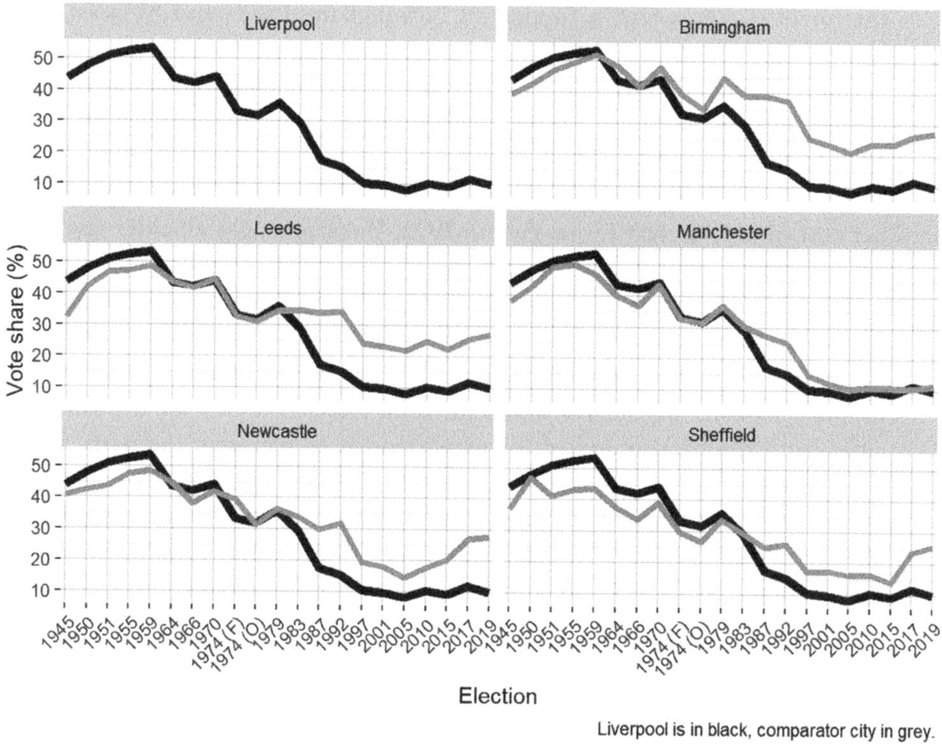

Figure 1.1: Conservative share of vote in general elections, 1945–2019

Source: Kollman et al. (2020) and Watson, Uberoi, and Loft (2021).

1.2.1 Liverpool in comparative perspective

Figure 1.1 shows the Conservative share of the vote in general elections from 1945 to 2019 for Liverpool compared to each of the five other cities. What is clear is that the Conservatives enjoyed a greater level of success in Liverpool than in the other cities until the 1960s, but by the 1980s Liverpool had become the least fertile ground for the party.

Generally, all cities saw Conservative vote share rise between 1945 and either 1955 or 1959, peaking at 53 per cent in Liverpool. From 1959 to the October 1974 election, the Conservatives suffered a slow decline of around 20 percentage points, before enjoying a rebound in the 1979 election. During this time, the Liverpool Conservatives went from clearly outperforming their comrades in other cities (1945–1959), to doing merely as well (1964–1979).

After 1979, Conservative support in these urban areas began to vary and the clear bunching pattern weakened. From the general election of 1983 to that of 1992 Conservative support in Birmingham, Leeds and Newcastle held up relatively strongly whereas in Manchester the party's support steadily declined, dropping from 37 per cent to 25 per cent. Sheffield ended up in a similar finishing position, although this occurred via a sudden decline in 1983, from 34 per cent to 24 per cent, before rebounding slightly in 1992.

Liverpool clearly experienced the greatest decline of all cities, from 34 per cent in 1979 to just 15 per cent in 1992. Unsurprisingly, all cities saw a decline in Conservative vote share in the 1997 election, which then levelled off for the 2001 general election. From 1987 onwards, Liverpool consistently underperformed in terms of Conservative vote share.

We see a similar — if more nuanced — pattern if we look at vote shares in local elections. Figure 1.2 shows the local election results for the same cities, with the background of the graph shaded to represent the party in government at the time of each local election. Local election results present a more varied voting pattern than general election results. We can see that in all six cities the Conservatives finished the period in a worse condition than they started it, but this hides several interesting points about Conservative performance in these urban areas.

Until 1971, Conservative vote shares in local elections followed a general pattern: swings towards or away from the Conservatives in one city tended to be matched by swings in the same direction — if not always of a similar magnitude — in the other cities. This reflects the influence national politics had on local election results. During this time, the Conservative vote share in Liverpool was often the highest — or one of the highest — in the cities examined.

However, after 1971 divergent trends began to emerge between the cities, and after this election the Conservatives underperformed in Liverpool relative to the other cities, in every year bar 1982. Liverpool was the only city not to see the Conservatives rebound to 40 per cent during the 1970s, attributable to the rise of the Liberal Party in Liverpool, which acted as an alternative opposition party to Labour. As Figure 1.3, below, shows, the Liberal rise in Liverpool during the 1970s was not matched in the other cities, although the Liberals did become a major force in Sheffield in the local elections following the 1992 general election.

Returning to Figure 1.2, we see commonalities in the local election results throughout the 1980s and most of the 1990s, in the direction, if not the magnitude, of swings towards or against the Conservatives. For example all six cities saw a swing towards the Conservatives in 1992, although the magnitude of this was muted in Liverpool, and then almost immediately all witnessed a large swing away from the Conservatives in 1994. After 1994 the Conservatives

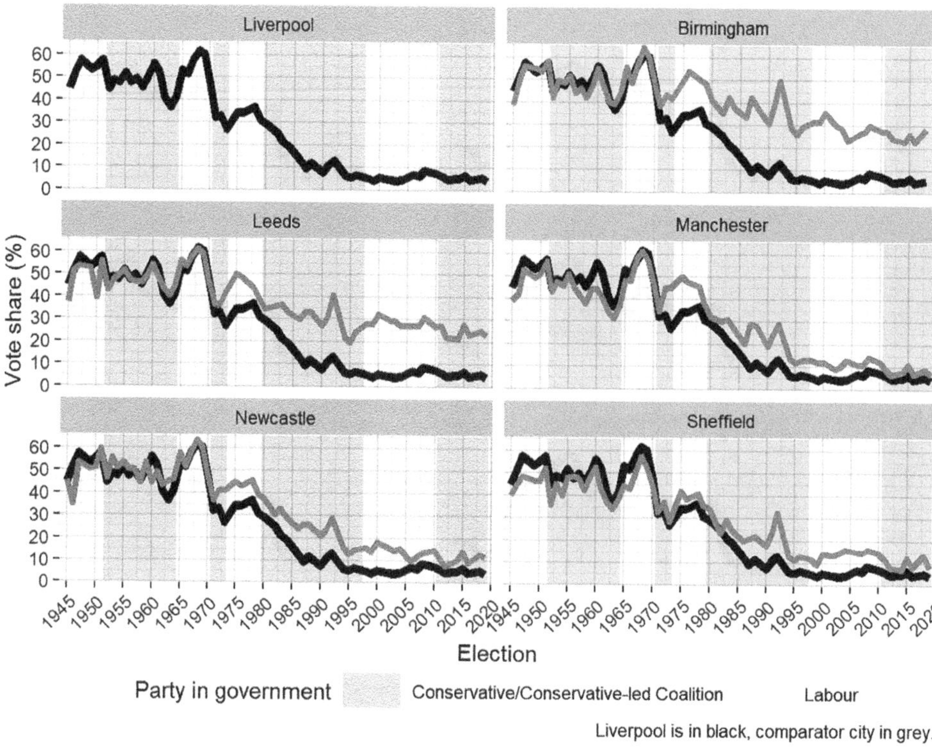

Figure 1.2: Conservative share of vote in local elections, 1945–2019

Source: Rallings, Thrasher, and Ware (2006); various sources collated by author. In Newcastle the Progressives were the main anti-Labour party until 1958, and whilst some candidates stood under the Conservative label the Progressives and the Conservatives never stood against one another. In Sheffield the Conservative Party was part of the Progressive Party until 1947, and then until 1962 stood under the Conservative and Liberal Unionist banner. Multi-vacancy elections can throw up some interesting problems, particularly in regard to turnout (and especially when individual parties fail to put up a full slate of candidates). In these cases, an estimated level of turnout has been calculated, by taking the votes achieved by each candidate, dividing by the number of vacancies, and then dividing by the ward electorate.

enjoyed a similar share of the vote in Birmingham and Leeds — between 20 and 30 per cent — and in Manchester, Sheffield, and Newcastle — between 5 and 18 per cent. This bunching persists to this day, and suggests there are structural differences between cities which need to be explored.

In both general and local elections we see a similar pattern: the Conservatives begin the period performing strongly in terms of vote share, in Liverpool compared to the other cities included here, but this performance then

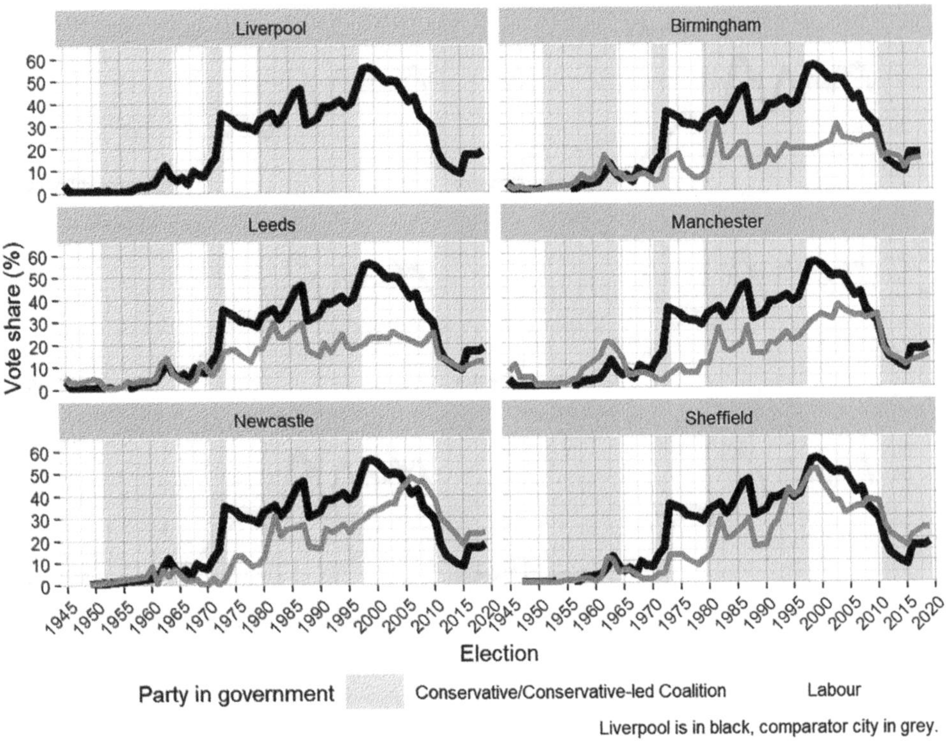

Figure 1.3: Liberal parties' share of vote in local elections, 1945–2019

Source: Rallings, Thrasher, and Ware (2006), Jeffery (2021), and various sources collated by author. Between 1981 and 1988 votes for the Social Democratic Party are included in these figures.

weakens by the 1980s at general elections, and earlier in local elections. Hence, Liverpool does seem to be a special case of Conservative decline, especially when examined through the lens of local elections. The next section will explore Conservative decline within Liverpool compared to other parties in the city.

1.2.2 Constituency-level decline

The most obvious place to look for evidence of Conservative decline in Liverpool is in constituency vote and seat shares.[1] This is done in Figure 1.4,

1 Seat shares, rather than the number of seats held, is the most appropriate metric given that the number of seats in Liverpool has changed over the years. As shown in Figure 1.5, there were eleven seats at the 1945 general election, nine from 1950 to 1970, eight from February 1974 to 1979, six from 1983 to 1992, and then five from 1997 to the present day.

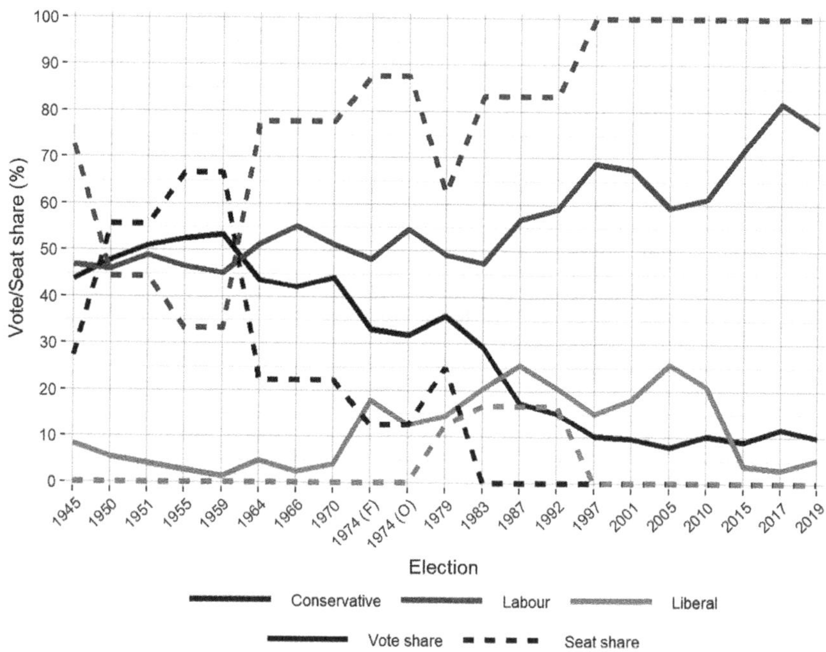

Figure 1.4: Vote and seat share in Liverpool's constituencies, 1945–2019

Source: Kollman et al. (2020) and Watson, Uberoi, and Loft (2021).

below, which shows that, from 1945 to 1970, Conservative vote share was consistently over 40 per cent in the city. However, from 1974 to 1983, the vote share dropped to the 30–40 per cent range, alongside a rise in the Liberal vote. Between the 1983 and 1987 general elections the Conservative vote share dropped from 29.3 per cent to 17.4 per cent and from 1997 onwards it hovered around 10 per cent.

At first glance this supports the popular claim that the premiership of Margaret Thatcher was the cause of Conservative decline in Liverpool. However, there are caveats: the Conservative vote share had been declining since the 1959 general election and the drop in Conservative vote share between 1970 and 1974 was nearly as large as the 1983–1987 decline, at 11 and 11.9 percentage points respectively. Thus, the entire blame for Conservative decline on a constituency level cannot be laid at Thatcher's door. Electorally, the Conservatives' position was weakening before her premiership.

Figure 1.5 puts constituency names to the numbers given above, with the list of Liverpool's constituencies shaded to represent the party that held it. The gap between certain elections represents parliamentary boundary

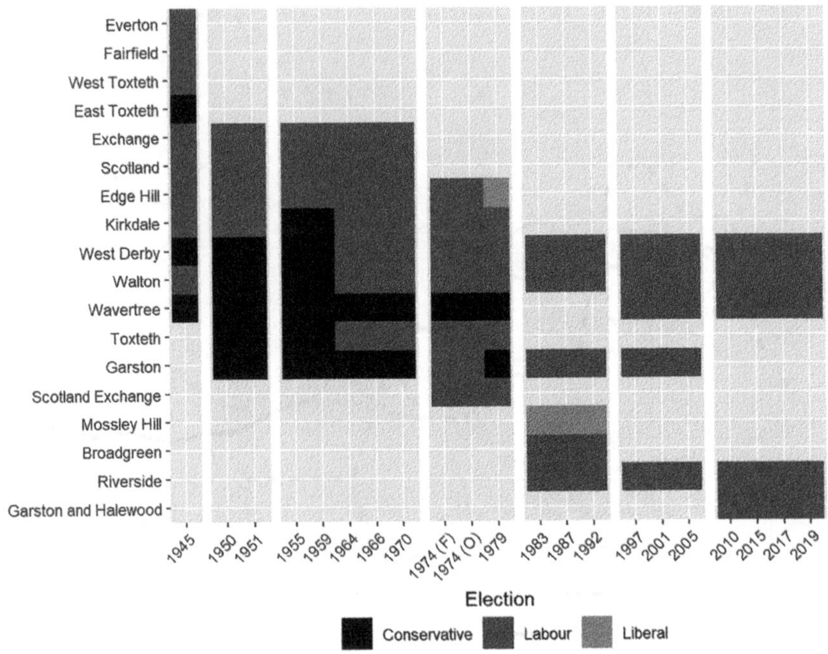

Figure 1.5: Liverpool constituencies by winning party, 1945–2019

Source: Kollman et al. (2020) and Watson, Uberoi, and Loft (2021).

reforms, and so while the constituency name might have remained the same the actual area a constituency covered may have changed slightly. This does not matter for the purposes of our analysis.

As mentioned previously, we can see two watershed elections. The first, in 1964, saw the Conservatives lose four constituencies they would never regain, whilst the second, in 1983, saw them lose their remaining two constituencies, Liverpool Wavertree and Liverpool Garston, for both of which the incumbent Conservative MP moved to contest other seats after significant and unfavourable boundary changes: Wavertree was split into the new Mossley Hill and Broadgreen constituencies, whilst the Garston constituency gained Speke ward (which returned a 78 per cent Labour vote in 1983). The Liberal dominance of Edge Hill (later Mossley Hill) was ended by boundary reform and Labour's 1997 landslide, leaving Liverpool with blanket Labour coverage across the city.

We can get a more nuanced picture of party support by moving away from percentages and instead towards the absolute number of votes cast (see Figure 1.6). This is also useful because it demonstrates clearly that the

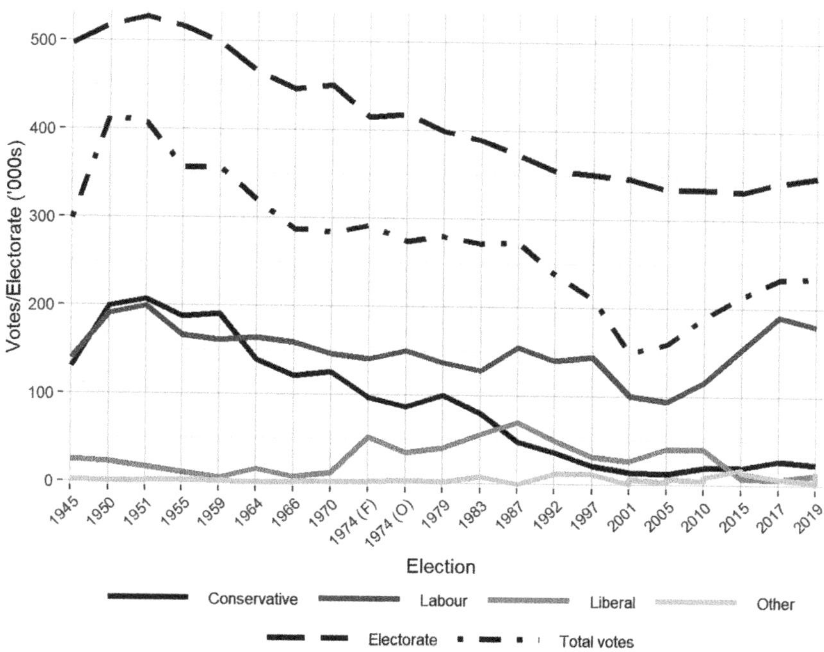

Figure 1.6: Number of votes for each party in general elections in Liverpool, 1945–2019

Source: Kollman et al. (2020) and Watson, Uberoi, and Loft (2021).

Conservatives experienced a marked absolute decline in votes as well as a relative decline in vote share.

Between 1945 and 2001 the electorate declined from a peak of 527,092 in 1951 to 347,488 in 2001, roughly 3,600 voters per annum, owing to a mixture of slum clearance and outward migration. The absolute number of votes received by both the Conservatives and Labour peaked in 1951, at 207,382 and 199,331 votes respectively. From that point, the Conservatives saw their vote decline to 125,868 in 1970, the final election before the Liberals began to enjoy success, compared to Labour's vote at 146,338.

After 1970, the Conservative vote continued to decline, dropping to under 50,000 in 1987 and 25,000 in 1997. By contrast, until 2001 Labour's vote hovered around the 150,000 level, despite the total electorate declining by 100,000. The Liberals only passed 50,000 votes in the February 1974 and 1983 general elections, after which their vote share again began to decline. Hence, after 1964, Labour dominated Liverpool on a constituency level.

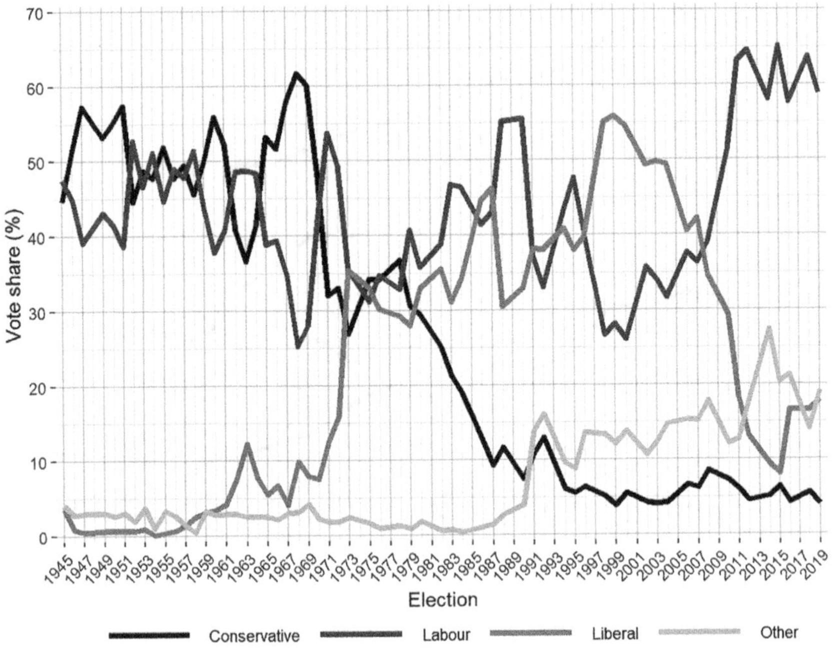

Figure 1.7: Share of votes for local elections in Liverpool, 1945–2019

Source: Rallings, Thrasher, and Ware (2006) and Jeffery (2021).

We can also see that the Conservatives' decline, in terms of the number of votes, began in earnest after the 1959 general election — again, long before Thatcher came to power — but did speed up in the 1980s, when the number of Conservative votes halved whilst the electorate shrank by only 20,000 voters. It is clear that the Conservatives suffered from both absolute and relative electoral decline at the constituency level, and that the reduction in the raw number of votes won was not solely the outcome of a shrinking electorate.

1.2.3 *Local-level decline*

If seat and vote share at the constituency level shows a one-way pattern of decline for the Liverpool Conservatives, an examination of local election results offers a more nuanced history.

Figure 1.7 shows the main parties' share of the vote for local elections in Liverpool, and Figure 1.8 shows each party's share of the seats. Here again we see evidence for three clear periods of Conservative electoral performance: success (1945–1972), decline (1973–1986), and irrelevance (1987 onwards).

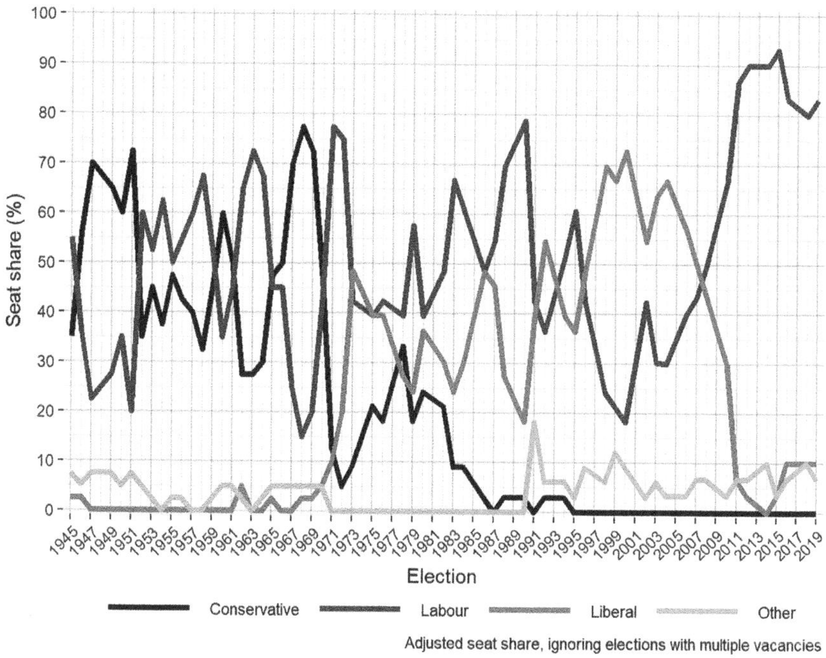

Figure 1.8: Share of seats for local elections in Liverpool, 1945–2019

Source: Rallings, Thrasher, and Ware (2006) and Jeffery (2021).

This first period, 1945–1972, saw the Conservatives do well when Labour did poorly, and vice versa. Party support was broadly cyclical, and as Chapter 7 demonstrates, often determined by national factors, namely the general popularity of the party in government. For example, the Conservatives did especially well in the late 1960s when Labour was in power, whereas Labour performed strongly towards the end of the Conservative Party's time in government in the early 1960s. Electorally, the Liberals were irrelevant.

The second period, 1973–1986, began with the Conservatives winning just 32 per cent of the votes cast — their lowest ever share up until this point — and ended with them winning 13 per cent of the vote. This was the period of decline for the party in local elections. However, the decline was not linear. For example, from their then-nadir in 1973, the Conservatives did experience a slight bounce back, for example in 1978 when they won 37 per cent and a plurality of the vote. This again shows the influence of national politics on local voting behaviour, with a tired Labour government boosting Conservative fortunes. Yet a plurality of votes did not translate into a plurality of seats: the Conservatives won 31 per cent of the seats from 37 per cent of the vote, compared to Labour's 40 per cent of the seats on 32 per cent of the vote. The role of electoral biases is explored in Chapter 4.

During the 1970s and early 1980s, Liverpool Council was a three-party polity with no party able to exercise overall control. Either the Labour Party, or the Liberals with inconsistent Conservative support, ran ineffective minority administrations. Conservative support became concentrated in the south of the city, with nearly half the party's vote situated in just 6 of the 33 wards in 1978. Unsurprisingly, this concentration of votes was reflected in a slow, if uneven, decline in seat share. The biggest drop for the Conservatives occurred between the 1982 and 1983 local elections, when they went from winning 21 per cent of the seats to 8 per cent, a drop of 13 percentage points — although the drop in vote share was just four points, from 25 to 21 per cent.

The final period began in 1987, when the Liverpool Conservatives became broadly irrelevant to Liverpool's politics. They were restricted to winning seats in Woolton ward, and after 1987 it became more common for them to not win at all than to win even one seat. The Conservatives won their final council seat in 1994.

Thus, in examining Conservative decline on a local level we must acknowledge two things. The first is that the story differs depending upon whether one looks at vote share or seat share. Vote shares give the impression of a party that dominated in the period up until 1970, then managed to adapt to the rise of the Liberals and remain competitive with the other two parties in the city for the next decade. After this, the Conservatives were still something of a presence electorally until the mid-1980s, achieving over 15 per cent of the city-wide vote. Conservative decline fully set in after this, with the party falling to under 10 per cent of the vote.

However, examining seat shares suggests that the Conservatives were regularly bested by Labour up until the 1970s, and that decline occurred in 1972, 15 years earlier than vote shares would suggest, when the party was reduced to just 13 per cent of seats in the council chamber. Moreover, the party failed to sustain its 1978 resurgence and the Conservatives effectively became a minor party in the city's politics thereafter.

The second factor of note is that the decline cannot be solely attributed to Thatcher, as although decline in both seat and vote share occurred under her premiership, both were already far below their post-war peak. In terms of vote share, the party fell from an average of around 50 per cent until 1970 (and even higher if support for its ally, the Protestant Party, is included), to 32.5 per cent between 1971 and 1979 inclusive. Even during the Thatcher era the average vote share was just shy of 20 per cent, which is significantly higher than the post-Thatcher average of 6.3 per cent. Similarly, in terms of seats won, the party fell from an average seat share of 50 per cent before 1970 (again, higher if the Protestant Party were to be included), to 21 per cent between 1971 and 1979 inclusive. Although during the Thatcher era this plummeted to an average seat share of 9 per cent, this was higher than the post-Thatcher average of 0.6 per cent. Hence, we cannot look solely to Thatcher to explain the Conservative decline, although her legacy rather than her premiership may well have been important in explaining the party's continued electoral irrelevance.

1.2.4 Aldermanic elections

Vote and seat shares do not, however, tell the full story of municipal politics in Liverpool. Until 1973 the city had an aldermanic system of local government under which 120 of the council seats were elected across 40 wards, and then a further 40 aldermen were elected by the 120 councillors, bringing the total number on the council to 160. These aldermen were elected in two groups, 20 every 3 years. Apart from being ineligible to vote for new aldermen, they had the same powers as elected councillors. Thus it is important to include them in any assessment of Conservative strength in municipal politics.

Figure 1.9 shows the political makeup of the council if just elected councillors were counted, versus councillors and aldermen (dotted line). We can see that, until 1953, the party with control of the council also had the greatest share of elected councillors. However, with the 1953 municipal election this changed: the Conservatives won 44 per cent of elected councillors to Labour's 54 per cent but due to the aldermanic system the Conservatives maintained control until 1955 (even though they were only sustained in power after 1954 as a result of the Protestant Party's two councillors and single alderman). When aldermanic elections took place in 1955 Labour was able to reduce the Conservative share of the aldermen from 68 per cent to 28 per cent, boosting its own share from 23 per cent to 70 per cent, thereby taking control of the council for the first time. The Conservative majority was, therefore, sustained for two years without a majority of elected councillors.

Labour dominance continued throughout the 1950s and when by-elections for aldermanic vacancies arose the Conservative share dwindled further, running contrary to the gentlemen's agreement that aldermanic replacements would be from the same party as the outgoing aldermen. In

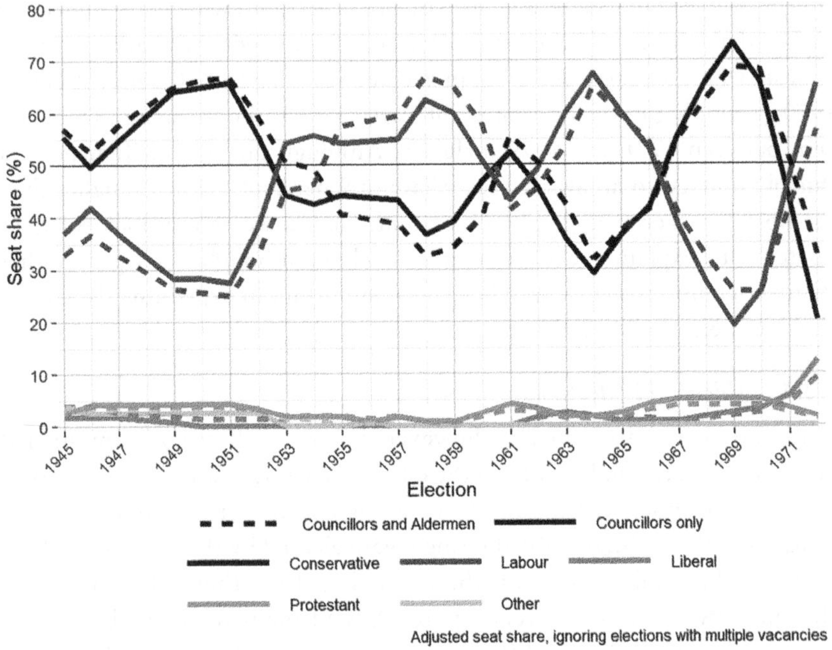

Figure 1.9: Seat share including and excluding aldermen, 1945–1972

Source: Aldermanic data are taken from *Liverpool Daily Post* on the day following each local election. Figures for aldermen are at the time of the local election — aldermanic elections usually took place a week after the local elections. Similarly, each year includes 'corrections' for the by-elections which took place in the previous year.

the 1958 aldermanic election Labour decided to remove the Protestant Party alderman too, harming the effective Conservative seat share. This continued until 1961, when the Conservatives saw their share of councillors rise to 53 per cent. Happily for the Tories, 1961 was an aldermanic election year and the party's narrow majority of councillors allowed them to increase their number of aldermen from 20 per cent to 65 per cent. This gave the Conservatives control until the 1963 election when the number of councillors' seats they won put Labour firmly in control; aldermanic elections in 1964 saw Labour re-establish its aldermanic majority, with 58 per cent of the aldermanic seats to the Tories' 40 per cent.

The year 1964 saw the start of the final hurrah for the Liverpool Conservatives. Their vote share began to rise and the 1967 local election saw them regain control of the council again, even before aldermanic seats changed hands in the subsequent aldermanic election a week later, which saw the Conservatives increase their aldermanic share from 40 to 53 per cent. The Conservatives continued to have a majority in elected councillors — peaking at 73 per cent in 1969 — until the 1971 election. Luckily for them, the final aldermanic elections took place in 1970, and the party used their dominant position on the council to boost their share of aldermen to 75 per cent.

In 1971 the Conservatives' share of elected seats dropped to 43 per cent but, sustained by aldermen, they held 51 per cent of the total seats. By 1972, however, their seat share had dropped to 20 per cent and their overall share on the council to 33 per cent. The Local Government Act 1972 saw the aldermanic system abolished and never again would the Conservatives control Liverpool's city council.

What this shows is that, save for 1953–1955 and 1971, the aldermanic system did not produce an overall council majority which differed from the majority of elected councillors. Similarly, in 1962 no party had a majority of elected councillors — the Conservatives held 46 per cent (49 per cent if the Protestant share is included) to Labour's 49 per cent — but the Conservatives had a narrow overall majority of 51 per cent, due to aldermen.

Thus, whilst the party's share of aldermen was often exaggerated compared to the number of seats won in elections, it was rare that this would sustain a party's council majority when elected councillors alone could not. This was largely because the aldermanic share of seats comprised just 25 per cent of the overall council total, which muted the impact they could have, and there was, usually, broad agreement that aldermanic seat shares should reflect elected councillor shares. We must look beyond the aldermanic system to explain how the Conservatives sustained support in the city.

1.2.5 Council control

As shown in section 1.2.4, council control depended upon both elected councillors and aldermen. Table 1.1, below, lists the leaders of Liverpool City Council, their party, the length of their leadership, and the party which controlled the council. A broad pattern emerges; between 1938 and 1973 control alternated between the Conservatives and Labour. After 1973, however, the Council underwent a decade with no party having overall control, and leadership passing between the Liberals and Labour. From 1983, save for a four-year period between 1992 and 1996, control alternated between Labour and the Liberals.

Table 1.1: Leaders of Liverpool City Council and party control

Council Leader	*Leader's Party*	*Years*	*Control*
Alfred Shennan	Conservative	1938–1955	Conservative
Jack Braddock	Labour	1955–1961	Labour
Maxwell Entwistle	Conservative	1961–1963	Conservative
Jack Braddock	Labour	1963–1967	Labour
Harold Macdonald Steward	Conservative	1967–1972	Conservative
Bill Sefton	Labour	1972–1973	Labour
Cyril Carr	Liberal	1974–1975	No overall control
Bill Smyth		1975–1976	
John Hamilton	Labour	1976–1978	
Eddie Roderick		1978 (May–Jun)	
John Hamilton		1978–1979	
Trevor Jones	Liberal	1979–1983	
John Hamilton	Labour	1983–1987	Labour
Tony Byrne		1986–1987	
Trevor Jones	Liberal	1987 (Mar–May)	Liberal
Harry Rimmer	Labour	1987 (May–Oct)	Labour
Keva Coombes		1987–1990	
Harry Rimmer		1990–1992	
		1992–1996	No overall control
Frank Prendergast		1996–1998	Labour
Mike Storey	Liberal Democrat	1998–2005	Liberal Democrat
Warren Bradley		2005–2010	
Joe Anderson	Labour	2010–2012	Labour
		2012–2020[a]	
Wendy Simon (acting)		2020–2021	
Joanne Anderson[b]		2021–	

[a] Since 2012 Liverpool City Council has been led by a directly elected mayor.
[b] No relation to Joe Anderson.

1.3 Explaining Conservative decline in Liverpool

This book challenges the idea that the Conservatives faced electoral decline in Liverpool because of the reduced importance of religious sectarianism, or because of the actions of the Thatcher government. The Conservatives enjoyed electoral success for such a long time, and the subsequent decline was too sudden, for a slow structural factor like the erosion of sectarianism to have been the cause. Similarly, decline began well before Thatcher became Conservative Party leader, let alone prime minister. Instead, there is a significant distinction between decline and irrelevance and they must be analysed separately as distinct periods in Liverpool's political history.

What is meant by decline? For the purposes of this book, decline will be used as shorthand for the decline of the Conservatives' share of the vote in local elections in Liverpool. Local elections have been chosen over general elections for two key reasons. Firstly, there were simply more local elections than general elections in Liverpool, and the greater number of wards allows for a greater range of socio-economic and electoral differences to be analysed than would be the case if we only examined parliamentary constituencies. Secondly, we see a greater variety in Conservative vote shares in local elections and a more nuanced pattern in Conservative support, which suggests a more interesting story than might initially be assumed through an analysis of just general elections.

The focus on vote share over seat share is justified by the fact that vote share is generally prior to seat share — in a democracy, voters must actually cast their vote before the results are known. Whilst voters may be influenced by the current seat shares of parties when they cast their ballot, this relationship is weaker than the direct relationship between vote share and seat share.

This methodological decision, however, does not mean general elections will be discounted in this analysis, nor does it mean that only vote shares will be analysed. Factors such as the local party organisation, the party's numerical strength in local government, and whether the party was in national government or not will be treated as independent variables, since all of these could play a role in explaining the decline in the share in the local vote in Liverpool.

As previously mentioned, the main aim of this study is to provide an account of Conservative decline in local elections in Liverpool and this is done through a tripartite framework focusing on success, decline, and irrelevance. In doing this, it serves as a detailed case study that fulfils two broader purposes.

Firstly, it provides a study of the changes in Liverpool's local party system and the drivers of the change from a two-party Conservative–Labour polity, to a three-party polity with the rise of the Liberal Party, and then the subsequent, new, two-party Labour–Liberal polity.

Secondly, this study makes a theoretical contribution to our understanding of the influence of socialisation, path dependency, and critical junctures in local party politics, as well as the importance of local identities in expanding or restricting the potential for success for political parties.

The first period in this history of Liverpudlian politics, that of success, occurred between 1945 and 1972. The root of pre-war Conservative success in Liverpool was, broadly speaking, based on the relationship between Protestantism and Conservatism. Conservative support derived directly from Protestantism. Despite the post-war shift towards class-based voting, Conservative voting in a working-class city like Liverpool was perpetuated by the socialisation of new voters in Conservative areas and was thus path dependent. Protestantism became the historical cause of Conservative voting in Liverpool, even though it was no longer directly relevant to voter behaviour for the majority of Liverpudlians.

The period of decline began in 1973 — not 1970, as might be suggested by a quick glance at the graphs above. This is because, until 1973, party support was broadly cyclical, with the Conservatives doing better when Labour was in power and vice versa. There is no reason why the Conservatives should not have enjoyed a resurgence when Labour's Harold Wilson became prime minister in 1974 — indeed, Conservative vote share was higher under the 1974–1979 Labour governments than it had been under Conservative Edward Heath's tenure as prime minister. Instead, this book argues that decline began in 1973 with that year's local election representing a critical juncture in Conservative fortunes in the city. The Local Government Act of 1972 resulted in a redrawing of ward boundaries, the removal of aldermen, and all-out elections to Liverpool City Council. In this key election, during the unpopular Heath government and while the Liberals were on the rise locally, the Conservatives won just 9 out of 99 seats and were damaged to such an extent that the narrative in local politics changed: the Liberals were now the main opposition to Labour. As a result, over time the Conservatives were squeezed by the first-past-the-post electoral system.

The irrelevance of the Conservatives in Liverpool has its origins in the Thatcher government's conflict with the Militant-controlled council in the

1980s. The argument here is that the conflict with the council added a strong element of anti-Conservatism and anti-Thatcherism to 'Scouse' identity. The decline of the Conservatives at the local level meant they were unable to mount an effective defence, or recreate a localised version of Tory Democracy, to counter or at least temper Thatcherism. Whilst wishing to avoid a counter-factual history, it is tempting to ask whether the Conservatives would still be a viable brand in Liverpool if Thatcher's government had compromised over the level of central government grant given to the city (especially since there were compelling arguments for an acknowledgement of Liverpool's very specific economic issues), if Michael Heseltine's attempts at urban regeneration had proved more successful and widespread, if the Liverpool Conservatives had been more willing to respond effectively to the Liberals' innovation of pavement politics, or if they had entered into a formal coalition with the Liberals in the early 1980s and governed on a platform of sound finances, housing provision, and urban renewal.

1.4 The structure of the study

To explain the Liverpool Conservative Party's decline in vote shares, this book is framed around a series of research questions, rooted in the exploration of Liverpool's electoral history undertaken in Chapter 2.

The first asks 'to what extent can Conservative decline in Liverpool be attributed to local party structures?' This will be explored in Chapter 3, which uses archival material to analyse the strength of the local party association and discusses the extent to which a poor party organisation contributed to the decline of the Conservatives in the city.

The second research question asks 'to what extent can Conservative decline in Liverpool be attributed to biases within the electoral system?', and is explored in Chapter 4. This chapter uses statistical methods to examine whether the Conservatives suffered from differential levels of abstention or electorate size, the distribution of the Conservative vote across the city, and the role of the Liberals in local elections. This is an approach which is rarely used in the examination of Liverpool's political history and it allows the study to address some of the received wisdom of Liverpool's psephology.

The third research question is 'to what extent can Conservative decline in Liverpool be attributed to changes in the city's demographics?' This is examined in Chapter 5, which draws on census data to explore the socio-economic bases of party support in Liverpool and identifies the types of ward which were more likely to vote for each party.

Following on from this use of census data is the fourth research question, 'to what extent can Conservative decline in Liverpool be attributed to migratory patterns?', which is addressed in Chapter 6. This uses census data to compare the demographics of those who left Liverpool with those who moved to the city. It also considers the profile of those who chose to travel to the city to work, in order to gauge whether the Conservatives had lost likely voters through migratory patterns.

Chapter 7 covers the penultimate research question, 'to what extent can Conservative decline in Liverpool be attributed to the breakdown of the link between Protestantism and Conservatism?' This chapter argues that the concepts of socialisation, path dependency, and critical junctures can explain Conservative success and decline, as outlined above.

Chapter 8 addresses the final research question, 'to what extent can Conservative decline in Liverpool be attributed to a specifically anti-Conservative identity widely held in Liverpool?' This chapter draws on the social psychology literature around identity formation and self-value to argue that the Scouse identity was transformed in the 1980s to become inherently anti-Thatcher and anti-Conservative, owing to the confrontation between the Militant-led Labour Council and the Thatcher government.

As such, this book will explore Conservative Party decline in Liverpool using a multi-method approach. In arguing that Conservative decline in Liverpool is best understood through a tripartite framework of success, decline, and irrelevance, this book brings a level of much-needed nuance to the study of Liverpool's political history.

2 Electoral politics in Liverpool: A brief history

There are numerous ways to classify the existing literature on the history of electoral politics in Liverpool and the decline of the Conservative Party, but for the purposes of this chapter the literature is split into four areas:

1. The transition from religion to class as the basis of party support
2. The changing demographics and economic structures of Liverpool
3. Party machines
4. Electoral structures.

2.1 The role of religion in Liverpudlian politics

This section will explore the Liverpool-specific literature on the relationship between religion and party support and the debate surrounding the shift towards a class-focused analysis of Liverpool's politics. The most common argument made by scholars of Liverpool's political history is twofold: firstly, that Conservative success in the city was based on stoking sectarian tensions to win the support of the Protestant working class, and secondly, that as the political salience of religion declined so too did the ties that bound the majority of Protestant voters to the Conservative Party. As these working-class voters realigned their interests along class lines, they switched to the Labour Party. A typical claim regarding Liverpool is that "among all Britain's cities, religion has dominated its political life and distorted it in a way that was unknown even in Glasgow — only Belfast can offer a comparison" (Baxter 1969, 1).

Liverpool's history has always been tied up with Ireland. The acquisition of Liverpool by King John, who granted it the title of borough in 1207, was in part to use Liverpool as a base to "convey troops and stores to Ireland" (Lacey

1907, 36). Roughly 600 years later, around the time of the Irish potato famine, the first major influx of Irish entered the city and supposedly "brought with them their unhealthy, seriously bigoted attitude towards Christianity which turned a decaying religious creed into a vigorous political force" (Baxter 1969, 1). Liverpool was not the final destination for most Irish migrants but those who settled in Liverpool were "dismissed as 'the dregs'... An underclass unable, unwilling or unsuited to take advantage of opportunities elsewhere, they retained a kind of Irishness which others were quick to shed or disown" (Belchem 1999, 128). The majority of the Irish who arrived were Catholic, creating an ethno-religious divide between Irish Catholics and Lancastrian Protestants, whilst Protestant arrivals, many from Belfast, "brought with them the traditions of the Orange Lodge" which would have a great impact on the political climate of the city (Baxter 1969, 210). In 1835 Hugh McNeile, an Anglican preacher, "founded the Protestant Association to link middle-class Anglicans with the Orange Order and with the Tories", whilst links were also maintained via the Orange Lodges. Day claimed "no potential Tory councillor could hope to achieve public office unless he was established, in McNeile's eyes, as a 'sound Protestant'" (Day 2008, 274).

The impact of Irish immigration on the economy and party machines of Liverpool will be explored below. However, it is generally accepted that until the early twentieth century the Conservatives drew the bulk of their support from the working-class Protestant population. Baxter claims that the Conservatives started their century-long domination of the council in the mid-1850s by "whipping up anti-Catholic feeling" (Baxter 1969, 210). Whilst broadly successful, the strategy of relying on Protestant support was not risk-free. Jenkins highlights how, unlike in Belfast, "Liverpool Tory Democracy was a political movement that lost control over popular sectarianism, a dynamic social force responsible for large-scale violence in the city" (Jenkins 2007, 177). The Conservatives used numerous vehicles to harness the working-class Protestant vote, the most prominent of which was the Liverpool Working Men's Conservative Association (LWCA, sometimes referred to as the WMCA), founded in 1867.

The LWCA was set up to be "specifically based in the working class, and even more precisely within the Protestant working-class. Catholics were excluded from membership, and the WMCA's strength was quite explicitly grounded in sectarianism" (Davies 1996, 227). The LWCA even required "members who have been guilty of 'consorting' with Catholics to confess their delinquencies and upon doing so they then receive a warning.

Catholics who have strayed in by chance are requested to leave the room" (Whittingham-Jones 1936b, 7–8).

The first priority of the LWCA was "to unite the friends of Conservative Principles in maintaining Protestantism", and "[i]n this transition lies the germ of the class prejudice which now animates all branches of the Conservative party in Liverpool" (Whittingham-Jones 1936b, 40). For Lees, "[w]ithout a strong sense of class community in Liverpool, the Protestantism and anti-Catholic Irish resentment filled the gap" (Lees 2011, 93). The exclusion of Catholics forms part of the case for the prosecution that the Conservatives played heavily on sectarian divides.

However, O'Leary argues that when Archibald Salvidge became leader of the LWCA in 1892 one of his first achievements "was the expulsion of the Orange Order from the formal Conservative organisation" whilst focusing on making it an organisation

> through which he could make the workingmen of Liverpool a formidable political force... to secure 'a great position in Liverpool, with a big name and lots of power, [to] make the city into a real democracy and show the masses how they can rule themselves'. (O'Leary 2004, 166)

Feeding into the argument that the Conservatives made their electoral pitch to Protestants is that the Labour Party only managed to get a significant foothold in the city following the demise of the Irish Nationalist Party (later called the Catholic Party and then renamed the Centre Party). As Peter Kilfoyle, Labour MP for Liverpool Walton (1991–2010) noted, "the working class was split along religious sectarian grounds between the Conservative and Unionist-supporting Protestants and the Labour-supporting Catholics" (Kilfoyle 2000, 1). Eric Heffer (Kilfoyle's predecessor as MP for Liverpool Walton, 1964–1991) agrees, and argues this sectarianism "tended to split the Labour vote" (Heffer 1991, 71). Labour's weakness within the Protestant working class is highlighted by Ramsay MacDonald who, following Labour's 1907 by-election defeat in Liverpool Kirkdale, reportedly said "It is astounding how in Liverpool whatever the issue appears to be at the start, you always manage to mobilize the full force of Orangeism. We'll never do any good here until that power is broken" (D.A. Roberts 1965, 49). This followed the Conservative tactic of playing "on the 'atheist' nature of 'socialist' policies", with local newspapers such as the *Protestant Standard* printing "claims that socialism would generate 'absolute infidelity' and 'the grossest immoralities'". Perhaps more importantly, however, was that the LWCA managed to mobilise

"500 canvassers in support of the Protestant Tory candidate" (Day 2008, 274–75).

Further evidence for the idea of an explicitly sectarian Conservative appeal can be found in the works of Whittingham-Jones, a Conservative activist in Liverpool who published a series of pamphlets in the 1930s decrying the sectarian nature of the party machine and its reliance on a narrow, religious electoral base, which she termed the 'Orange Caucus'. Whittingham-Jones claims that the

> Liverpool Tories discovered that the talisman to electoral victories was the "Protestant ticket," and, so well did they learn their lesson that, long after it has ceased to be infallible they persist in thinking the magic of "No Popery!" is still sovereign on Liverpool hustings. (Whittingham-Jones 1936a, 37)

This allegedly led to a situation in which

> [t]he Conservative party in Liverpool suffers a cruel deprivation in the exclusion of (a) the Big Business community; (b) the Catholic workingman; (c) the thousands of non-sectarian electors of all classes whom the Caucus deliberately avoids bringing in. (Whittingham-Jones 1936a, 8)

In the pre-1945 era, then, the Conservatives were linked to the Protestant vote and Labour to the Catholic vote. There is a debate, however, surrounding the extent to which the Conservatives made their appeals along explicitly sectarian religious lines. This falls into two camps: supply-side critiques (i.e. what the Liverpool Conservative Party offered to the voters) and demand-side critiques (what the voters wanted). The literature's focus on a sectarian appeal to Protestant voters ignores the broader policy content of the Conservatives' electoral appeal to voters.

O'Leary is the most sceptical proponent of the traditional sectarian argument, seeing in it an attempt by left-wing scholars to explain away Liverpool's failure to conform to a class-based analysis. She argues that

> [s]ince Liverpool did not fit the 'dialectical materialist' mould, the city was presented as the exception that proved the rule. Religion became the new dialectic as historians juxtaposed the Protestantism of Liverpool's indigenous population with the staunch Catholicism of the geographically segregated and culturally insulated Irish migrant community, to discover an intriguing working-class dichotomy. (O'Leary 2004, 157)

However, O'Leary blasts this reading as a "rather one dimensional, sectarian account of Liverpool's political history", in which "militant denominationalism in the city had retarded the natural development of a unified working-class consciousness and, consequently, the forward march of Labour" (O'Leary 2004, 158). Similarly, the

> Conservative Party's political hegemony has been explained, almost exclusively, as a direct consequence of pre-existing religious affiliations and popular sectarian identities amongst the electorate… the overstated link between Church and party has nevertheless resulted in a rather one-dimensional, reductionist reading of Liverpool's political history. (O'Leary 2004, 159)

Instead, she argues that "[i]t is surprisingly difficult to locate any explicit appeal to sectarian identities within the formal public discourse of Liverpool Conservatism during the late nineteenth century", and those that did occur

> were generally of minor significance, restricted to specific historical junctures, and invariably coaxed from reluctant Tory candidates who were prevailed upon by extreme Protestant organisations or indicial Protestant demagogues. For the period down to the First World War, the dominant Tory electoral cry in Liverpool was that of Democratic Conservatism. (O'Leary 2004, 159)

Similarly, despite claims of the Conservatives running the city in the style of an American political machine, with 'boss politics', terms "loaded with innuendo, implying profiteering, criminality and jobbery on the part of Liverpool's Tory councillors", O'Leary finds no evidence that ethnicity or religious affiliation played any part in the allocation of housing (O'Leary 2004, 163).

Furthermore, a range of scholars have referred to O'Leary's concept of 'Democratic Conservatism', although the labels often vary. O'Leary points to a range of policies which fall under 'Democratic Conservatism', including the party's "reputation as a pioneer in the sphere of Victorian housing reform", especially under Salvidge after 1900, the extension of polling hours to assist the working classes, and a programme of "municipal socialism" including the purchase of Liverpool's tramways in 1897, the building of a passenger railway tunnel in 1886, and the Mersey Tunnel, opened in 1931, which were "celebrated as triumphs of practical Tory Democracy" (O'Leary 2004, 168). An example of this school of thought was Salvidge's

> pressing for a "fair wage clause" to be inserted into all Corporation contracts, a policy which was opposed by the official Conservative leader Sir Thomas Hughes — the measure passed with support from Liberals and Irish Nationalists, but in the course of the heated debate Salvidge had alleged that Sir Thomas Hughes had never been known to advocate anything in the interests of the workingman. (D.A. Roberts 1965, 16)

In a similar vein, Belchem argues that Protestant workers were not simply driven by anti-Catholic prejudice, but rather by an attempt to "protect their 'marginal privilege'" through a "compound of populism, protectionism and Protestantism" which enabled Tory political hegemony to persist in Liverpool (Belchem 2000, xvi–xvii). This was a "constitutional" Conservativism, based on "economic management through a strong and responsive executive, arbitrating between the needs of government and of society in taxation and tariffs, and recognising the interdependence of classes and interests in the distribution of national income", in opposition to the dogma of free trade (Belchem 2000, 170). Later, he argues that whilst there was indeed "a pejorative stigmatizing" of the Irish in Liverpool, "Tory sectarianism was complemented by civil progressivism, a prototype 'municipal socialism' pioneered by 'Tory Democrat' Alderman A.B. Forwood" (Belchem 2006, 17–18).

Less positively, Smith argues the party had adopted "the Belfast cry of 'Social Reform but no Socialism'", a programme of municipal reform and "jobs for the Protestant boys" alongside token accommodations to the nationalist Catholic-Irish leadership, especially on issues of housing (Smith 1984, 39). As such, for these scholars the Conservative appeal was based on ideology and policy, rather than an aggressive, solely sectarian, platform. Indeed, Roberts notes how in the 1907 municipal election the Conservatives appealed to anti-socialism, rather than anti-Catholicism, and thus they "appealed to the whole religious vote, both Protestant and Catholic. The results proved the success of these tactics" (D.A. Roberts 1965, 49).

Similarly, Sir Thomas White, the leader of the Liverpool Conservatives following Salvidge's death in 1928 — and like Salvidge also a publican — attempted to woo the Catholic vote in the 1929 general election campaign, his first real test as leader. The main effect of this was to turn younger Orangemen to Labour, without convincing "many Catholics that the Conservative party was no longer the party of anti-Catholicism". Although at this point Roberts argues "White had inherited most of Salvidge's centralized power but little of his political acumen", by 1934 White had become "an able tactician" able to see through Protestant Party leader Reverend H.D. Longbottom's proposed deals, which "for a maximum gain of 10,000 militant Protestant votes concentrated in a few particular wards" ignored "many more Catholic votes which could be won for the Conservatives, spread over many wards" (D.A. Roberts 1965, 111–24). These are not the actions of a rabidly Protestant sectarian party.

This point is also supported, inadvertently, by Lane. He pushes the common line that "[t]he key to Tory success was religion" but acknowledges that this was supported by an ability to deliver the goods and, once the Conservatives lost their ability to deliver these goods, be they housing or the protection of marginal privilege for Protestants, the party lost the working-class vote (Lane 1978, 340). Lane later argues that, ultimately,

> it is actually doubtful that Tory manipulation of anti-Catholic sentiment among the Protestant working class had much electoral impact… Recent research, however, persuasively suggests that it was Tory gerrymandering of ward and constituency boundaries rather than sectarianism which mainly turned the trick. (Lane 1997, 110)

Thus, for Lane, the key to Tory success was religion, except when it was gerrymandering; it certainly was not delivering the goods; but when the goods were not delivered the Tories lost votes!

The strong-sectarian thesis common in the literature also ignores the demand side, or what Protestant voters (who made up the majority of Liverpool's electorate) wanted. Roberts' judgement is that

> Salvidge was often criticized for using religious issues in election campaigns. He was not the last Conservative leader to do this… he would not ignore the religious prejudices of its members — prejudices with which he sympathized rather than shared. (D.A. Roberts 1965, 108)

This approach to sectarianism was shared by White, who — unlike Salvidge — was actually a member of the Orange Order. According to Roberts, White argued that it was inadvisable for the Conservatives to "shed their sectarian skin", because

> [w]hether we like it or not… there are many thousands of electors in Liverpool who will, if the need arises, put Protestantism before their politics, and it would simply be madness on my part if I told the people of Kirkdale, Everton, or West Toxteth, that the Conservative Party has ceased to care for religion or for Protestant interests. (K.D. Roberts 2015, 233)

Further to this, it is important to recognise that Protestant working-class voters had individual agency; as Belchem argues, they were not "passive instruments... manipulated at will by the Tory caucus" (Belchem 1992, 11). Bohstedt likewise claims that "[s]ectarianism was not simply elite manipulation of the masses. The elites did not create it. Plebeian Protestants used the Conservative bosses to advance their own interests more than vice versa" (Bohstedt 1992, 204). As a result, "local Tory bosses were frequently compelled to adopt policies and practices at odds with the orthodox political economy of mainstream middle-class conservatism" (Belchem 1992, 11).

As such, it is unfair to claim that the Liverpool Conservatives were solely responsible for stoking sectarian tensions; instead, they were responding to a marked demand from the public. Wildman argues that the Tory democrat image was a conscious reaction to the rise of Labour within the city (Wildman 2012, 126), and thus should be seen as a way of responding to class-based demands without requiring sectarianism.

For Baxter, the Conservative appeal was not to religious piety but to welfare provision and jobs:

> The working classes of Liverpool are not renowned for devoutness and it is hard to conceive of a division as deep as it was, caused by religion. Christianity seemed rather to be the excuse — the way a division caused by other influences manifested itself. Nationalism was an obvious alternative cause and doubtless it contributed, but a more fashionable reason would be economic. (Baxter 1969, 2)

In this reading, the attraction of sectarian bodies like the Orange Lodge was because they provided a quasi-safety net. The Protestant working class "desired an organisation that offered its own welfare schemes and mutual fellowship, comparable to what their Irish counterparts found in the Roman Catholic Church", whilst the Irish Catholics "were perceived as alien intruders and economic rivals in a situation where competition for work was already fierce" (K.D. Roberts 2015, 4). Simply put, many Conservative voters voted for the party which would do the most for them. As Baxter argues, "[t]he Conservatives, with consummate skill exploited the economic and social anxieties of the workers, dividing Protestant from Catholic, and securing the support of the former for themselves" (Baxter 1969, 1).

Roberts outlines the weakness of the traditional reading of the role of sectarianism and voting in Liverpool, arguing how even the Protestant Party was unable to stand on narrow religious platforms, pointing to the 1904 municipal election where it was forced to broaden its appeal "to take in any workingman who might be inclined to vote for a prospective Labour candidate", a policy which Roberts terms a success (D.A. Roberts 1965, 40). Similarly, in 1919 Catholics found the issue of secular education "less important than their depressed economic condition, and their dislike of the attitude of Council [*sic*] or the [police] strikers of August" (D.A. Roberts 1965, 78). In 1921, the "unemployed Protestant" would not "put his economic before his religious interest" (D.A. Roberts 1965, 87) but by the end of the 1920s "[f]ew election addresses of the Conservative and Labour candidates mentioned religious topics" (D.A. Roberts 1965, 94).

We also see a similar focus on economic issues in the 1924 West Toxteth by-election, when many "younger Orangemen, especially ex-servicemen, [have] ceased automatically to obey the patriotic appeal, and voted for the Labour party on economic grounds" (D.A. Roberts 1965, 97). The lesson seems to have been learnt. By 1925 Salvidge is quoted as saying "I am a Protestant, your candidate is a Protestant, but in council the question of religion does not enter into the arena" (D.A. Roberts 1965, 103). Even as far back as 1903 — when the Protestant Party first stood in Liverpool's municipal elections — Salvidge believed that "the Protestant ticket was not the sole answer in mobilizing the working classes for the Conservative vote", but rather the issue of tariff reform "would appeal more consistently (and with less danger) to the working classes of the city" and so be more effective (D.A. Roberts 1965, 33). It seems that Protestantism has never been a master key with which the Conservatives could open the door to electoral success; Kilfoyle's and Heffer's claims that the Conservatives simply played on sectarianism are too simplistic.

In addition to economic appeals, Roberts argues that the Catholic–Protestant divide was not so much about religion as identity. He finds the "level of genuine observation to the doctrine was not the overriding factor. It was about identification and belonging" (K.D. Roberts 2015, 260). For Lane, Conservative supporters were "at best, notional Protestants but who were very definitely opposed to Irish Catholics" (Lane 1987, 138). This allowed the Conservatives to play on a 'them' versus 'us' narrative which allowed for the rallying of votes; had there not been a Protestant versus Catholic narrative, it is possible the party might have found another divide, although this might have been less electorally salient and thus less useful in terms of winning Protestant votes. For Smith, the politically salient cleavage in Liverpool in the early twentieth century was between Irish Catholicism and Lancastrian Protestantism: "Catholicism came to dominate Irish Nationalism and to take precedence over the Labour beliefs of working class Catholics" as evidenced by the 1907 Kirkdale by-election (Smith 1984, 46). This, however, was the exception rather than the rule. Indeed, the Tories and the Irish Nationalists "appealed for local working class support on the basis of their social reform platform as well as on the basis of organized prejudice" (Smith 1984, 40). Sectarian appeal on both sides, to the extent that it existed, was only ever one piece of the jigsaw of electoral success.

The suggestion that identity was a stronger driver of voting behaviour than religious belief is supported by events following the establishment of the Irish Free State. Stanley Salvidge, Archibald's son, argues that following the Irish Free State agreement and the protection of Ulster, the Conservatives' working-class coalition "was never again quite the same reliable force. The old incentive of 'Loyalty to Ulster' had gone, and more modern cries of a class-conscious Labour movement were reaching the ears of a younger generation" (K.D. Roberts 2015, 238). Thus it appears that it was not religion, but rather policy or identity which kept many loyal to the Conservatives. The role of changing identities and their link to Conservative support in Liverpool is explored in Chapter 8.

Further, claims that the Conservatives simply played on sectarian divides fails to recognise that Liverpool Protestantism was not "an homogenous political force" (Davies 1996, 227). Militant Protestantism, expressed through the Protestant Party, the LWCA, and the Orange Lodges, was stronger in the north of Liverpool. Davies attributes this to the greater evangelical presence in these areas, whereas in the south of the city "dissenters were marginally in the majority, and reduced the influence of the more extreme elements of Protestantism" (Davies 1996, 228). This shows that the relationship between Protestantism and Conservativism was conditional and geographically varied. If the Conservatives were as sectarian as they are made out to be in the traditional literature, then they would not have lost the wards in the Netherfield and St Domingo area by being outdone on sectarian appeal. However, at the turn of the twentieth century, and also in the 1930s

> Tory democracy was deserted by the Protestant working class in the north end of the city — in the Netherfield/St Domingo area — for a more explicit Protestant Party. Sectarianism, pure and simple, was what was required there, not municipal reform. (Davies 1996, 37)

Davies comes to a similar conclusion for Labour in the interwar years as O'Leary's for the Conservatives, finding that "religious sectarianism was almost certainly not as important as twentieth-century convention has made it out to be, but it was still relevant", and that the Conservatives only used anti-Catholic sentiment in a few wards, where even there "the sectarian appeal was not a major factor consistently throughout the inter-war years". Labour's electoral nadir in the city, in 1930 and 1931, is found to be down to national crises rather than local sectarianism (Davies 1996, 233).

One final point regarding the role of sectarianism and the Conservative machine in Liverpool is that it was not unheard of for Catholics to be members of the Liverpool Conservative Party, nor indeed Liverpool Conservative MPs. The heavily Catholic — and heavily working-class — constituency of Liverpool Exchange was dominated by Labour's Bessie Braddock after her victory in 1945, but before then it had been represented by the Catholic Conservatives Sir James Reynolds (MP 1929–1932) and Sir John Shute (MP 1933–1945). Tiernan argues that Braddock's victory in 1945 — as a left-wing atheist — was attributable to "complacency by the businessmen", insofar as only 2,292 business votes were recorded cast, out of a registered 26,732. This sub-electorate voted overwhelmingly Conservative, and Braddock won by just 665 votes. This shows that issues apart from sectarianism could be the reason why the Conservatives won — or lost — seats in Liverpool. Similarly, in the 1951 general election the Catholic trade unionist John Tiernan was selected as the Conservative candidate in Liverpool Exchange (Tiernan 2017, 4). This is a real-world example of the sectarian-political divide being less clear-cut than the literature makes it out to be.

As such, the standard claim that electoral politics in Liverpool was solely driven by religious belief is an oversimplification. Whilst religion was indeed a factor behind party support in Liverpool, it was never the sole factor, nor was it even the most important in many elections.

2.1.1 The decline of the political salience of religion

Mirroring national trends, religion began to decline in electoral salience in Liverpool during the first quarter of the twentieth century. Wald outlines how class began to override religion around 1918, pointing to Butler and Stokes' finding that "the pre-1918 cohort was apparently the last electoral generation for whom religious influences were paramount" (Wald 1983, 68).

This claim is supported by attendance figures at explicitly sectarian organisations. Throughout the interwar period the Orange Order and the LWCA lost support to the trade unions and Labour clubs, whilst churches — especially Protestant churches — were becoming emptier, and their political and electoral significance was increasingly limited to the Kirkdale and Exchange divisions (D.A. Roberts 1965, 118). As previously mentioned, in 1934 Sir Thomas White, Liverpool Conservative Party leader, turned down a deal with the Protestant Party which envisaged the Conservatives taking a "firmly anti-Catholic line" in order for the Protestants to withdraw from the municipal election, based on the assumption that the Protestant vote was only significant in a few wards, and on a city-wide level would not make much difference (D.A. Roberts 1965, 124). He was right; the Protestants stood in eight out of forty wards, winning just one seat and costing the Conservatives another three.

By 1945, the LWCA and the Orange Lodge were apparently "no longer very important" and the new leader of the Liverpool Conservatives, Alfred Shennan, "was less sympathetic to their claims than White or Salvidge would have been" (D.A. Roberts 1965, 142). Similarly, on the left, Bessie Braddock declared that "she would not watch their [Catholic] interests at the expense of working class interests as a whole" (D.A. Roberts 1965, 143). Roberts argues that in the 1950 municipal election, "[o]utside of the St Domingo, Netherfield, Brunswick, North Scotland, [and] Exchange wards, where either Protestants or Independent Catholics were standing, there was no mention of any religious question, housing and other shortages being the most discussed topics" (D.A. Roberts 1965, 151). Even the Protestant Party, which survived until the early 1970s, was tolerated by the Conservatives because of "their anti-socialist attitude" (D.A. Roberts 1965, 144), and the Independent Catholic councillors in the early 1950s also based their appeal on anti-socialism rather than religion (D.A. Roberts 1965, 154).

Baxter describes the 1950s as "years of 'normalisation' for voting behaviour in Liverpool as the electoral pendulum moved in a manner almost identical to the rest of the nation" (Baxter 1969, 125). Heffer notes how, by 1964, only "small pockets of Protestant Unionism still existed" where generally older voters refused to vote Labour because they "did not vote Papist" (Heffer 1991, 110). Ramsden identifies 1964 as a watershed moment (Ramsden 1996, 230), with Roberts outlining how the constituencies won by Labour, including Kirkdale, Toxteth, Walton, and West Derby, which had been safe seats for the Conservatives, were "mainly Protestant areas, with sizeable Orange contingents" (K.D. Roberts 2015, 240).

Miller and Raab show that on a national level religion was still important but mainly when considered through the lens of class; in 1963 class was a much better predictor of party support than religion, but religion still accounted for within-class differences. Conservatives tended to do poorly amongst Nonconformists (especially middle-class ones) and Catholics, but well amongst Anglicans, although the relative advantage had decreased compared to the 1920s (Miller and Raab 1977). As such, it may be premature to claim that religion was no longer important, but rather the way in which religion was important had changed.

Every now and then, however, there would be attempts at playing the religion card. Taaffe and Mulhearn recount an experience in 1983, when the Liberals issued a leaflet in the Vauxhall ward with the heading "Why no Catholic can vote Labour on Thursday", which

> carried a picture of the Pope with the statement: 'Who would have thought that just after twelve months after the Holy Father's historic visit, the Labour Party would want to close our Christian schools'... Several nuns told Labour canvassers that they had come out to vote Labour, because the Liberals 'dared to insult His Holiness by using his name for cynical manoeuvres'! (Taaffe and Mulhearn 1988, 79)

Similarly, in the 1992 general election the Walton constituency, which included areas where the Orange Lodge was traditionally strong, saw a Protestant Reform candidate stand and win just 393 votes (0.8 per cent), fewer than Screaming Lord Sutch's 546 votes (1.4 per cent) for the Monster Raving Loony Party in the constituency's 1991 by-election (K.D. Roberts 2015, 239–40).

Roberts argues that the "orthodox opinion" on the cause of the decline of sectarianism was attributable to the postwar slum clearance undertaken by both Labour and Conservative councils (K.D. Roberts 2015, 21). However, the importance of slum clearance "appears to be assumed rather than proven" (K.D. Roberts 2015, 211).

For many, slum clearance was seen as a deliberate policy of the council, especially Labour councils, to break up Protestant estates. Day conducted a survey of Orange Lodge members in Liverpool, and found that 60 per cent of those polled thought slum clearance was the main reason for the decline of the Order, whilst some believed the policy was an example of 'ethnic cleansing' pushed by Jack and Bessie Braddock (Day 2008, 277). Waller argues that "[i]n the slums removed for the highway to a second Mersey tunnel, sectarian identities were buried" (Waller 1981, 349).

Roberts challenges the idea that slum clearance caused the decline of sectarianism, arguing it is

> too simple an explanation for the corrosion of a social, religious, economic, xenophobic, tribal, and traditional dispute that had raged for nearly two centuries... [However,] in breaking up the old 'Orange strongholds', the Protestant Party could no longer rely on a micro-majority of supporters to

> keep them in office. Yet, it is probable that this powerbase would not have survived regardless of rehousing. (K.D. Roberts 2015, 401)

Roberts points to the fact that "clearance also took place in both Glasgow and Belfast, areas which retain strong sectarian traditions to this day" (K.D. Roberts 2015, 215). Furthermore, as outlined above, most scholars consider the decline of religiously influenced voting behaviour to have been completed before 1964, but slum clearance was only partially completed by then (K.D. Roberts 2015, 241). Accordingly, slum clearance does not seem a satisfactory explanation for the decline of sectarianism, or indeed the decline of religiously influenced voting behaviour. It came about much too late, and only affected certain parts of the city; why would slum clearance in Everton affect voting behaviour in the Smithdown or Church wards? Any effect it did have could only have been marginal to the Conservatives' electoral performance in Liverpool. Roberts also discounts the idea that "the vigour of ecumenical projects" is to thank for the decline of sectarianism, arguing that the bulk of sectarian tension had dispersed by the time Archbishop Worlock and Bishop Sheppard began their ecumenical work in the city in the 1970s and 1980s (K.D. Roberts 2015, 255).

For Roberts, the most important reason for the decline of sectarianism was not slum clearance, but rather "a change in attitudes towards theology, coupled with the development of a common identity, the new 'religion' of which became football" (K.D. Roberts 2015, 412). This identity emerged "in response to Liverpool 'being downtrodden by the rest of the UK', slowly morphing from divergent Irish Catholic and Orange Protestant sects to an overarching 'Scouse' character" (K.D. Roberts 2015, 23). Belchem argues that "Scouse is a recently invented tradition, a cultural response to the city's decline", which emerged in part as a result of the success of Merseybeat and Liverpool's football teams (Belchem in K.D. Roberts 2015, 408). This identity cannot explain the decline of the Conservatives in Liverpool, as it would have occurred too late in the day. It can, however, explain the continued irrelevance of the party, and will be explored in greater detail later.

Ultimately, however, it was not the decline of Protestant and Catholic labels that is important, but rather the decline of an exclusive link between religion and political party. As stated above, the difference between the two groups was rarely down to doctrine, but rather a consequence of relative economic position or identity. Gradually these labels began to lose their exclusivity, and it became increasingly normal, for example, to be Orange and Labour. Roberts argues that by the mid-twentieth century Liverpool saw "the dual assimilation of both identities [Irish Catholic and Lancastrian Protestant] into the newly emerging and dominant local character of 'Scouse' which had the most profound effect of subjugating sectarian vehemence" as people began to "look beyond religion towards other forms of fulfilment" (K.D. Roberts 2015, 321).

This brief history of the decline of religious sectarianism and its influence on voting behaviour shows that sectarianism could not have been the sole cause of Conservative support in the postwar period for two reasons. Firstly, it was never the case that religion was the sole issue driving Conservative support. Religion only became important when tied up with other issues, usually education or Irish home rule. When religious factors were less salient, more mundane municipal debates took their place and the Conservatives could still win. Secondly, if sectarianism was the main driver of Conservative support, then the number of Tory voters should have declined much earlier than it did, or at least the Conservatives should have done well only in areas where sectarianism was still a potent force, namely in the north of the city. Instead, on a municipal level the Conservatives did well across Liverpool in the 1960s, peaking with 87 elected councillors following the 1969 local election. Thus, whilst 1964 may appear a watershed general election at which Marx replaced God, the pattern of voting behaviour at the local level shows a great deal more nuance. The Conservatives still managed to put up a decent showing in Liverpool, in terms of seat share until the 1970s, and in terms of vote share until the 1980s. Thus, the claim that religion was the key driver of the decline in Conservative vote share is unsustainable. The relationship between sectarianism and postwar Conservative support will be explored in Chapter 7.

2.2 Economic and demographic change

Academic studies often link Conservative decline to Liverpool's changing demographic and economic structures. It is well known, for instance, that Liverpool's economic development was tied up in the fortunes of its port. For Lacey, the "story of the growth of the Dock Estate is the story of the rise of Liverpool" (Lacey 1907, 57). Boland argues that Liverpool's development began with the slave trade, and continued as it became the "Gateway to Empire" during the Industrial Revolution (Boland 2008, 356–57). For Parkinson, "[t]he story began with the port" (Parkinson 1985, 9).

Following the port's brief resurgence in the Second World War, Wilks-Heeg argues that Liverpool was poorly placed to take advantage of rising trade with the "EEC and other West European countries", as Liverpool's merchants found they were able neither to exploit new markets nor to remain competitive in old markets (Wilks-Heeg 2003, 45–47). Similarly, containerisation, alongside the decasualisation and decline of dock labour (falling from 13,500 in 1965 to 10,000 in 1972, and to 2,000 by the mid-1980s) also played a role in the decline of the employment opportunities in the port (Lawton and Pooley 1986, 74).

Despite this, Merseyside enjoyed a brief 'Golden Age' which saw employment peak in the mid-1960s. However, this peak was soon followed by decline. Between 1966 and 1978 employment in the city fell by some 20 per cent (compared with national and regional declines of 5 and 12 per cent respectively), and between 1978 and 1981 employment fell by a further 18 per cent (Meegan 2003, 58). Whilst regional policy successfully attracted firms to Merseyside, it had "mixed success" in retaining it as the global economy slowed (Meegan 2003, 59). Boland concurs, arguing that "[t]he global economic restructuring of the 1970s and 1980s dealt a huge blow to the Merseyside economy and Liverpool's in particular. Many firms either closed down or relocated. The city suffered employment haemorrhage, poverty, population loss and declining GDP" (Boland 2008, 357).

Parkinson argued at the time that "decline has turned into collapse… In the 1980s, the city is economically marooned: it is in the wrong place, based on the wrong kind of economic activity with an outdated infrastructure and an underqualified labour force" (Parkinson 1985, 9). Further, owing to the "mainly semi- and unskilled, casual, irregular and poorly paid" labour prominent at the docks, "a core of skilled workers did not develop because manufacturing never took off in Liverpool" (Parkinson 1985, 10–11).

Liverpool's poorly unionised docks were never Labour strongholds. The party did better in

> wards where significant numbers of non-waterfront workers were based, and in the support of predominantly craft unions. Labourism, the dominant political strand in the national labour movement, was not the intuitive home of waterfront workers in Liverpool. (Davies 1996, 234)

However, with the decline of the docks and the growing relative importance of manufacturing in Liverpool's economy, trade unionism received a shot in the arm as the "Liverpool working-class began to show more solidarity and trade unionism helped to politicise the Liverpool electorate… Labour and trade union militancy was not merely a product of activism, it was a consequence of Liverpool's declining fortunes as a city" (K.D. Roberts 2015,

245). Similarly, Davies argues that public sector unionism became much more important in Liverpool in the 1950s and 1960s (Davies 1999, 19).

However, it is worth highlighting McKenzie and Silver's findings that in the 1960s "trade unionists and their dependents vote Conservative only somewhat less often than do non-unionists" (McKenzie and Silver 1968, 128). Further, they argued that working-class Conservatives could be categorised as either 'deferentials' or 'seculars'. For deferentials "the merits of the Conservative party are defined in terms of its intrinsic qualities — what it is; for seculars, in terms of its policies — what it does" (McKenzie and Silver 1968, 213). As such, and related to Liverpool, secular Conservatives were much less likely to support the Conservatives when they experienced economic distress. McKenzie and Silver found younger voters were more likely to be seculars too, meaning that as time passed there were fewer working-class voters on whom the Conservatives could depend to support them regardless of their economic situation.

However, the increase in manufacturing in Liverpool was not without its downside. For Parkinson, the weakness in Liverpool's economy was that

> its manufacturing is dominated by a small number of very large absentee employers... By 1985, seven large firms controlled almost half of all the 47,000 manufacturing jobs in the city. And between 1981 and 1985 these seven firms had shed 30 per cent of their jobs.

These firms tended to be established because of regional policy during the 1950s and 1960s, and made "investment and disinvestment decisions in terms of national and international, not local, markets" (Parkinson 1985, 11–12). Frost and North agree, arguing that these were "run by business-people with no commitment to the city" (Frost and North 2013, 16). For Ridley, "as new technologies allow multinationals to operate fewer plants, they exclude Liverpool, on the periphery of Europe" (Ridley 1986, 128).

In considering housing, Lawton and Pooley argue that slum clearance meant "[p]rivately rented accommodation was virtually eliminated in redeveloped inner areas. In Everton Ward, for example, corporation dwellings increased from 23 to 97 percent of housing stock, and in Netherfield Ward from 14 to 86 percent" (Lawton and Pooley 1986, 77). Relatedly, McKenna notes that those who were moved in an early, prewar wave of slum clearance faced new problems, as these families tended to be larger, but incomes remained low and they were moved far from the docks: "[f]amilies barely able to feed themselves found it impossible to pay travelling expenses" (McKenna 1991, 186). This new structure of hardship would be important in forcing people to reassess their interests through an economic, rather than a religious, lens.

By the 1980s Liverpool's economic prospects were bleak: "[h]igh unemployment, overdependence on declining industries and a shortage of skilled labour thus gave Merseyside the classic features of a declining economy" (Lawton and Pooley 1986, 70). Liverpool faced a high level of outward migration, offsetting "relatively high natural growth" as the population declined by nearly 300,000 between 1951 and 1981 (Lawton and Pooley 1986, 75–77) and an economy increasingly reliant on public sector employment, accounting for a third of the jobs, a higher proportion than in other cities (Ridley 1986, 130).

Thus, in the 1983 general election — when the Conservatives lost their last two parliamentary seats in the city — Liverpool was already beset with economic problems. Whilst the traditional argument is that the Falklands War led to a surge in the polls for the Thatcher government, work by Sanders et al. argues that the 'Falklands bounce' has been overdone in the literature, adding roughly 3 percentage points to the popularity of the Conservatives, and only from May to July 1982 (Sanders et al. 1987, 286). Instead, they argue that Thatcher's victory in 1983 was due to an economic revival, which explains why there was no such bounce back in places like Liverpool. Although this reading has been challenged (Clarke, Mishler, and Whiteley 1990), the broader argument that economic trajectories are important is also supported by Savage, who claims that

> it may not matter so much in explaining political partisanship whether you live in a working-class or middle-class town; what does matter is whether it is expanding or not... most of the towns which have deviated from previous Tory traditions appear to have suffered considerably more decline than is common nationally. (Savage 1987, 70)

As Parkinson notes, "Merseyside has had the highest rate of unemployment of any English conurbation in every decade since the 1950s". This suggests that the Conservatives had the ability to do well despite the relatively higher levels of unemployment. However, during the 1970s "the rate of unemployment in Liverpool quadrupled from 5 per cent to 20 per cent" and by "1985 it was 27 per cent, double the national average" (Parkinson 1985, 13). Similarly, until the Thatcher era, the

> city's economic misfortunes did not have a major direct impact upon the health of the municipal economy itself, because high levels of public

> expenditure and a relatively generous government grant system protected the local authority from the most severe financial effects of structural decline. (Parkinson 1985, 9–10)

As a result, Liverpool had previously been insulated from the effects of its poorly performing economy.

These changing demographics are important. In national elections, Heath et al. note that voting is "contagious", that is, "[h]ow you vote may depend on how the people round you vote" which tends to "accentuate the prevailing patterns of political support" (Heath, Jowell, and Curtice 1985, 76). Similarly, Miller finds that the effect of class polarisation on voting behaviour is greater on the area level than the individual level (Miller 1978, 258). In the case of Liverpool, this would suggest that as those groups with a greater propensity to vote Labour (or at least not vote Conservative) — such as those in social housing, the working class, and the unemployed — become a higher proportion of the electorate the areas they reside in are also more likely to vote non-Conservative as these neighbourhood effects grow. Whiteley et al. have come to a similar conclusion (Whiteley, Seyd, and Richardson 1994, 191–92).

The importance of economic decline for Conservative decline is also true for Scotland. Seawright and Curtice note how "bringing home the economic bacon is as powerful a 'Scottish card' as any the party can play" (Seawright and Curtice 1995, 339). They theorise that a similar factor has "probably influenced the Conservatives' fortunes in England" too, as, after 1955, much of Northern England "shared much of the relative economic disadvantages of Scotland" (Seawright and Curtice 1995, 342). As such, the role of changing demographics, and of migration, present a potential area for exploration. This is done in Chapter 5 and Chapter 6.

2.3 Party machines

The history of Liverpool's political parties is one of 'boss politics': of overpowerful individuals at the centre of effective party machines. For Kilfoyle, Liverpool politics has been dominated by a number of city bosses, "typified by the Conservative leaders Arthur Forwood, Archibald Salvidge, Thomas White and Alfred Shennan, and then Labour's Jack Braddock" (Kilfoyle 2000, 22). Heffer argues that this was due to Liverpool's character. The "semi-anarchic" city and reliance on a port-based economy have created a "strongly belligerent civic chauvinism", and have given the "twin impulse toward autocracy and flamboyant individualism" which has bled into the politics of the city (Heffer in Carmichael 1993, 388). Bealey found a similar impulse in his study of Newcastle-under-Lyme, arguing that "the character and style of leadership in any sort of society have a great influence on the flavour of its politics" and "continue to provide it long after the social basis of their pre-eminence has ceased to be in a preponderance amongst the electorate in their areas" (Bealey, Blondel, and McCann 1965, 409). This section will explore the literature on Liverpool's political parties and their effects on voting behaviour.

2.3.1 *The Liverpool Conservative Party*

The modern Liverpool Conservative Party can trace its origins back to 1848 when, chastened by defeat in 1847 (where the two Tory MPs for the Liverpool constituency were defeated by a Peelite and a Liberal), the Tories reorganised. Their motto was 'The Church, the Throne and the People. Ships, Colonies and Commerce', and they "placed protectionism above Protestantism" (Belchem 2000, 169). The success of the Liverpool Conservatives amongst the working class of Liverpool can be traced to the LWCA, set up in response to the Representation of the People Act 1867, which extended the vote to the town's artisans. The LWCA's aim was to "unite the friends of Conservative principles maintaining Protestantism", with Catholics forbidden membership (D.A. Roberts 1965, 5).

The Liverpool Working Men's Conservative Association was a rather ineffective body until Salvidge, who joined it in 1885, became its chairman in 1892. He held this position until 1928, and is without doubt the key prewar figure in the history and development of the Liverpool Conservative Party. Known as the "King of Liverpool", Salvidge was a publican who wasted no time in reshaping the LWCA into an effective electoral machine, pushing for "what Disraeli would have called the 'Tory Democracy'" (D.A. Roberts 1965, 22).

In 1918 Salvidge became leader of Liverpool City Council, and in 1919 he extended his power over the Liverpool Conservative hierarchy by also becoming chairman of the Liverpool Constitutional Association, all while remaining chairman of the WMCA. Salvidge was thus in a completely dominant position within Liverpool Conservatism (D.A. Roberts 1965, 77). However, as noted by his son, Stanley Salvidge, "local Unionism had for so long been looking to him, not only for its impetus and inspiration, but for much of its policy and direction, that the appointment [as Liverpool Conservative leader] appears to have been regarded as little more than a matter of form" (Salvidge 1934, 170). Still, his original power base in the LWCA was beginning to weaken — as general elections in the 1920s showed, the appeal and electoral reward of the LWCA was declining. A *Liverpool Daily Post* leader on the Conservative defeat in the 1919 municipal election argued that the decline of the LWCA was partly to blame:

> [Twenty-five] branches are still left open, but even now they are little better than skeletons of their former selves. The war is the cause of the apathy; Tory jingoism died on the battlefield. The young are not joining the Liverpool Workingman's Conservative Association, they are becoming Trade Unionists instead. (D.A. Roberts 1965, 79)

There is no doubt, however, that the LWCA was an effective electoral machine in its prime, able to mobilise canvassers in their hundreds (Day 2008, 274–75).

The extent to which Salvidge played on sectarian divides is debatable and has been explored above. However, Salvidge struggled to contain the passions of the militant Protestants. Indeed, the wider party was aware of "institutional weaknesses" amongst the working class, even in their strongholds. As Jarvis argues, following the First World War "the militant Orange caucus politics of Archibald Salvidge's Liverpool fiefdom had become a source more of embarrassment than of pride" (Jarvis 1996, 71).

By the time of Sir Thomas White's death in January 1938, it is clear that the Conservative Party machine still remained dominated by a key central figure. Of course, that is less of a problem when that figure is competent and, although the LWCA had declined in importance, the party machine was still able to 'get out the vote'. However, an overreliance on a key central figure can, and in the case of the Liverpool Conservatives did, mask deeper organisational issues.

Firstly, the Liverpool Conservative MPs "were kept in an unusually subordinate role, which caused some frictions, although this system declined after the sudden death in 1928 of the 'city boss', Sir Archibald Salvidge, 'left everything in absolute chaos'" (Ball 2013, 151). An example of Salvidge's power, and the influence of the LWCA, at the turn of the twentieth century was that he forced the MP for Liverpool East Toxteth, A.F. Warr, into making a grovelling apology in the press for resigning his membership of the LWCA, by threatening the loss of his seat (Salvidge 1934, 35–36). Similarly, Walter Long, MP for West Derby (and President of the Board of Agriculture, a cabinet-level position), was deselected in 1899 for not subscribing to the policy of "church discipline" (Waller 1981). Secondly, the party's financial health was reliant on "a perilously narrow basis of funding", with Salvidge complaining that "the number of contributors is very small, and the same persons respond almost every time" (Ball 2013, 183).

This is not to say that Salvidge and White were at fault in developing such a centralised system, or that they were wholly responsible: Ball outlines how in other major cities such as Birmingham, Manchester, and Glasgow there also were city-wide Conservative associations which dominated individual division parties, which in turn "acted more as its branches; this was particularly the pattern... where there were strong central bodies dominated by a cohesive business and social oligarchy" (Ball 2013, 151).

Whittingham-Jones also presents an account of the shortcomings of the local Conservative candidates, branding them "dull, incompetent speakers, who fail equally to impress the intelligent or to excite the ignorant" and concludes that until the "calibre of Conservative candidates is greatly improved the Socialist advance on municipal government will advance unimpeded" (Whittingham-Jones 1936a, 10).

However, as outlined above, the Liverpool Conservatives did make an appeal beyond simple sectarianism. Part of this sprang from the fact that the Conservative machine in the city had very strong roots in its local communities. Indeed, this placed the Conservatives in direct contrast to the city's Liberal Party at this time:

> While Liverpool Toryism displayed the characteristics of a party of 'social integration', the Liberals remained socially exclusive (and hence politically disabled), safeguarding the integrity of their advanced principles from contaminating contact with drink, ignorance, and vulgar prejudice. (Belchem 2000, 175)

The reason for this rapport with the electorate can be traced to the membership of the Liverpool Conservatives. Both Baxter and Lane argue that Conservative councillors were drawn from a cadre of middle-class small-business owners, rather than the great business magnates seen in the Liberal Party (Baxter 1969, 14; Lane 1997, 106). The LWCA would also have helped to bridge the gap between the worker and the party, in spite of the unstable nature of port employment. Lane credits these organic links — as always, along with the sectarian card — with providing a solid working-class base of Conservative voters. This can perhaps be epitomised in Salvidge himself — a "self-made local brewer and publican" who would be just as comfortable mingling with the working class as the business class (O'Leary 2004, 166). Further evidence of the links between Tory grandees and the working class can be seen in the local football clubs, set up "thanks to the patronage of 'King John Houlding' of Everton, a self-made publican and Tory councillor" in order to cultivate associations with the working class (O'Leary 2004, 168).

The above literature, and the debates within it, sheds light on the shape and character of the Liverpool Conservative Party before 1945: an effective political machine rooted in the local community. The structural weaknesses of the party, namely its small financial base, power centralised in the leader, and the formal exclusion of Catholics from its organisational life, could be — and indeed were — ignored in light of the machine's remarkable success. For Baxter

> [t]he Conservative Party had a long tradition of tight organisation both on the Council and in the city at large... When the first Labour representatives reached the City Council they found not only their own tiny organisation, but the more respectable Nationalist and Liberal Parties too, in the shadow of what was probably the most formidable provincial Conservative organisation of its time. (Baxter 1969, 155)

The analysis in Chapter 3 will explore the extent to which the Conservative Party machine in Liverpool continued to help or hinder the winning of votes.

2.3.2 *The Liverpool Labour Party*

The modern Labour Party in Liverpool came into existence in 1917, and began its first year of "normal political activity" in 1918 (Baxter 1969, 6). However, beginning with its birth as the Independent Labour Party (ILP), Merseyside proved "to be an extremely weak area for the party" (Davies 1999, 6). The literature identifies numerous interrelated reasons why the Labour Party was less successful than its Conservative rival or Labour counterparts elsewhere: religion, factionalism, boss politics, the structure of Liverpool's economy and trade unions, gender, and political and electoral structures.

2.3.2.1 *Labour as a Catholic party*

The first area highlighted in the literature regarding the Liverpool Labour Party and its relative lack of success in the twentieth century is the role of religion, specifically the reasons why Labour came to be identified with Catholic interests. Until the 1930s, the Irish Nationalist Party — in its various guises — could rely on holding around 14 seats on the council from Catholic-dominated areas. Its appeal declined rapidly with the formation of the Irish Free State in 1922 and so the party changed its name to the Irish Party, and then the Catholic Party, to boost its appeal. Following the First World War, Davies reports that "some prominent members began to throw in their lot with the Labour Party" and many voters found themselves in a situation where there were two Catholic candidates to vote for (Davies 1999, 11).

Scholars of this period credit the intervention of the Archbishop of Liverpool, Dr Richard Downey, with the decline of the city's Catholic party. In 1928 Downey declared his opposition to the use of the term 'Catholic' to describe any particular political party and banned priests from standing for election or being heavily involved in electoral politics. This led the Catholic Party to change its name yet again, this time to the Centre Party, and then for most of the party's candidates to stand down in favour of Labour (D.A. Roberts 1965, 107). Finally, the Labour Party's significant gains in the 1929 general election led to "wholesale defections to Labour" (Davies 1999, 11). By this point, Catholics had become a recognisable bloc in the Labour Party (Baxter 1969, 212). This merging

> handed over to the Labour Party a substantial body of politically active working-class people who were not socialist; who indeed were not in politics for class reasons at all, but were involved for nationalist and religious reasons — motives that were basically irrelevant to the Labour Party. (Baxter 1972, 106)

This was not overly problematic for the Labour Party, since during this time "the Catholicism of many electors and elected came before their Socialism. Labour inherited rather than won Nationalist seats" (Waller 1981, 324). Indeed, the strength of the Catholic vote is highlighted by the anecdote that, in the 1931 general election, the only seat which Labour did not lose in Liverpool was the "the imperishably Catholic Scotland division" where the incumbent, David Logan, "was confident of beating all-comers, 'from the Prime Minister downwards'" (Waller 1981, 328). Logan's predecessor was T.P. O'Connor, the Irish Nationalist Party candidate, who had been the MP from 1885 until his death in November 1929 and in every general election since 1918 been elected unopposed.

Whereas in other parts of the country Labour did deals with, and often cannibalised, the Liberals on a local level, there was no such Lib-Lab policy in Liverpool. Hence Lane argues that the Labour Party in Liverpool did not inherit "the radical wing of the Liberal Party" but rather "acquired the conspiratorialism of Irish politics as practised in England", providing the foundation for the "flavour of Tammany Hall" within Liverpool Labour (Lane 1978, 341). Indeed, the "Catholic faction was unaccustomed and indeed unsympathetic to ideas of participating membership", and had "a horse-trading approach to political organisation, where things were arranged through nods, winks and favours done for friends, relatives and constituents", which undermined the vitality and development of the party's organisation and led to its withering in the postwar years (Lane 1997, 111). Electorally, the influence of the Catholic bloc meant that Labour was on the wrong side of public opinion on the key issue of subsidies for Catholic schools. This retarded the party's growth, especially in the 1937 and 1938 municipal elections (Baxter 1969, 79–82).

Baxter argues that the Second World War "dampened down" religious attitudes within the party, pointing to a decision by a Protestant councillor to join Labour, whilst during the postwar years "Catholic influence declined considerably" as ward reorganisation and slum clearance killed "many old traditions" and "helped to break the habits of the past" (Baxter 1969, 214–19). The end of religion's salience in the Liverpool Labour Party can be seen in the victory of atheist Jack Braddock, supported by the non-Catholics, over Catholic-backed Luke Hogan in the party's 1950 leadership election (Baxter 1969, 214). Roberts talks about this issue as a divide more between right and left than between Catholics and non-Catholics (D.A. Roberts 1965, 149).

For Kilfoyle, vestiges of the Catholic-Labour machine could still be seen in the 1970s, when he claims "the Catholic church continued to influence the Labour Party in pockets of Liverpool" (Kilfoyle 2000, 8). Similarly Parkinson argues that "[t]hroughout the 1970s, the old guard, right-wing Catholic faction were a powerful minority force in the Labour group" and, in 1978, were able to "stage a brief coup and depose the existing old left leader, John Hamilton, and replace him with their own candidate, Eddie Roderick" (Parkinson 1985, 24). However, similar to the leadership election in 1950, it is unclear whether this was a Catholic coup, or a right-wing coup in response to the leftward swing of Labour under the influence of a rising Militant (Parkinson 1985, 24).

It is important not to exaggerate the Catholic-Labour relationship. Whilst there were strong trends towards Catholics being involved in, and voting for, Labour, it was by no means a majority Catholic party. Roberts, for one, argues that once Irish home rule had been secured, and Ulster was 'safe', many "saw signs of Orangemen turning to the Labour party". Similarly, an Orange Rally in 1919 aimed at dissuading Orangemen from joining the Labour Party saw crowds react with hostility to anti-socialist speeches (D.A. Roberts 1965, 79–80).

2.3.2.2 *Factionalism and 'boss politics'*

By the 1930s, the Catholic caucus formed a solid right-wing bloc, and often entered into alliances with the "predominantly moderate wing based in the Trades' Council". This alliance was opposed to a "disparate left wing minority" which held its strength in the divisional and ward parties. This minority could be split into two further sub-groups: the ILP and the ex-Communist bloc (Davies 1999, 11–12).

It was this factionalism that arguably laid the groundwork for boss politics to emerge within the Labour Party: by splitting the Party into groups, such as "the 'ins' and the 'outs', the 'establishment' and the 'anti-establishment', rather than 'right' and 'left'", it created a situation where the "uncommitted were forced to choose between alternative leaders rather than alternative policies" (Baxter 1969, 62). This is coupled with the fact that many of Liverpool Labour's councillors lacked a decent education and the capacity for independent, critical thought, and thus could be bought off with minor positions such as "Membership of the Parks and Gardens Committee" (Baxter 1969, 2).

Similarly, the inability of leaders such as Jack Braddock to control the Catholic caucus led to a situation where it was easier to bribe them with positions or threaten them with deselection than to convince by debate. The fact that many councillors who would serve in the 1960s cut their teeth in these fractious times is important, because it is here that the groundwork was laid for "Cook County, U.K. — Liverpool's answer to America's political bosses" under Braddock (Baxter 1969, 62).

Following ward boundary reforms, the all-out municipal elections in 1953 brought new councillors to the Labour Party who had little experience of Labour's historic religious divides. The older generation of councillors — who were steeped in Catholic-Socialist infighting — provided the main opposition to Braddock, whilst the younger generation were more supportive of the leadership. This cleavage deepened throughout the 1950s. However, the Conservative victory in 1961 swept away many of the Labour old guard, who were replaced in 1963 with a new generation of Labour councillors. Although factionalism continued, it was no longer based on religion (Baxter 1969, 148–51).

Kilfoyle argues that this is too optimistic a reading of events. In the 1960s "[t]he local church was in league with a number of large Labour families in the Vauxhall–Scotland area, running what amounted to a Catholic political mafia" (Kilfoyle 2000, 7–8) whilst "Braddock's strength lay in the north end of the city" (Kilfoyle 2000, 23). This perspective is important, because it highlights the geographical determinants of faction support in Liverpool Labour and how different factions could continue to survive despite being defeated in the council chamber.

The literature treats Jack Braddock as the "archetypal working class 'Boss' figure" (Elcock 1981, 439). Kilfoyle describes him as "a real 'Boss Hogg' who, with his formidable wife and consort Bessie... oversaw politics in the city with an iron grip, and by methods coated in the language of contracts and contacts, reeking of returnable favours" (Kilfoyle 2000, 2). By combining the positions of "Chairman and Leader of the Labour Group, Chairman of the Finance Committee of the Council and for a time also Chairman of the Liverpool Trades' and Labour Council", Braddock had a level of control over patronage held by "[n]o other British city leader", and a similar level of power over policy development and setting the annual budget (Elcock 1981, 441–44).

The limited literature on Liverpool Labour has highlighted that the party inherited a 'boss politics' like that of the Salvidge-White Conservative Party, born out of the factionalism of Labour's prewar era. The effect of boss politics is not simply academic — it led to moribund local parties and out-of-touch representatives, which not only undermined the strength of the Labour Party on a local level, as those who were the 'wrong sort' were kept away from the party machines, but also undermined the effectiveness of Labour as an effective municipal administration. This lay the groundwork for the rise of both the Liberal Party within the city, and of the Militant Tendency within the Labour Party.

2.3.2.3 *Economic structures and Liverpool trade unionism*

It would be an incomplete argument to treat religion, factionalism, and boss politics as the only reasons for Liverpool Labour's unusually slow rise to power in the city. The literature also points to the city's economy as a factor that hindered the development of Labour in Liverpool.

Firstly, the idea that Liverpool would be a natural breeding ground for socialism must not be taken for granted. Smith notes that "Glasgow working men were good socialists but lousy rioters; Liverpool working men were quite the reverse" (Smith 1984, 50). Davies quotes a prominent labour organiser in the city, Mary Bamber, who argued "Liverpool was the last place God made so far as industrial solidarity was concerned" (Davies 1996, 17). Davies also argues that, Catholic areas aside, Labour "fared less successfully in those areas where casual, port-related employment was predominant" (Davies 1996, 234).

Furthermore, Smith argues that local Tory hegemony shaped the trade union movement, encouraging it "to distance itself from Labour politics". The ILP in Liverpool went so far as to call themselves a 'people's party' and 'collectivists', as "concessions to the Tory distinction between Labour and socialism", reflecting just how powerful a sway Conservatism had over Liverpool's political culture (Smith 1984, 40–42). These tactics produced "a weak and divided Labour movement until Liverpool's economy was itself restructured", highlighting the importance of the structure of the economy for the political system of Liverpool (Smith 1984, 50). Belchem agrees, claiming that "Labour solidarity... did not extend into class-based political mobilization", with sectarian divides trumping class as "the traditional partisan divisions" (Belchem 1992, 9). Moore comments that "[i]n the absence of an independent working-class tradition, the new unions turned for leadership and guidance to an eccentric 'Tory' philanthropist" (Moore, in Belchem 1992, 5).

Kilfoyle argues that, owing to the structure of Liverpool's economy — specifically its lack of artisan and manufacturing base — the unionist left lacked "the vanguardist skilled workforce of other cities" that traditionally raised "the consciousness of the semi- and unskilled sections of the population". This absencewas important, because it ensured that the "workerist attitudes set a context for a political class in Liverpool that had no real intellectual content and was wholly producer orientated" (Kilfoyle 2000, 9).

Belchem argues that, after 1945, the shift from a maritime to a manufacturing-based industry, coupled with an unusual predominance of strike-prone industries, contributed to the development of a more militant unionism in Liverpool (Belchem 1992, 19). Davies highlights how factories in the new manufacturing industry had to be unionised from scratch, and often involved workers who had not belonged to unions before. This aided union recruitment whilst retaining "the process of democratisation of the union movement that was taking place on the docks" (Davies 1999, 18). Roberts agrees, arguing that this shift in the structure of the economy created "greater possibilities for the development of trade union affiliation as vehicles of political education and class consciousness", whilst trade unionism and the "acute industrial crisis" of job losses within the city throughout the 1970s and 1980s helped to politicise the working class (K.D. Roberts 2015, 245–46).

Parkinson hints at this too, suggesting that, in the 1960s and 1970s, the decline of the traditional industries and their unions, and their replacement with more militant local public sector unions, led to an "important shift in the power of the unions within the Labour party" (Parkinson 1985, 25; see also Davies 1999, 19).

As an aside, however, it is important to note that the structure of the economy also meant that "Liverpool was an unlikely site for popular Toryism", where the casual labour market contrasted with the "large manufacturing plants in which Tory employer paternalism was to flourish best". As Trench and Beard state, "[i]n Liverpool, almost alone amongst the provincial cities of the kingdom, the intercourse between masters and men, between employers and employed, ceases on payment of wages" (Belchem 2000, 156).

Thus, the structure of the economy can be seen as an important factor explaining the lack of Labour success, the reasons why the party developed the way it did, and why unions with a more militant approach were able to rise within its ranks after the Second World War.

2.3.2.4 Gender

In Liverpool, the interplay between gender and the Catholic faction was also important for explaining certain weaknesses in Liverpool Labour's support. On a national level, Ball points to evidence that working-class women were more likely to vote Conservative than their husbands or brothers, and prone to appeals which crossed class boundaries (Ball 2013, 117). Similarly, trade union life was "heavily masculine in focus, excluded women from power and often from employment" and politics "at a local level were often tinged with misogyny and could seem aggressive and confrontational" (Ball 2013, 119).

Unsurprisingly, in Liverpool local tensions also took on a religious edge. The arrival of the Catholic caucus, which rapidly formed a majority in the Labour group on the council, began to shape policy. One example is a motion in 1936 to renew the annual grant to a mothers' welfare clinic in the city centre. Luke Hogan, the leader of the Labour Party — and the Catholic caucus within the party — opposed this, as the clinic was "one of the few institutions in the city where women could get advice on birth control". The final vote saw 15 Labour members, 4 Protestants, 5 Liberals, and 48 Tories vote in favour, whilst 34 Labour, 4 Independents, and 3 Tories voted against. Davies describes this as "a curious alliance of left and right [which] triumphed over the majority Catholic caucus in the Labour group" (Davies 1996, 176–77).

This speaks of a wider tension between socialist women and the Catholic-dominated Labour Party, in which "many issues of importance to women were seen as non-party issues and were therefore left to a free vote by Labour councillors, [which] only served to magnify this major political problem for women in the party". This often negated the benefits of joining the Labour Party in Liverpool for women, since "however effective they might have been within the party organization, their efforts could always be negated by the decisions of the Labour group". The only alternative route to power was by election to the council itself, which proved difficult for most women in the party (Davies 1996, 176). Labour also did worse in areas where "women voters were more prevalent" (Davies 1996, 188).

In Liverpool, the Labour Party became more open to women as the economy moved away from port to factory and public sector unionism, within which women were more prominent. As Davies highlights,

> significant numbers of women workers were involved in many of these industries, and the gender-balance of the trade union movement was permanently altered as the old dock-based sectors declined and the new manufacturing sectors grew. Issues such as Equal Pay now took on a new priority, as the women workers at Ford's showed. (Davies 1999, 18)

We have seen that the prewar Labour Party also suffered from organisational and electoral weaknesses, and a structure which left it open to factionalism and strong — although not necessarily effective — leadership. How this influenced the postwar Labour Party — and, more importantly for this study, Conservative electoral prospects — is explored in Chapter 7.

2.3.3 *The Liverpool Liberal Party*

The third party in Liverpool's body politic was the Liverpool Liberal Party, which emerged from the local Whig party. In contrast to the Liverpool Conservatives, the politicisation of sectarianism and the emergence of Irish nationalism led to the Liverpool Liberals becoming the party of Catholic interests in the city.

The Liverpool Liberals "were generally richer merchants, ship owners, and brokers who had supported the abolition of slavery — a highly unpopular position in slave-trading Liverpool — and who advocated social philanthropy and religious equality" (Dye 2001, 379). As such, their appeal to the working classes of the city was limited, especially after the Liberal Party "supported the Union Government in the American Civil War", which severely impacted Liverpool's trade in cotton (and hence working-class employment). This was seen as "anti-civic" by the Protestant working class, who were already angry about the (Unitarian-dominated) Liberal leadership's support for Roman Catholic rights (Kennedy 2009, 7 fn. 22). These factors all contributed to the party's poor standing in the Protestant working-class community, and this was further compounded by the fact that "the Liberal merchant elite in general neither worked hard at elections nor saw the need to do so" (Waller 1981, 13), and instead worried that electioneering would introduce "a disreputable rabble into the respectable game of politics" (Dye 2001, 379).

Jenkins highlights how, as early as 1844, "the interests of Liverpool's Catholic Irish were represented within the Liberal minority on the Council by the middle class Catholic Club" (Jenkins 2006, 104). The Catholic Club was set up by Richard Sheil, the first Catholic to be elected to Liverpool Town Council, in 1858; he sat as a Liberal. It was intended to be a counterweight to McNeile's Protestant Association and resulted in the extension and solidification of "the Liberal alliance: prosperous middle-class Catholics, Irish and otherwise, were brought together in continuing support of Liberal candidates drawn from Unitarian and progressive ranks within the mercantile elite" (Belchem 1999, 133). The Club "modelled itself after the politically moderate wing of the British Catholic Institute: it sought to defend Catholicism while remaining inoffensive to Protestants", and thus fitted in well with the respectable face of the Liverpool Liberal Party (Dye 2001, 379).

Belchem, however, outlines how the Catholic Club was unable to convince "rich merchants and Liberal councillors" to support home rule, and as a result shifted its focus to electing Irish Nationalist councillors, specifically in the Scotland and Vauxhall wards. This move was successful, since "the Liberal political elite kept distant from the lowly constituents and their crude conviviality", but "Catholic priests and Irish nationalist politicians displayed a willingness to compromise with the street and the pub". This embrace of the "parish and pub-based ethnic infrastructure facilitated an effective challenge to the traditional Liberal alignment" (Belchem 1999, 140).

The election of a Home Rule councillor in 1875 — defeating an incumbent Liberal councillor — and further victories in subsequent local elections shocked the Liberals into an alliance between "respectable Home Rulers and the Liberals, with Irish Nationalists sitting on the Liberal Executive" (Jenkins 2006, 104). This alliance, however, was much weaker than in the past: there was a new desire amongst Irish Nationalists "to eradicate all vestige of patrician Liberal dependence, to provide self-sufficient protection for the Catholic working-class community against the dominant Tory political machine" (Belchem 1999, 141). Further, as the leadership of the local Irish National Party passed to the Liverpool-born second-generation Irish, "it displayed less interest in the fate of Ireland than in the immediate needs of the local Catholic community in housing and employment" (Belchem 1999, 141).

As such, the Liberal Party's Catholic base was squeezed by the Irish Nationalist Party. Evidence of this can be seen in the approach of brothers Austin and Frank Harford — Liverpool-born and educated, successful businessmen and both Irish Nationalist councillors for South Scotland ward (Austin was elected in 1898, Frank in 1899) — who "developed a form of community politics which depended first on a large network of confidants able to produce the goods, and second on the continued estrangement of the Liverpool Irish from other (class-based) political formations". This evolved into 'Nat-Labism', a "cross-class political formation that proved more resonant and enduring than conventional Lib-Labism elsewhere" (Belchem 1999, 142).

It was not just the Irish Nationalists who were focused on low politics — Catholic Irish Liberals also shared this interest. Dye argues that although most Catholic activists "were nominally Whig-Liberals because of the party's tradition of religious toleration, their political work sought primarily to aid Liverpool's large and growing Catholic population, not to advance English party interests" (Dye 2001, 364).

Despite this, by the start of the twentieth century "there remained a connection between Catholicism and Liverpool Liberalism", seen, for example, in the positions taken by Liberal associations in Everton, Kirkdale, and Walton. All three "took an unshakeably pro-Home Rule line. The Walton Liberal Association, for example, affirmed its 'total support for Home Rule'" (Kennedy 2011, 531).

This was helped somewhat by the rise of the temperance movement, which gave the Liberals a new, non-sectarian issue to campaign on. There was a movement within Liverpool which saw the rise of pubs and "illicit drinking houses", and the subsequent crime and social problems, as a consequence of deliberate Conservative policies that favoured the interests of prominent Conservative publicans over public health and safety. This issue allowed the Liberals to break the stranglehold of the Conservative Party in the 1890s (Kennedy 2009, 7–8).

On the national level, during the early years of the twentieth century, Dutton notes how "the Liberals' failure to adopt more working-class men as parliamentary candidates emerges as a fundamental error. Many working men had been driven to Labour not in the quest for socialism but simply to secure representation of their own class interests" (Dutton 2013, 51). We can see evidence of this in Liverpool in the interwar years — after home rule was secured and the need for an explicit Irish Nationalist party diminished, Nat-Labism rapidly evolved into simple Labour support for many Irish Catholics who, as outlined above, were not very socialist in their world-view.

During the interwar years, the Liberals were further undercut by the Irish Nationalists in Catholic areas and by Labour in working-class Protestant areas. Moreover, the national Liberal leadership still saw politics in terms of "major international and domestic issues", rather than local ones, or low politics (Dutton 2013, 124). By 1945 the Liberal Party in Liverpool was irrelevant, at least until the late 1960s.

2.3.4 *Party machines and the impact of campaigning*

There is a long-running debate in psephology regarding the extent to which local campaigning makes a difference to election outcomes. If local campaigning does not make much of a difference, then it does not particularly matter whether the Conservatives were weak on the ground in Liverpool. If, however, campaigns do make a difference, then the health and vibrancy of party machines becomes very important when we seek to explain the party's electoral performance.

The traditional view of the impact of local party campaigns in individual constituencies during general elections was that it was nothing more than a ritual, which had "little success in changing political attitudes" (Kavanagh 1970, 87). Voters in the mass-media age, it was argued, got most of their political news from the national media, namely the press, the radio, and television (Pattie et al. 1994, 470). For many scholars, the futility of local campaigning in the postwar period was demonstrated by the phenomenon of the uniform swing, where swings from Labour to the Conservatives, or vice versa, were replicated across the whole country, often with little local variation. Pattie and Johnston argue that, in the traditional view, "the constituency campaign had become a means for keeping local party activists busy, for giving them a feeling of participation in the party's struggle (or more cynically, to prevent the devil of party discord from finding work for idle hands!)" (Pattie and Johnston 2003a, 305).

The Nuffield series of general election analyses is perhaps the best example of the downplaying of local campaigning (Pattie and Johnston 2003b, 384). For example, in the 1987 general election analysis Butler and Kavanagh argue that "the anachronistic local rites of canvassing and public meetings... are thought not to have any real bearing on results" (Butler and Kavanagh 1988, 211). Similarly, they concluded after the 1992 general election that it was "hard to pinpoint any constituencies where the quality of one side's efforts made a decisive difference", nor could they "locate evidence of great benefits being reaped by the increasingly sophisticated and computerised local campaigning" (Butler and Kavanagh 1992, 245). In addition, despite a growing literature proclaiming the importance of local campaigning — explored below — Butler and Kavanagh came to the same conclusion after analysing the 1997 general election: national politics, specifically the impact of party leaders, "would largely swamp local endeavours" (Butler and Kavanagh 1997, 210).

The Nuffield study was not the only site of opposition to the thesis that local campaigns matter. In analysing the 1997 election, King argued that "all the evidence suggests that the campaign was largely irrelevant" (King 1998, 179), whilst Crewe argued that even if Labour had not bothered to campaign, they "would have still won by a mile. The election was decided long before the campaign by events in the first half of the 1992 parliament" (Crewe in Whiteley and Seyd 2003, 302).

Indeed, the narrative that there is little relationship between local campaigning and constituency vote shares can be traced backed to McKenzie, who, according to Whiteley et al., gave rise to this "conventional wisdom" (Whiteley, Seyd, and Richardson 1994, 244). McKenzie's analysis covered a small sample of constituencies, and found no relationship between the size of the local Labour Party and Labour's vote share (McKenzie 1963, 544). However, upon closer inspection Whiteley et al. found that McKenzie had misinterpreted his own data, and a supposed negative correlation between these two variables was actually positive (Whiteley, Seyd, and Richardson 1994, 244).

Furthermore, since 1992 a new orthodoxy has emerged within the literature on local campaigns (Fieldhouse and Cutts 2009, 368). Various studies have shown, through a variety of methodological approaches, that the level of campaign activity can both boost a party's vote share and suppress rival parties' shares (Fisher, Cutts, and Fieldhouse 2011, 816–17).

Pattie and Johnston outline three key methodological approaches to examining the impact of local campaigns in the British context: firstly, constituency campaign spending as a proxy for campaign effort; secondly, surveys of voters, party members, or campaigners to gauge campaign intensity; thirdly, surveys of party election agents. They argue that all three methods produce evidence of a strong correlation between levels of campaign intensity and electoral outcomes (Pattie and Johnston 2003b, 384).

For example, in examining the Labour campaign in the 1987 general election, Seyd and Whiteley report that the greater the level of activity by a constituency Labour Party and the greater the amount of voter canvassing, the greater the swing to Labour between 1983 and 1987. They argue that if every constituency Labour Party had "recruited an additional 100 members prior to the 1987 election, and each of these increased the activism score by an average of 8.5 points", the party would have increased their vote share by five percentage points (Seyd and Whiteley 1992, 197–98). Similarly, Pattie et al. show campaign spending returns are a useful proxy for campaign activity, and that "an effective and energetic local campaign can make the difference between winning and losing. Political parties ignore the work of their local members at their electoral peril" (Pattie et al. 1994, 479). Whiteley et al. conclude, based on their analysis of the 1987 election, that "[t]he conventional wisdom that general elections in Britain are dominated by the national campaigns to the exclusion of any local influences is not supported" (Whiteley, Seyd, and Richardson 1994, 250).

For Johnston and Pattie, the 1992 general election provides a good example of what happens when parties get it wrong: they find that "the Labour Party's relatively low spending in Conservative-held seats may have substantially disadvantaged its electoral prospects" (Johnston and Pattie 1995, 270). They also find differential effects for incumbent and challenger parties: "incumbent-party campaigning is less effective than that by challenger parties", whilst spending money advertising candidates, in addition to expected levels of general activism, results in a higher party vote share (Johnston and Pattie 1998, 685).

Even in the 1997 general election, in which even the national campaign was seen to have had little effect on the outcome, local campaigns are found to have had a strong effect. Whiteley and Seyd's statistical analysis finds that had Labour done no campaigning at all, they would have ended up with 72 fewer seats than they actually won, whilst if they had campaigned at twice the intensity than they actually did they would have won 69 more seats. Even starker are the results for the Liberal Democrats: whilst doubling their campaign activity was projected to net them 23 more seats than the 46 they actually won, not campaigning at all would have resulted in winning just 3 seats. Whiteley and Seyd conclude that "[t]hese figures suggest that campaign effects are really quite strong" (Whiteley and Seyd 2003, 320).

Pattie and Johnston find a similar pattern: those who received a visit from Labour on the doorstep during the 1997 general election campaign were 1.6 times more likely to vote for the party than those who did not, whilst those who were door-stepped by the Liberal Democrats were 1.7 times less likely to vote for Labour. This effect, however, does not translate to telephone canvassing, which did not have a statistically significant impact on voter behaviour (Pattie and Johnston 2003a, 315).

A similar effect is identified for the 2001 general election, which is summarised by Pattie and Johnston as "[t]he more active a party is in campaigning in a seat at election time, the more likely is it that an individual living there will vote for that party in the election" (Pattie and Johnston 2003b, 412). Furthermore, they show that parties are strategic in where they campaign, insofar as they tend to campaign more actively in marginal seats than safe or unwinnable seats, and that individuals are swayed by constituency votes. Whether it is through genuine conversion, or through convincing voters of the merits of tactically voting for a particular party, they find that "the more active a party was in a seat, the more likely it was to win over new voters from electors living there who had not previously intended supporting the party" (Pattie and Johnston 2003b, 412).

It is also clear that, in 2001, the more the Conservatives and Liberal Democrats campaigned in a constituency, the more likely people were to vote for them, and the less likely to vote Labour. The effects of Labour campaigning, however, did not serve to dampen Conservative support (Denver, Hands, and MacAllister 2004, 302). This is partly because Labour were already expected to win in 2001, and "after 1997 had disappointed some of the party's core supporters. Labour campaigners may, therefore, have found it more difficult to galvanize voters through local campaigning" (Denver, Hands, and Fisher 2002, 91–92). As such, whilst the literature shows that local campaigning can be important in determining electoral outcomes, the national context is still clearly a mediating factor.

These factors all played a role in the 2005 general election too, with Fieldhouse and Cutts finding that all parties were increasingly rational and strategic in where they campaigned, and that each party's campaign effort "had the effect of suppressing the performance of opposing parties", apart from Labour's failure to hurt the Liberal Democrats' performance (Fieldhouse and Cutts 2009, 388). In the 2010 general election, a similar pattern was identified: "[f]or each party, it is apparent that more intense constituency campaigning did indeed appear to yield electoral payoffs, though the impact varies" (Fisher, Cutts, and Fieldhouse 2011, 822). The study by Johnston et al. found that "[l]ocal campaigning is a carefully crafted activity and it delivers. People sympathetic to a party's political programme and who get messages from it just before they vote are more likely to give it their support than those who are not contacted" (Johnston et al. 2012, 328–29).

However, as the three major (national) parties all focus on marginal seats — especially those where they are in first or second position — Pattie and Johnston warn that "constituency campaigning may produce a sort of stand-off between the parties locally, where each party's efforts are to a large extent neutralised by its rivals' counterattacks" (Pattie and Johnston 2010, 502). Ironically, as each party gets better at constituency campaigning, the actual effect of that campaigning might diminish. This, however, is mediated by a party's national popularity. For example, Fisher et al. find that "electoral context can condition the effectiveness of campaigns — if a party is particularly unpopular, its campaigns are less likely to be effective", and this was the case with the Liberal Democrats in 2015. Despite this, however, the Liberal Democrats' defensive local campaigns meant that they held on to more seats than otherwise would have been the case (Fisher et al. 2018, 284).

Accordingly, it is necessary to recognise that local campaigns have become increasingly important. Whitley and Seyd argue that this has been facilitated by the decline of partisan attachment among voters, while the variability in party support across the country — in contrast to the idea of uniform swing — means that voters are now more likely to be convinced to support a different party by a local campaign (Whiteley and Seyd 2003, 306). Furthermore, as voters make their mind up about who to support closer to the point of casting their vote, there is greater scope for influence (Fisher, Cutts, and Fieldhouse 2011, 816).

To what extent is this argument relevant to postwar Liverpool, when nationally it is argued that the British electorate had a high level of partisan alignment? As Pattie and Johnston maintain, constituency campaigns serve two purposes: to "mobilise committed supporters, and to win over floating voters" (Pattie and Johnston 2003b, 383). As such, even if Liverpudlian voters were highly loyal to their parties, local campaigning could still be important as a mechanism to mobilise voters.

2.4 Rules of the electoral game

As has been hinted at above, electoral rules and institutions have long played a role in Liverpool's political history. Before 1953, Liverpool's ward boundaries had last been redistributed in 1895, and research by Davies suggests that Labour's advance in municipal politics was hampered by these out-of-date ward boundaries. As a result, although the Conservatives dominated the council chamber until the early 1950s they were being outpolled by Labour as early as 1926. Indeed, in

> the ten years between 1926 and 1935, despite a massive setback in 1930 and 1931, Labour actually gained more votes than the Conservatives on seven occasions... The discrepancy between seats held and votes won certainly suggests that there were elements of the electoral system which disadvantaged the Labour Party. (Davies 1996, 89)

Further, Labour's seat share was always worse than its electoral support warranted, whereas the reverse was true for the Conservatives. Davies finds that minor parties were also overrepresented in the 1930s (Davies 1996, 93–94).

This bias towards the Conservatives was extended by the expansion of the city. In 1938 Garston and Croxteth "had six seats between them on the council, and a combined electorate of 28,956" whilst

> Fazakerley, Allerton, Childwall and the two Woolton wards, all strongly Tory, had thirteen seats, and a combined electorate of 31,650. The new Tory voters of the suburbs had been allocated almost exactly twice as many seats per head as the new Labour voters. (Davies 1996, 100)

Furthermore, the prewar slum clearance programme saw dwellings built outside the city boundary. In 1939 4,082 houses were built outside Liverpool, roughly 12 per cent of the total built that year, housing about 8,000 working-class voters and roughly equivalent to "one ward with three councillors and an alderman on the council" (Davies 1996, 100). It is not hard to see how Labour was systematically restricted in assuming its full potential in municipal politics by the structural effects of ward boundaries. Even the small advantage gained in inheriting Nationalist wards, which were declining in population, "did not compensate for under-representation in the rest of the city" (Davies 1996, 102).

The effect of the ward boundaries can be seen following redistribution in 1953: despite polling 5,000 fewer votes than the Conservatives,[1] Labour won a majority of seats — 65, to the Conservatives' 53 and the Protestant Party's 2 — but the Conservatives maintained control through aldermen. However, following the aldermanic election in 1955 Labour took control of the council for the first time. Davies argues that Labour was constantly underrepresented in terms of aldermen in the interwar years, owing to "conscious manipulation" by the Conservatives in seeking the overrepresentation of smaller parties (Davies 1996, 110). However, nationally, after 1945 Labour's previous indifference towards the aldermanic system "turned to blatant abuse", so much so that the Conservatives now wanted to abolish the system (Davies 1996, 157).

There is evidence that the Conservatives in the postwar years were less opportunistic than might be suggested by the above. Minutes from the Liverpool Constitutional Association show that, in 1961 when the Conservatives had a majority of councillors and were deciding on how to

1 This figure is adjusted to take into account that each ward had multiple vacancies, by using the figures for the highest-ranked candidate for each party in each ward.

divide aldermanic seats between the parties, there was a general agreement that Labour should be given some seats. The minutes report a Mr Lewis stating "there should be no gang warfare" whilst Mr Macdonald Steward, later leader of the Liverpool Conservatives, "would like to do something to show that we were Conservatives and that even in politics decency still mattered". The motion to give two seats to Labour was passed, by 43 votes to 15 (Liverpool Conservative Association 1964).

Finally, the inclusion of business voters distorted the franchise, especially when contrasting their inclusion with the "exclusion of council tenants living outside the city boundaries [which] shows the bias inherent in the system" (Davies 1996, 126). Plural voting survived until 1969 in local elections, despite being removed from the parliamentary franchise in 1948. The small number of plural voters could have a significant — and pro-Tory — effect on outcomes, especially in some of the very small city-centre wards. During this period, wards were distributed based on both population and rateable value, meaning that the city centre was "inevitably over-represented" (Davies 1996, 126). Baxter gives an example of this from 1950, contrasting Croxteth and West Derby, which had "33,509 and 31,444 electors respectively, while the two smallest wards, Castle Street and Exchange had 860 and 1,575 electors respectively — only 68 of Castle Street's electors lived in Liverpool" (Baxter 1969, 109).

As such, Davies claims that on a local level "[t]he relative weakness of the Labour Party in Liverpool compared to other parts of the country were almost certainly exaggerated by the electoral system" (Davies 1996, 132). However, these disadvantages were reduced on a parliamentary level, owing to differences in the process of boundary revision, the franchise, changes in divisional demographics, and the aldermanic system not applying (Davies 1996, 147). This provides a clear explanation of why Labour were much more successful on a national level than on a local level, but it does not detract from the central question of this study — after all, both Labour and the Conservatives still enjoyed periods of large vote shares in postwar Liverpool, regardless of how these were translated into seats.

Furthermore, Davies makes clear that institutional factors were not the only important consideration when assessing Labour's electoral weaknesses. Firstly, its inability to recognise the problem was itself a major problem:

> the Labour Party seems hardly to have appreciated the contribution that the distortions of the electoral system may have made to its poor performance. Religious sectarianism was always the first excuse that

> Labour leaders turned to when faced with electoral disappointment, to the extent that they seemed blinded to any other possible reason. (Davies 1996, 158)

Secondly, "Labour never challenged the validity of the aldermanic system itself... In fact, the Labour group on the council seemed far more concerned about selection procedures for the purely honorary position of Lord Mayor" (Davies 1996, 159). For this reason, Lane's claim that Conservative success was a result of "Tory gerrymandering of ward and constituency boundaries" is an exaggeration (Lane 1997, 110). There was no active attempt by the Conservatives to change ward boundaries, rather a reluctance to meddle with a situation which provided them with an electoral benefit.

Ultimately, Davies claims that Labour "failed to confront the problems of the local electoral system, and at times was compliant with them". However, and more importantly, the party

> was poorly organized, structurally weak, and frequently divided internally by religion, occupation, gender, and political ideology... The party was unimaginative in its attempts to meet the political needs and demands of important sections of the local working class... However unfavourable the historical circumstances were for the Liverpool Labour Party, plainly it failed to cope with them adequately in this period. Structure and agency, then, were both intertwined in explaining the development of Liverpool Labour. (Davies 1996, 234–35)

Thus we can see that in the prewar period the impact of ward boundaries on electoral outcomes was significant, even if it was not the only important factor. However the role of the electoral system on postwar Conservative decline so far has not been examined in the literature and is clearly an avenue for research. This will be examined in Chapter 4.

2.5 Gap in the knowledge: It isn't (just) religion/Thatcher

As this chapter has shown, the scholarly work on the postwar Liverpool Conservative Party is limited and sketchy, especially in comparison to the pre- or interwar periods. Most often, information regarding the Liverpool Conservatives must be gleaned from studies focusing on other aspects of Liverpool's politics, or studies which focus on the Conservative Party more broadly. Although this makes the task of studying Conservative decline in Liverpool more difficult, there is ample scope to apply concepts and analytical frameworks from fields beyond those used in the literature on Liverpool. The remainder of this chapter will outline the key concepts and theories that will be used to explain Conservative decline in Liverpool.

As outlined at the conclusion of Chapter 1, this book argues that the concepts of socialisation, path dependency, and critical junctures are vital in explaining Conservative success and decline in Liverpool. The relationship between these concepts and the case of the Conservatives is explored in detail in Chapter 7, but essentially the argument is that the historic cause of Protestantism gained the Conservatives support originally, and this support was perpetuated by socialisation, which meant that new generations of voters were Conservatives long after Protestantism ceased to be salient. This followed a path-dependent process, until the critical juncture of the 1973 local election.

Path dependency and socialisation are key concepts in understanding the causes of Conservative decline in Liverpool, and whilst they are often thought of in isolation, they are interrelated phenomena. Path dependency can be understood as "social processes that exhibit positive feedback and thus generate branching patterns of historical development", which, once established, become self-perpetuating so that an increasingly larger shock is required to change course (Pierson 2004, 21). Pierson terms this "inertia", and explains "[o]nce such a process has been established, positive feedback will generally lead to a single equilibrium. This equilibrium will in turn be resistant to change" (Pierson 2004, 44).

Socialisation, on the other hand, is the process whereby an individual's beliefs, outlooks, and other related values are shaped by the environment in which they find themselves. There is considerable evidence to suggest that the most important period of socialisation — where an individual is most receptive to environmental cues — is during their formative years (D. Green, Palmquist, and Schickler 2002, 107–8; Hooghe 2004, 334). This idea is prominent in the literature on voting patterns in Britain. Butler and Stokes found that "[c]hildren of parents who were united in their party preference were overwhelmingly likely to have absorbed the preference at the beginning of their political experience" (Butler and Stokes 1974, 51). Furthermore, Ball argues that "people form their views shortly before or during their young adult years, between the ages of around fifteen and twenty-five, and thereafter do not greatly vary their fundamentals" (Ball 2013, 120). Thus, we can establish a relationship between the social context in which an individual is brought up and their propensity to vote in a certain way.

There is great analytical value in understanding the phenomenon of socialisation within a path-dependency framework. Returning to Pierson, we see that path-dependency arguments

> rest on what Stinchcombe has termed a conception of 'historical causes'... some initial event or process generates a particular outcome, which is then reproduced through time even though the original generating event or process does not recur. (Pierson 2004, 45)

This concept of historical causes is essential for understanding Conservative success in Liverpool (the first stage in the tripartite historical framework used in this book) since it explains, to some extent, why such a heavily working-class city resisted Labour and provided fertile ground for the Conservatives. In Liverpool this historical cause is religion, or more specifically for the Conservatives, Protestantism. This set the broad framework for electoral politics in Liverpool, until the 1973 local election became a critical juncture which changed the narrative of the city's local politics and eroded the importance of the historical cause of Protestantism, and led to the period of Conservative decline in Liverpool. Hogan describes critical junctures as "an event, prior to which a range of possibilities must exist, but after which these possibilities will have mostly vanished" (Hogan 2006, 664). After the 1973 local election, as shown in Chapter 7, the possibility of the Conservatives being the main opposition to Labour had mostly vanished, especially in the context of the first-past-the-post electoral system.

This leads to the final part of the tripartite framework: irrelevance. Chapter 8 draws on the social psychology literature around identity formation and self-value to argue that the Scouse identity was transformed in the 1980s to become inherently anti-Thatcher and anti-Conservative, primarily as a response to the confrontation between Liverpool's Militant-led Labour Council and the Thatcher government, within the broader context of the city's economic, societal, and reputational decline.

The concept of identity is hard to define. For Hogg and Abrams, identity is simply "people's concepts of who they are, of what sort of people they are, and how they relate to others" (Hogg and Abrams 1988, 2). Fearon goes further in defining it, arguing that in fact there are two different understandings embedded in the concept of identity: "social" and "personal". Social identity refers to "a social category, a set of persons marked by a label and distinguished by rules deciding membership and (alleged) characteristic features or attributes", whilst a personal identity "is some distinguishing characteristic (or characteristics) that a person takes a special pride in or views as socially consequential but more-or-less unchangeable" (Fearon 1999, 2). It is important to note that these are 'sticky', or slow to change; "[n]o one can unilaterally change the content or rules of membership for a social category; this can only be accomplished through collective action that recoordinates beliefs and expectations" (Fearon 1999, 20).

Clearly, there is no necessary link between the social and personal conceptualisations of identity, but in the case of a Scouse identity, the two elements are related. Indeed, it is difficult to hold a Scouse 'personal' identity without meeting (some of) the membership rules required to have it as a 'social' identity (at least, to some extent). Further, it is personal identity that Fearon argues is important in understanding how just how identity influences action — for example, voting. He defines personal identity as

> a set of attributes, beliefs, desires, or principles of action that a person thinks distinguish her in socially relevant ways and that (a) the person takes a special pride in; (b) the person takes no special pride in, but which so orient her behavior that she would be at a loss about how to act and what to do without them; or (c) the person feels she could not change even if she wanted to.

With regard to point (a), it is argued that "identity can typically be glossed as the aspects or attributes of a person that form the basis for his or her dignity or self-respect. Used in this sense, 'identity' has become a partial and indirect substitute for 'dignity,' 'honor,' and 'pride'" (Fearon 1999, 11).

As such, an understanding of identity as the basis of an individual's dignity or self-respect allows us to understand more clearly just how it can affect an individual's behaviour. Ultimately, decisions to act in a certain way are based on social norms — that is, informal understandings which are "(a) shared by other people and (b) partly sustained by their approval or disapproval" (Elster 1989, 99–100).

These norms, and their applicability or validity, are themselves inherently shaped by identities. For Fearon, an explanation of actions based on social identity essentially "amounts to saying that the person was following a norm associated with the category", in the general form of "[m]embers of category X are supposed to do (or ought to do) Y in situations A, B, C" (Fearon 1999, 27).

With regard to a personal identity, there is also a strong drive to act following the norms bestowed by one's social identity, namely what Fearon terms 'internalisation':

> One might believe that following the norm is the right thing to do, whether because of early socialization or one's independent judgement and experience. Relatedly, one might want to follow the norm because one would think badly of oneself otherwise — failing to follow the norm would undermine one's pride, dignity, or self-respect. (Fearon 1999, 28)

Hence, we can see why, theoretically, individuals follow certain norms if they think that either the rules of their social identity group disallow alternatives (for example, the notion that 'real' Scousers don't vote Tory) or that not doing so would reduce feelings of their own self-worth (e.g. feeling as though they were betraying their city).

Identities, however, are not fixed. They are socially constructed, and hence changeable. The concept of social identity theory allows us to apply a conceptual framework to help us better understand the drivers of change in Scouse identity, and how this plays a role in Conservative irrelevance in Liverpool.

2.5.1 *Social identity theory*

Social identity theory was first articulated by Tajfel and Turner as an attempt to understand just how, and in what ways, perceived membership of a social group influences one's behaviour. For the purposes of this analysis, a group is defined as

> a collection of individuals who perceive themselves to be members of the same social category, share some emotional involvement in this common definition of themselves, and achieve some degree of social consensus about the evaluation of their group and of their membership of it. (Tajfel and Turner 1979, 40)

Intergroup behaviour is essentially "any behaviour displayed by one or more actors toward one or more others that is based on the actors' identification of themselves and the others as belonging to different social categories" (Tajfel and Turner 1979, 40). The case of a Scouse identity meets both criteria. At the root of social identity theory is the belief that "identification is a motivational need for some positive distinctiveness, which is believed to be satisfied through social comparisons to heighten differences between groups" (Greene 1999, 394). Thus, there must be some positive aspect of a social identity, *vis-à-vis* other social groups.

Tajfel and Turner's framework is based on three broad assumptions:

1. Individuals strive to maintain or enhance their self-esteem and they strive for a positive self-concept.
2. Social groups, and the membership of them, are associated with positive or negative value connotations. Hence, a social identity may be positive or negative according to the evaluations of those groups that contribute to an individual's social identity.
3. The evaluation of one's own group is determined with reference to specific other groups through social comparisons in terms of value-laden attributes and characteristics. Positive comparisons between in-group and out-group produce high prestige; negative comparisons between in-group and out-group result in low prestige. (Tajfel and Turner 1979, 40)

As a result of these assumptions, Tajfel and Turner derive three theoretical principles. Firstly, individuals aim to "achieve or to maintain positive social identity". Secondly, positive social identity is "based to a large extent on favourable comparisons that can be made between the in-group and some relevant out-groups". Thirdly, when a "social identity is unsatisfactory, individuals will strive either to leave their existing group and join some more positively distinct group and/or to make their existing group more positively distinct" (Tajfel and Turner 1979, 40).

In the case of a group holding a threatened or negative social identity, there are three potential routes for change. The first is termed "individual mobility", and involves an individual, rather than the whole group, aiming to move from a lower to a higher status group. Tajfel and Turner specify that this is a "personal, not a group, solution". The second route is social creativity — which, it is argued in Chapter 8, the Scouse identity followed — and involves "redefining or altering the elements of the comparative situation" — essentially changing the basis of the comparison. The third method is social competition, which involves direct competition with the outgroup (Tajfel and Turner 1979, 43–44).

This theory suggests that it is clear that group identity can indeed shape behaviour, including voting behaviour, and that these group identities are not fixed — in fact, there are various routes available for individuals and groups to change their identity. This presents a promising avenue for understanding Conservative irrelevance, which has continued until this day.

2.5.2 *Lessons from Scotland*

Scotland is a good starting point for an analysis of the relationship between identity and Conservative voting, as it shared the key elements of religious sectarianism and Protestant-led Conservative support. As will be shown below, Conservative decline in Scotland can be attributed to an anti-Conservative and anti-Thatcherite element within a new Scottish identity that was not present during earlier periods of Conservative success.

Seawright and Curtice argue that

> [i]f devolution and independence are wrapped in the thistle and the saltire, unionism, it is argued, was associated with equally powerful symbols of Scottish culture, the Union Jack, militarism and the British empire… These were of course symbols that appealed to Scotland's indigenous Protestant community rather than its immigrant Catholic population. It provided the Conservatives with a social base in the Protestant working class which, with the exception of Merseyside, was unavailable in England. (Seawright and Curtice 1995, 324–25)

However, in examining the work of Kellas, Dyer outlines how the decline of the 'Orange factor' — namely, Protestantism — "can only offer a partial explanation" of Conservative decline, because not all areas in Scotland had a Protestant/Orange divide (Dyer 2001, 30). Whilst those areas that did have the divide saw the steepest decline in Conservative strength, "the central feature is a substantial Tory retreat nationwide" and "a general collapse of working-class Conservatism" (Dyer 2001, 36).

Although Kendrick and McCrone recognise that Conservative support for devolution and pro-Scottish rhetoric did help them electorally, they argue it is "unlikely that this factor alone was sufficient to explain the Conservatives' consistently good performance in Scotland in comparison with England in the elections of 1945, 1950, 1951 and 1955" (Kendrick and McCrone 1989, 594–95). Instead, it was the Conservative appeal to the Protestant working class that delivered their better-than-expected performances in Scotland, based on "a complex of interrelated elements such as Protestantism, Orangeism and Unionism under the canopy of a strong sense of British national and imperial identity" (Kendrick and McCrone 1989, 595). Similarly, Kidd argues that whilst secularisation was important for realigning the basis of voter choice from religion to economics/class, other factors were also important, namely that "with the retreat from Empire, common standards of welfare, rather than any shared pride in the projection of power, provided the most compelling basis for British unity, a social narrative that was much easier for Labour to exploit" (Kidd 2012, 62).

These studies point to a common strand: whilst religion was an important factor in delivering the Conservative vote, it was tied up in the concept of identity. Kendrick and McCrone argue that the Conservatives performed more strongly than might have been expected in the Scottish socio-economic context by "centring on religion and a particular form of Scottish identity", and that "the enfeebling of this bloc and the weakening of its links to Conservatism underlay Conservative electoral decline in Scotland" (Kendrick and McCrone 1989, 596). As is explored below, the Conservatives in Scotland became perceived as an "English" party, and thus can be seen as the 'other' to the Scottish identity (Seawright and Curtice 1995, 333–34; Curtice 2012, 120). This leads Seawright and Curtice to the conclusion that

> Unionism then had two sources of strength. One was an affinity with Protestantism and our evidence suggests that there is no sign that this has disappeared. The other was an ability to appeal to powerful symbols in Scots culture which gave the party a Scottish identity irrespective of its stance on devolution. This is the crucial ingredient the party has lost. (Seawright and Curtice 1995, 334–35)

For Finlay, the Conservatives' emphasis on the Empire appealed to the "imperially minded" Scots, but it was their "inability to adapt pragmatically to the changing socio-economic circumstances of the 1960s that undermined traditional Tory notions of patriotism and paternalism", and they "fumbled around in reaction to the growth of Scottish Nationalism" (Finlay 2012, 39). The ability to appeal to Scottish identity is of vital importance in a country where, in 1992, when asked to select 'something that is very important to you when you think of yourself', 'being Scottish' was mentioned almost as frequently as being a parent, and "45 per cent of respondents referenced their 'Scottishness'; just 11 per cent their 'Britishness'" (Massie 2012, 139). Curtice reaffirms the argument that an inability to appeal to Scottish culture and identity is the reason for the lack of Conservative success in Scotland, rather than ideology or opposition to devolution (Curtice 2012, 118).

Mitchell and Bennie also argue that, in Scotland, anti-Conservatism is linked to Scottishness and a Scottish identity (Mitchell and Bennie 1995, 102). Curtice argues that the Conservatives have "an image that is at odds with the predominant sense of Scottish identity" (Curtice 2012, 124) whilst Massie finds that "[t]he Tories remain a toxic brand in Scotland" and, similarly to Liverpool, "[t]here has been no active 'decontamination' project, merely the hope that the Conservatives' Scottish radioactivity will decay naturally. Alas, it seems to have a very long half-life" (Massie 2012, 138).

Hassan comes to a similar conclusion, arguing that "as the 1980s wound on, [Scotland] began to see Toryism and the Thatcher government as distinctly 'anti-Scottish'" (Hassan 2012, 78). He maps the consequences of this, and his findings are redolent of the Liverpool experience: "Scottish politics have become dominated by a narrow spectrum of political debate around a social democratic politics centred on Labour versus the SNP which has not been vibrant, pluralist or challenging" and that a process of "delegitimising, dehumanising and caricaturing the Scottish Tories" has resulted in the weakening in "the breath and health of our politics" (Hassan 2012, 86). Ultimately, Hassan claims that "[t]he false collective memory syndrome of Thatcherism allowed part of Scotland to place the blame for our problems on one factor, to paint a black-and-white past (and, thus, present and future) and luxuriate in the power of victimhood" (Hassan 2012, 87). It is hard to not see parallels with Liverpool. Interestingly, the referendum on Scottish independence and the response of the Scottish National Party to the referendum on membership of the European Union gave the Scottish Conservatives a base upon which to bounce back electorally, something which has not been the case in Liverpool.

Wyn Jones et al. have come to a similar conclusion for the case of Wales, where "[a]nti-Conservatism, it seems, has become part of the constellation of Welsh national identity" as a result of the Conservatives being seen as "a fundamentally 'English' party" (Wyn Jones, Scully, and Trystan 2002, 243). Randall argues that this problem is also applicable to northern England, highlighting a 2007 Populus poll in which

> 37 per cent of Northern respondents felt the party 'understands and speaks for people in my part of the country as much as any other part of Britain'. Some 64 per cent agreed the party 'is more the voice of people in the SOUTH of England than of the whole country', while 50 per cent considered the party 'to have a patronising attitude to people in the North of England'. (Randall 2009, 187–88)

Furthermore, Randall argues that that the party lacks "authentic Northern voices, suffers from a poor image in the North, a relatively weak organisational base and a shortage of policy proposals that speak directly to Northern voters", retarding attempts by the Conservatives to address these problems or to craft a new identity for the party (Randall 2009, 192).

This brief examination of the literature on identity and Conservative decline in Scotland highlights that the religious argument has been overplayed. Protestantism was just one aspect of the Conservative appeal to voters, but the most important was to appear compatible with a broader Scottish identity. The fact that the Conservatives lost the ability to tap into that identity can be ascribed as the reason for their decline. This suggests that the idea of a Scouse identity is indeed a worthwhile path down which to travel to understand Conservative irrelevance in Liverpool.

The next chapter will explore the first potential explanation of Conservative decline in Liverpool: the role of party organisation on electoral success.

3 The Liverpool Conservative Party machine

Electoral success, at any level, requires winning a sufficient number of votes to garner a sufficient number of seats. As already outlined, the Liverpool Conservative Party machine was traditionally very good at winning an impressive segment of the popular vote across the city. This chapter will explore the extent to which this remained the case after the Second World War.

As shown in Chapter 2, local campaigning can make a difference to election results and hence a strong local party organisation can be an effective tool for winning elections. In the interwar years, organisations like the LWCA provided the lifeblood of the Liverpool Conservative Party, both through providing members and also by encouraging those members to campaign for local Conservative candidates (Day 2008, 274–75). By 1945 the link between the LWCA and the Conservative Party had declined in importance, and had "all but disappeared by 1968" (Davies 1999, 21). Nevertheless, the example of the LWCA — and its beneficial impact on the Liverpool Conservative Association — shows the importance of a strong local organisation.

However, before we move to an analysis of the health of the Liverpool Conservative Party machine it is important to consider how the health of a local party influences its electoral success.

Firstly, the key personnel in the local party matter for electoral success, insofar as they represent the local face of the party in the city, and also have responsibility for planning and executing campaigns, and maintaining a healthy organisation. As Ball notes, local leadership was vital for organisational success, and "in districts where such leadership did not exist or held back from involvement, it was an uphill struggle to maintain an effective organization" (Ball 2013, 150). In the case of Liverpool there is certainly evidence that the key personnel in the local association were not always positive or effective leaders.

Secondly, the organisational structure of the local party itself is an important influence on electoral success, to the extent that it is able to encourage members to join, to campaign, or to donate to the party — for example, in an area with a large number of working-class voters a Conservative Trade Unionist branch might be an effective way to encourage more members and increase campaign activity. Similarly, once recruited, a vibrant organisation offering members key social or political benefits would be more likely to keep those members enrolled — and active — than a poorly organised local party branch. The quality of local party organisation varied both across Liverpool and throughout the period of examination.

Thirdly, the financial health of the local party organisation can also play a role in electoral success. Although partly a function of party membership (and the wealth of those members), a financially healthy party can spend more money on campaign material or members of staff, which can boost the professionalism and effectiveness of campaigns. The more effective a campaign, the more votes we would expect a party to get.

Thus the party organisation, whether conceptualised in terms of key personalities, the structure of the organisation itself, or its financial position, all have clear theoretical links to the phenomenon under examination here: the electoral success of the Liverpool Conservative Party.

If we could attribute Conservative decline in Liverpool to organisation we would expect to see a strong Liverpool Conservative organisation in the early period of analysis, from 1945 to 1970, which would become increasingly weak through the 1970s and onwards. The material for the bulk of this analysis will come from the Conservative Party Archive, especially correspondence relating to the Liverpool constituencies. However, owing to the limited archival material available, we are only able to examine the period up to 1968. This is sufficient to show that the Liverpool Conservative Party was rarely a model of organisational efficiency, and that any explanation that attributes Conservative decline to organisational weakness has to account for the fact that the party was electorally successful in periods when its organisation was weak. In short, the archival research in this chapter undermines the case for a causal link between party organisation and electoral results.

Instead, what is presented is an argument that the Conservatives in Liverpool did well despite substantial organisational weaknesses. These weaknesses include personal rivalries and petty vendettas from the top of the local party downwards (in some cases leading to threats of violence against central party staff), poor organisational practice, underdeveloped sections of the party machinery (especially the Women's and Trade Union wings), poor financial health, and consistent strategic errors in campaigning.

A good starting point for this analysis is 1948, when the local party was gearing up for the 1950 election. The state of the party organisation was laid out by Stephen Pierssené, the general director of Conservative Central Office (CCO) from October 1945 to August 1957, in a letter to Mr Watson, another member of staff at the CCO. He argued that the Liverpool Conservative organisation faced six key issues, which they — especially Alderman Shennan, the leader of the party at the time — would not agree to fix without financial support. These were:

(a) the absence of mass membership,

(b) ineffective organisation at Divisional level,

(c) tendency to concentrate too much power at the centre,

(d) inadequate income, and the absence of properly organised money-raising activities,

(e) lack of qualified agents, organisers and missioners, and[1]

(f) The archaic rules. (CPA 1948b)

However, despite these significant weaknesses in the Association's structure, the party was still able to do well. David Maxwell Fyfe, the then MP for Liverpool West Derby, credited the chief agent, Mr Mayhew, with the fact the Conservatives won five of their six target seats (and came close in the sixth). The results in Liverpool were seen to be substantially better than those for any other large borough in the North (CPA 1950).

This neatly sums up the paradox of the organisational aspect of the Liverpool Conservatives: organisationally, they faced a range of problems, just one of which could have been sufficient to torpedo electoral efforts, but despite this they still managed strong performances measured by share of votes and, usually, seats.

1 Missioners were paid party staff, who were responsible for enrolling "more members... producing an accurate canvass, picking up voter concerns, and distributing literature, especially in the marginal seats" (Bale 2012, 19).

3.1 Personalities

Liverpool has a long history of boss politics which originated from time of Alderman Salvidge's leadership. This strong leadership model continued within the Liverpool Conservative Party as well as within Liverpool's politics more generally.

The first issue of personality relates to a lack of professionalism within the party. There was lack of trust between key members of the Association and CCO — not unique to Liverpool by any means — an internal memorandum noted that "it was very necessary to have a witness present from our side as otherwise the Liverpool people might well deny that they had agreed to any particular conditions that they afterwards found unpalatable" (CPA 1948c).

Similarly, the Association had a habit of keeping Central Office out of the loop on key decisions, such as adopting candidates. Whether this was a purposeful snub by the Liverpool Association or incompetence is not clear, but there are numerous complaints of this occurring. Brigadier James Rawcliffe, the CCO agent for the north-west area, claims that although Mayhew "in many ways is quite helpful and co-operative... the statement that he has kept this office closely informed about candidates is quite untrue so far as spontaneous action on his part is concerned" (CPA 1949a). Further, there were complaints that Central Office was left to find out about candidate adoption via the press, rather than via the Association (CPA 1949b).

These problems of personality clashes persisted during the Liverpool West Derby by-election in November 1954. In a letter from Conservative MP Iain Macleod, the then minister of health, to Lord Woolton, Party chairman, the former complained about the treatment he received on a visit to the city for the by-election campaign. The root of his complaint was that he had been "snubbed"; neither the Liverpool nor the West Derby agents came to meet him and the constituency chairman only met him by accident. Macleod — by no means a stuffed-shirt — then went on to complain that "[h]e enquired what my name was and, on being told that it was Macleod, asked whether I was a Member of Parliament". Macleod claimed that "I have never met with anything approaching the discourtesy that I did last night". Overall, he believed that the focus of the Association was on May's council election, rather than the by-election. This perhaps reflects the fact that at this point the Liverpool Association was still organised by ward parties, rather than constituency parties as was the norm elsewhere in England (CPA 1954c).

In response, the general director claimed that "Liverpool has always been isolationist and difficult to deal with", whilst the *Daily Telegraph* noted that

> [e]ver since the days of the late Sir Archibald Salvidge the leaders of the Conservative party in Liverpool have shown hostility towards any intrusion into their affairs by Central Office. The local association in West Derby, I hear, even refused to allow the Central Office to see the candidate's election address until after it had been printed. (CPA 1954b)

This claim is supported by the party's by-election report, prepared by Mr A.N. Banks, the north-west area agent at this time; under the title 'Initial Difficulties' the report claims that "[a]t the outset there was some resistance on the part of the City of Liverpool Office to the Central Office Agent and his staff taking part in the By-Election Campaign" with little consultation "about publicity plans, the preparation of the introductory leaflet or the election address". Despite these differences though, Banks was able to gain control and direct the campaign. He finished his report by claiming that "[i]n spite of initial difficulties" he ended up with "a united, happy and hardworking team at the Central Committee Rooms" (CPA 1954a).

Thus, we can see that for the first decade in the post-war period, personalities could still be a hindrance to the success of the Liverpool Conservative Association, especially as a result of a poor working relationship with Central Office. However, according to Banks, the replacement of Alderman Shennan by Ernest Stacey marked "the end of an epoch as far as the Liverpool organisation is concerned and that we may be able to look forward to Liverpool conforming more closely with the general pattern". Similarly, the replacement of Mayhew with his deputy, a Mr W.G. Hanlon, as chief agent in Liverpool was met with relief by Banks, who wrote "I have more confidence in him than I had in his predecessor" (CPA 1956a, 1956b).

It would be tempting to look upon this era as a new start in Liverpool–Central Office relations, but this does not seem to have been the case. In a 1956 confidential report on the City of Liverpool Constitutional Association, which included an analysis of Stacey's character, Banks wrote that Stacey

> is keenly interested in the organisation, he demands efficiency and can get things done. He is not a self seeker and although he is highly critical he has the interests of the Party at heart. He enjoys the confidence of the business and professional community in Liverpool and has helped in no small way to build up the finances of the Association during the last few years... He has been much more co-operative with the Area during

> the past two years than any other Liverpool Officer in memory. He is a member of the Area Finance and General Purpose Committee and has attended meetings regularly.

On the other hand, he

> is not however an inspiring leader and tends to annoy people by his dictatorial and intriguing methods. His attitude towards everything is that all men are fools except Stacey... There seems to be some doubt as to whether he will be able to hold on to the Chairmanship and it is possible that he will be opposed in the future. (CPA 1956a)

Thus, an element of boss politics lived on in the Liverpool Conservative Association, bringing with it the associated problems of overcentralised control and petty resentments.

Furthermore, rather than ending personality clashes, Stacey seemed to perpetuate them. Banks recounted an event in August 1957 at which, during a meeting with Stacey and the chief agent about cooperation between Liverpool and the wider area party, Stacey announced that Liverpool wished to cede from the area, although "in his ignorance of the structure of the Party Organisation he had not realised the full impactions of his decision". Later, when the chief agent had left the room, "Mr Stacey uttered a personal threat" to Banks. Banks argued that the underlying cause of this ruckus was that Stacey was aggrieved at being passed over in the Birthday Honours List in June of that year, and at failing to be elected to the National Union Executive Committee at the area annual meeting (CPA 1957a). Stacey only withdrew the threat "when it became clear that this would exclude [the Liverpool Association] from the Party Conference and the services of Central Office" (Ramsden 1996, 100).

Similarly, there were complaints that Stacey had also been rude to north-west area chairman, Colonel Douglas Glover, who

> encountered Mr Ernest Stacey in the Harcourt Room at the House of Commons and the latter administered a calculated snub. Colonel Glover subsequently wrote to Mr Stacey about the occurrence and suggested that they should meet in Liverpool for a talk during the recess [a request which was declined]. (CPA 1957b)

Although these issues seem fairly minor, they hardly suggest that Stacey had the temperament required to lead a major political party in a major British city. He could be brash, impulsive, and willing to resort to threats, which did not bode well for relations within the Association. There is evidence that tensions were mounting in some of the constituencies, especially Liverpool Exchange, where a group of people hostile to Stacey managed to get themselves elected to all divisional offices in 1958 (CPA 1958c). It is also fair to point out that what is recorded in these archives is only a small sample of the number of meetings and personal interactions Stacey would have had to undertake as leader of the Association; nonetheless it is perfectly plausible that this represents just the tip of the iceberg in terms of reckless and inappropriate behaviour.

Stacey ceased to be chairman of the Association at the end of 1965, and was replaced by Macdonald Steward, who had been a councillor since 1953 alongside being the MP for Stockport South from 1955 to 1964, when he lost his seat and instead became leader of the council. Macdonald Steward appeared to bring a new way of thinking to the post, for example pushing for a reset in relations with the press, which "were bad in Liverpool chiefly by decision of the previous Chairman". There was an element of professionalisation of the media campaign, which involved the use of party lines and warmer relations with press and television (CPA 1966b).

Overall, Macdonald Steward was more suited to a leadership role than Stacey. There are no reports of calculated snubs or divisional uprisings under his leadership and he openly rejected sectarianism as a political strategy (D.A. Roberts 1965, 155–56). Instead, while he occupied the chair, it is claimed that the ethos of the party changed, from the Tory Democracy of Forwood, Salvidge, and White, to a concern "with the Protestant work ethic of business efficiency and time management" (Kilfoyle 2000, 37). In some ways this foreshadowed the shift the national party would take briefly under Heath, and then more aggressively under Thatcher. For Waller, Macdonald Steward "espoused business efficiency and comprehensive planning, not nationality or religion" (Waller 1981, 250).

This section has shown how the personalities of those at the top of the Association, rather than structural issues, had served to undermine the effectiveness of the party, be it aloof chief agents failing to maintain good links with Central Office, or chairmen showing a weak understanding of the importance of organisation, fundraising, or networking. The real-world effect of this personality clash was laid bare in the weak start to the West Derby by-election in 1954.

3.2 Organisational issues

Ramsden claims that Liverpool was "in an earlier period a by-word for modern Tory organisation" but in the early post-war period "had been very backward" (Ramsden 1995, 115). Following the end of the Second World War the Liverpool Conservative Association was beset with organisational problems. Maxwell Fyfe notes that

> [t]he Conservative organization in Liverpool was something less than perfect; there was only one central agent, and other agents for the eleven divisions were recruited solely for the election campaign, with the inevitable result that divisional organizations lapsed completely between elections, of which there had not been one since 1935.

Indeed, so desperate was the situation during the 1945 general election campaign that Maxwell Fyfe found it necessary to hold three meetings a night, two in his own constituency of West Derby and one in another (Maxwell Fyfe 1964, 83–84). Despite this, his vote share dropped by 4 per cent from its 1935 level.

One of the main issues was that, as mentioned in section 3.1, unlike Conservative associations elsewhere Liverpool was organised through ward parties rather than constituency parties. This was probably reflective of the fact that in the past municipal politics had been seen as much more important than national politics and real status and civic pride could best be garnered by representing Liverpool on a local, rather than a national, level.

In a memorandum on the problems of the Liverpool Association, written by Pierssené in October 1948, it was claimed that there were two main organisational problems in the city. Firstly, the Association needed to become a federation of constituency parties, rather than having wards as the basic unit. The aim of this was to "overcome the bias in favour of Local Government as opposed to the Parliamentary aspect". Secondly, the positions of chairman of the association and leader of the municipal party — i.e. the party in the Council chamber — should also be split, although this was recognised as "dangerous ground" which "should NOT be pressed initially". The estimated total cost to Central Office of these reforms was £5,940 (roughly £163,000 in 2022 prices) (CPA 1948c). This would have covered agents, an office, and missioners, who would have helped the Association to build up a membership, "which does not now really exist" (CPA 1949b). The fact that Central Office was willing to spend such a large sum of money shows the importance to which they attached to the Liverpool Association.

Despite the urgency placed on these reforms by Central Office the issue was still ongoing four years later in 1952, with the general director claiming that "[t]he Liverpool Association is in very low water" — even though the party had won 58 per cent of the vote in the 1951 municipal election. Moreover, the fact that the Association was in debt and had requested help allowed Central Office to attach conwditions to financial assistance (CPA 1952b). These conditions involved the Liverpool Association recognising the primacy of the constituency as a unit of organisation, as well as requiring constituency branches to make more of an effort at raising funds, including basing party membership on a subscription and the appointment of full-time certified agents to all constituencies, starting with the marginal ones (CPA 1952a).

These rules were finally adopted at the 1954 annual meeting, with the result that "that the organisation in Liverpool will now conform more closely with Party organisation generally" (CPA 1954d). However, it is unclear whether these reforms made much difference. As John Tilney, MP for Liverpool Wavertree, stated in a letter to the then chairman of the Conservative Party Edward du Cann, following the 1964 general election,

> [t]he Liverpool Conservative Association was rescued by Central Office from bankruptcy and £17,000 debt at the end of the Shennan era... the L.C.A was saved on the understanding that the Chairmanship and Leadership of the Council should be divorced. This happened but with one brief interlude the Conservative fortunes in Liverpool declined. Many people think that this is due to two people being responsible for local policy, and that the local political hierarchy changes too slowly. (Tilney 1965)

Further, Tilney bemoaned the lack of enthusiasm of the political clubs in Liverpool for campaigning — although he observed this was a nationwide trend. Thus, we can draw one of two conclusions from this: either the organisational reforms had a negative and detrimental effect on the ability of the Association to campaign effectively, as suggested by Tilney, or they made no difference to the ability of the Association to campaign and as such were merely cosmetic. Lending weight to the latter conclusion is the fact that this complaint about the weakness of the Association came just before the Conservatives produced some of their best local election performances ever, including holding 73 per cent of elected council seats by 1969. As such, it seems that this organisational change at the top was not the cause of Conservative decline in the early 1960s, but rather the previously noted phenomenon of voters tiring of the party in national government and voting accordingly in local elections.

Further challenging this narrative of ineffective reorganisation is a report by Banks in 1956, written in his capacity as north-west area agent, where he outlined the state of each of Liverpool's constituency parties across a range of key indicators. On a Liverpool-wide level, he noted that the Association had about 500 direct subscribers, with a minimum subscription of 2s 6d, but the party was not very good at collecting this money. There had been moves towards giving responsibilities to constituency parties, but the effectiveness of ward campaigning was dependent upon the type of club in the wards, which would pose a problem as these types of club were becoming less politically engaged. However, as Banks noted, they did play an important part in party organisation, with almost every ward possessing a club which acted as the hub for ward committees.

In his view, the city could boast a decent Young Conservative branch, with good personnel, but there was still "plenty of room for improvement in the organisation and the membership could be much larger". Moreover, there were still weaknesses in the Liverpool Conservative network: the Women's Federation did not meet regularly and was not a very effective body, with women tending to be excluded from leadership roles (CPA 1956a). Interestingly, there is evidence that this was never really addressed. A decade later, in 1966, the new Central Office agent for the north-west area, Mr Webster, wrote "I am most anxious that the Women's Organisation in Liverpool should be improved for it has been very much played down for many years now" (CPA 1966b).

Furthermore, there was no Conservative Trade Unionist committee in the city and just one division had a divisional Conservative Trade Unionist body. This was clearly a glaring omission in the Associational structure, especially in a city with such a large union presence as Liverpool. This was recognised by Banks, who noted that a trade unionist organiser had been sent to the city "to work up the movement". Finally, the Association was weak with regard to 'political education', an idea which "Liverpool has not taken to", although there were hopes that a new area political education officer would help to change this (CPA 1956a).

However, in his conclusions Banks comes back to the paradox at the heart of the Liverpool Conservative Association's organisation:

> It has employed the minimum of professional help, has had the services of voluntary election agents for both Parliamentary and Local Government elections and until recently no effort has been made to enlist members or carry out any of the organisational methods to which the Central Office attaches so much importance. Its Women's, Y.C. and C.T.U. sections are well below the average, there is no marked register and the amount of canvassing and doorstep work carried out is negligible. Yet it has achieved better Parliamentary results than any other large city and was the last of the large cities to lose Conservative control of the City Council. (CPA 1956a)

The litany of failures of the Liverpool Conservative Association goes on, and yet the party still managed to be a dynamic, effective electoral force. For Banks, this was because "Liverpool has a very strong Conservative tradition on which it has relied far too long", which ties in with the argument made regarding socialisation in Chapter 7, "but that combined with good organisational methods there is no reason why very much better results should not be achieved in the future" (CPA 1956a).

Tables 3.1, 3.2, and 3.3 outline the key aspects of divisional organisation. Without going through the tables in full, it is worth noting that Banks' subjective view of the three agents who were involved with the Liverpool association was that only two were good, whilst Binns was described as an "agent of limited capacity... within limits he is doing a reasonable job" (CPA 1956f). Binns was responsible for both Kirkdale and West Derby, both marginal seats (Kirkdale had a Conservative majority of 2,747 in 1959 whilst West Derby had a majority of 3,333 — both were lost to Labour in 1964). Indeed, even the MP for Kirkdale, Normal Pannell, complained that Binns was "most unsatisfactory" and that, after Binns retired, the division was left with no agent for several months (CPA 1956d). The fact that both marginal constituencies were left without an agent highlights further organisational defects.

Table 3.1: Findings from the 1956 report on Liverpool's constituencies for Edge Hill, Exchange, and Garston constituencies (CPA 1956a)

	Edge Hill
Agent	No agent, under city office control.
Chairman	MR MOORE: "He is not in any way outstanding."
Hon. treasurer	MR GARNER: "Not much use as a treasurer."
Finance	Dependent upon city resources, but some effort made towards raising money.
Membership	No subscribing membership.
Propaganda	Directed from the city office.
Active workers	Shortage of active workers but stalwarts assist at election times.
Women	Largely concerned with social activities.
Young Conservatives	Four ward branches: total membership 92. No divisional council.
Trade unionists	No CTU activity.
Clubs	Three clubs, which provide meeting places for ward activities.
Other	

Exchange	*Garston*
MR ROSE: "a very satisfactory agent" (see Toxteth)	No agent, under city office control.
MR CHESHIRE: "He is an average chairman."	CLLR BIDSTON: "A very able chairman… considered as a possible successor" to Shannon as chairman of LCA.
Division covers the business and commercial centre so it does not collect subscriptions but has an arrangement with the city association.	Dependent upon city resources, but some effort made towards raising money.
No subscribing membership.	No subscribing membership.
Good nucleus of active workers in Abercromby and St James's wards. They function well at election times and are closely associated with the clubs.	Several workers associated with wards and clubs who canvass at elections. Also provide mutual aid to marginal wards/seats elsewhere.
Largely concerned with social activities.	Largely concerned with social activities: "Seem to have no place in the organisation except… working at election times."
Five branches: total membership 148. Some progress is being made.	Three branches; total membership 134. Slight drop during the past year.
No CTU activity.	No CTU activity.
Three clubs, around which most political activity revolves.	Four clubs, much of the political activity revolves around them.
	MP: SIR VICTOR RAIKES: A good constituency member, visits the constituency regularly and holds a monthly "surgery" for electors.

Table 3.2: Findings from the 1956 report on Liverpool's constituencies for Kirkdale, Scotland, and Toxteth constituencies (CPA 1956a)

	Kirkdale
Agent	MR BINNS (see West Derby).
Chairman	CLLR CRAINE: "Keen but not in any way outstanding."
Hon. treasurer	
Finance	Association income is being built up through collection of subscriptions, an autumn fair, divisional dances, and whist drives.
Membership	Attempt being made to introduce a membership scheme.
Propaganda	Directed from the city office.
Active workers	A number of active workers at election times.
Women	Branches in the wards but no divisional Women's committee. No record of membership.
Young Conservatives	Four branches: total membership 230. Making some progress.
Trade unionists	No CTU activity.
Clubs	Three clubs; most of the political activity centred on the clubs.
Other	MP: CLLR PANNELL: "Neither a good speaker nor a good mixer but takes his duties very seriously. A good constituency member and holds regular surgeries."

Scotland	*Toxteth*
No agent, under city office control.	MR ROSE: "Making considerable progress in building up the organisation."
MR SHAW "is a poor and ineffective chairman."	MRS PROCTOR, OBE, JP: "82 years of age and has held the Chairmanship for the past five years. She is much too old for the job, particularly as it is now assuming much more importance."
MR W. MARTIN: "He is treasurer in name only."	MR BURLEY: "Of very limited capacity. He is ably assisted by a finance officer, Mr A. Rushton."
Entirely dependent upon city resources.	A finance committee has "taken in hand the building up of a constituency income" via a garden fete and an autumn fair.
No subscribing membership.	No membership figures available.
Directed from the city office.	Produces own news-sheet three times per year.
Very few active workers in this constituency.	A number of active workers are available at election times, centred on ward clubs. Attempts being made to obtain more active workers to operate between elections.
Women's branches in the two wards and a Women's club.	Largely concerned with social activities; not very effective and they consist mostly of older women.
No branches.	Three ward branches: total membership 189. Not much progress recently. No CTU activity.
Three clubs in which ward meetings are held.	Six clubs, which perform useful work for the Party and provide the centres for ward activities.
DIFFICULTIES: "This division consists of a slum dockside area of Liverpool and includes a large foreign element. It is extremely difficult to achieve anything in the way of organisation."	MP: MR BEVINS: "He is a local man, residing in the division, and is in constant touch with local affairs."

Table 3.3: Findings from the 1956 report on Liverpool's constituencies for Walton, Wavertree, and West Derby constituencies (CPA 1956a)

	Walton
Agent	MR ALLEN: "Doing a good job." (see Wavertree)
Chairman	CLLR BRADY: "A good type of chairman although he is inclined to be impulsive at times."
Hon. treasurer	MRS A.W. LOWE: "Wife of the treasurer of the city association and adequately performs the limited duties of her office."
Finance	Dependent upon city resources, but some effort made towards raising money.
Membership	No membership figures available.
Propaganda	Publishes a quarterly magazine.
Active workers	A number of good workers in this division; it is probably the best organised in the city.
Women	Best in the city but it functions on a ward basis and there is no divisional committee.
Young Conservatives	Three ward branches: total membership 190. Slight drop during the past year.
Trade unionists	A divisional council meets regularly. Eleven factory groups, including two Conservative shop stewards.
Clubs	Three clubs, which provide meeting places for party meetings and are politically active.
Other	MP: CLLR THOMPSON: "He keeps in close touch with the Party organisation in Liverpool and is a member of the City Council. He is a good constituency member."

Wavertree	*West Derby*
MR ALLEN: "A good organiser and knows what is required." (see Walton)	MR BINNS: "An experienced agent of limited capacity... within limits he is doing a reasonable job." (see Kirkdale)
CLLR ROGERS: "He is a live wire and is a good leader."	MR GRAY, MBE: "I found him extremely helpful. He has the reputation of being an agitator and is rather outspoken and tactless at times."
	MR H.R. BUTLER: "proved very helpful since he took over the treasurership a few months ago."
Dependent upon city resources, some effort made towards raising money, with a house-to-house collection of funds in progress.	Dependent upon city resources, but some effort made towards raising money.
No membership figures are yet available as a result of recent efforts.	Small subscribing but efforts are being made to enrol members.
Directed from the city office.	Directed from the city office.
Attempts to enrol active workers to carry out the new scheme of organisation.	A nucleus of workers in three of the four wards and they can be relied upon at election times. Gillmoss Ward is very "red" and there are no workers available.
Largely concerned with social activities.	Largely concerned with social activities.
Three branches: total membership 190. The position is static.	Three branches: total membership 178. The position is static.
No CTU activity.	No CTU activity.
Three clubs, which provide the centre of political activity in the division.	Three clubs, provide ward headquarters, and most of the political activity.
MP: MR TILNEY: "He is a good constituency member and is in the constituency almost every week-end."	MP: MR WOOLLAM: "He is a very good constituency member who knows how to nurse his constituency."

We can see the intertwined influence of personalities and organisational issues in the case of an agent for Kirkdale. In July 1956, it was noted that under Mayhew "the City association has not accepted as a necessity the principle of a full-time agent in each constituency" (CPA 1956e). In September 1956 Banks reported that Stacey

> is quite adamant that he will not have an agent in Kirkdale at the present time even if financial help was offered... [because Binns] did so much damage that two of the ward associations would resign if another agent was introduced into the division.

There was, however, a Central Office missioner in Kirkdale who was doing very well, and a glimmer of hope for Central Office, with Stacey "prepared to accept" an agent in Edge Hill — where Labour had a 1,100 majority in 1955 — and "if an agent proved successful in this division he might be prepared to transfer him to Kirkdale later on" (CPA 1956c).

As such, we can see that key personalities in the Association — including Stacey and ward chairmen — were actively undermining the ability of associations to develop through the use of agents. We can see the beneficial effects of agents in later reports on the Liverpool Association: in October 1957 in a letter to the general director, the Party's national deputy chairman Oliver Poole reported that "the idea of having constituency Agents has only recently been adopted in Liverpool. The result has been a great improvement in the [West Derby] constituency organisation" (CPA 1957c). Further, in a report on the Kirkdale constituency, written by Banks in December 1958, he noted that "[t]he organisation is in good heart and the Tuebrook ward has been re-organised. There has been a great improvement in all sections of the association since it has received the full-time attention of an agent" (CPA 1958a).

In a report on West Derby, he noted that "[o]utstanding progress has been made in the past six months" as "[n]ew Ward Branches have been formed at Dovecot and Gillmoss, the latter being a large Prefab Council estate" where two years earlier it was claimed no workers could be found. Similarly, "[t]wo new Y.C. Branches have been formed" and following a recruiting campaign, in which the women's wing did "a wonderful job", "[o]ver 100 Conservative Trade Unionists were located and an excellent D.C.T.U. was later formed" (CPA 1958b). These results were nothing short of astounding, and go to show the difference that a good, dedicated agent could make to a divisional party. This makes the opposition of the leader and ward parties even more damaging and outlines the lack of rationality in some of the actions of key players in the Association. However, despite these advances, in the 1959 general election Kirkdale saw a swing towards the Conservative of just under 2 per cent and West Derby of under 1 per cent, a warning that the effects of good constituency organisation should not be overstated.

Banks also wrote that five of the nine divisional chairs were lacking in some way. The Edge Hill chair was described as "not in any way outstanding", whilst the chair of Exchange was "an average chairman". Mr Shaw, of Scotland division, was "a poor and ineffective chairman", Cllr Craine, the chair of Kirkdale, is "keen but not in any way outstanding", whilst Mrs Proctor, chair of Toxteth, an OBE and a Justice of the Peace, was "82 years of age… much too old for the job, particularly as it is now assuming much more importance". As well as poor chairs, three of the six divisions that had treasurers were saddled with sub-par ones: Toxteth's Mr Burley was seen as "of very limited capacity" whilst Walton's Mr Garner was simply "not much use as a treasurer". Mr Martin, in Scotland, escaped personal criticism by being "treasurer in name only" (CPA 1956a).

These examples point to a personnel problem in the Liverpool Conservative Association, in the 1950s at least. Further, divisional funding was generally from the city office and no division was able to provide a membership list. Not only was this detrimental for collecting subscriptions, it also reduced the ability of the Association to bring in new people, who could support or replenish the organisational structures. We can also see weaknesses in the women's wing of the organisation, which existed mainly as a vehicle for social events and in practice provided women in the city with little opportunity to get seriously involved in Tory politics (perhaps reflected in the fact that only one officer named in all nine of the reports was female). Similarly, only one constituency, Walton, had a Conservative Trade Union branch. The Young Conservatives wing seemed to be stronger across the divisions, barring Scotland, although as Banks noted there was room for improvement with only one ward passing 200 members. However, there was a recognition within the members of the council in 1953 that "the Labour Party had got a strangle hold on the youth of Liverpool", with the Socialists assiduously leafletting the Liverpool Boys Association, reaching audiences of 2,000 to 3,000 youths. Further, Councillor Curtis claimed that

> we, as a party, have taken only a financial interest, and are insufficiently interested to most Youth Clubs in our wards [*sic*]. We are making a stick with which to beat ourselves in 4 or 5 years time [*sic*]… as there was a Youth Club in practically every ward in the City, councillors should

> approach the warden, who would arrange for the Councillor to assist the work in some way. (Liverpool Conservative Association 1953)

By 1954 there were claims made at a meeting of the organisation committee of the Liverpool area council of the Young Conservative Association which suggested that the Young Conservative representation, in numbers at least, was not insignificant, with their annual report claiming

> it is IMPERATIVE that if we are to counter the terrific wastage which occurs from year to year that we as an Organization must RECRUIT EVERY WEEK if we are to maintain our proud title of being the largest Political Youth Organization in Liverpool. [capitalisation in original] (Liverpool Conservative Association 1954)

These two pieces of evidence suggest that although there were decent numbers in the Young Conservative branches they were not used as effectively as they might have been.

Finally, the number of clubs, which formed the hub of social and campaign activity, looked quite strong; no division had fewer than three. However, it is important to remember that these clubs were still formally excluding Catholics from membership. This had been a bone of contention for some time, with minutes from a meeting of Conservative members of Liverpool City Council in 1947 discussing whether the ban was appropriate. A passionate argument was made by Councillor Prout, who believed that to "really fight for the good of the country" a debate on whether it was right to exclude Catholics from membership was necessary. Some councillors were uncomfortable with the fact there was a religious link to the LWCA at all, with Councillor Haswell arguing that "[h]e wanted the Conservative Party to be representative of all religions. He did not think this discrimination was good for the Party". However, it was recognised that this was for the clubs to decide, and that the Party had no control over them. Alderman Shennan stated that

> the Workingmen were determined that they [Catholics] should not join them socially... the members with one voice said that they were going to stand by the tradition of the W.M.C.A., and that they would retain the preamble even if it meant disaffiliation from the Association of Conservative Clubs. (Liverpool Conservative Association 1953)

Further, it was noted that Catholics could still join the political aspects of the association, including ward and divisional parties. In Banks' report on the Liverpool Association nine years later in 1956 he noted that "[r]eligion is still a factor in the Liverpool politics but Roman Catholics are not now so rigidly excluded from office in the Party" (CPA 1956a). Interestingly, by 1962 the chair of the Exchange divisional party had three requirements for the next Conservative candidate. Firstly, that he be a Roman Catholic, secondly that he be "fairly local", and thirdly "not too smart" (CPA 1962a).[2] This does show that, although formal bars to Catholic membership existed in the social clubs, this was not always accepted on the explicitly political side of the party. However, potential Catholic activists would surely have been wary of getting involved, and the desire for a Roman Catholic in Exchange likely reflected a rational appreciation of the religious makeup of the division as much as it did a desire to open up the party.

It is worth noting the rapid post-war decline of the Liverpool Working Men's Conservative Association, which by 1964 had just two functioning branches. As Davies states, the LWCA "so powerful a force in Liverpool since its foundation in 1868, had all but disappeared by 1968" (Davies 1999, 21). This correlated with the decline of other organisational representations of sectarianism, including the Orange Order, the Protestant Party, and the Protestant Association, which "no longer held sway over the local Conservatives... The Order's lack of political organisation was a reflection of a changed reality" (Day 2008, 282–84).

Overall, the divisional reports paint a picture of a hit-and-miss association, with some wards drastically outperforming others, in terms not only of the quality of personnel and volunteers but also the vibrancy of other wings of the party, such as the Conservative Women's organisation or the Conservative Trade Unionists branches. There is also no evidence of sharing best practice between the constituency parties. However, this variation does not seem to have affected general election results in 1959, when the Conservatives won six of the city's nine constituencies. Again, we see direct evidence that poor associational structures do not seem to have had much of an effect on the party's fortunes when it came to general election results.

There is also evidence that a shift to a focus on constituencies rather than wards had some detrimental effects. A report on the municipal elections of 1962 shows that in the two wards where the Liberals won a seat, St Michael's and Church, defeat was attributed to poor ward organisation. In St Michael's,

2 It is not clear whether "smart" in this context referred to the intelligence of the candidate or how well they dressed. For a largely working-class constituency like Liverpool Exchange it would not be surprising for the latter to be the case.

where the Liberals won with a majority of just 164, the candidate claimed that "[d]ue to [the] fact that members have looked upon Ward as 'safe' for many years, Organisation has become lax". The same can be seen in Church, where there was a "[l]ack of any adequate organisation" and an "[u]nfavourable comparison by the electorate with vigorous canvassing by Liberals". There was a similar response from the Broadgreen ward, which managed to remain Conservative-held but with a majority reduced from 2,240 to 663. They found a "[l]ack of enthusiasm among workers", as well as the "[i]ntervention of Liberal, who polled 1133 votes — 90% of this figure estimated as from Conservative supporters [*sic*]" (CPA 1962c).

Further evidence that the reorganisation in the 1950s failed to solve the Association's problem comes from a letter from the then temporary leader Macdonald Steward to du Cann, who argued that

> the situation here is considered to be unsatisfactory... I am trying... to inject some life into the existing Organisation. Unfortunately, the position had been allowed to run down to a very low level and nothing short of a complete revision of structure will meet the long term needs. (CPA 1966a)

The scale of the losses in the 1964 general election, and the dire financial needs of the Association, led to Central Office finally being able to bring Liverpool under its oversight (Ramsden 1996, 270).

Accordingly, by the 1960s the idea of the Liverpool Conservatives being run by a 'city boss' on the level of Salvidge or White had disappeared, brought about by the bosses' own failures. As Anthony Howard states, following the poor result in the 1964 Scotland by-election — examined below — "[t]he years of glory have departed for the Liverpool Conservatives and even their days of autonomy seem to be numbered" (Howard 1964, 138).

Thus, organisational issues were a persistent problem for the Liverpool Conservatives. If it was not poorly suited leaders at the top, it was often ineffective office-holders in the middle, or run-down ward parties at the bottom. One of the reasons why the Liberals were so devastatingly effective against the Conservatives from the early 1970s onwards was that the Conservative local parties were run down and thus poor campaign machines, unresponsive to the needs of local people. However, until their opponents got their act together, the fact that the Liverpool Conservative Party itself suffered from poor organisation did not seem to matter much at all.

3.3 Financial issues

The Liverpool Conservative Association began the period under study in a problematic financial situation. In 1948 Central Office had no idea about the state of the Association's finances, so much so that any help given by CCO would be dependent upon the provision of "a full statement of the present financial position of the Association, including disclosure of reserves both of real and personal property, the statement to be audited or otherwise satisfactorily vouched for", as well as allowing the Board of Finance to view the Association's records. Even "in event of a breakdown of negotiations the Representatives of the Board will in any case be sent to Liverpool within six months" (CPA 1948c). This represented a serious assault on the traditions of associational autonomy, which serves to show just how bleak the Liverpool Association's financial prospects were.

Financial aloofness had material consequences for the effectiveness of Liverpool's divisional and ward parties. Rawcliffe, then Central Office agent for the north-west area, denied a request made by the chair of the Exchange constituency party for a missioner because the city had been uncooperative over fundraising, as well as the fact that boundary reform made Exchange a non-competitive seat (CPA 1948a).

Ramsden states that "only in 1953 did the city party make ordinary membership dependent on the payment of a subscription, 'in addition to political conviction'", but notes that by 1956 "the city party was still calling special meetings of large subscribers to raise money for much of the city's basic organisation" (Ramsden 1995, 115).

In his 1956 report, Banks outlined the two main changes made regarding fundraising. Firstly, the collection of direct subscriptions operated under what is termed the "shepherd system", under which "a doctor is selected to collect from doctors, an architect from architects". However, not much success had been made in the collection of small subscriptions. Secondly, the party had begun selling advertising space in the *Liverpool Diary*, published annually by the Association. This seems to have been successful, with Banks reporting that "[a] considerable sum of money has been raised during the past two or three years which has enabled a large bank overdraft to be repaid and a start to be made on building up a reserve fund" (CPA 1956a).

Following these reports, little is mentioned of the Association's financial situation, which suggests that the problem had, broadly speaking, been solved. The fact that the Association was in the red for a significant number of years does not seem to have hindered campaigning efforts; there were no reports of campaigns being hamstrung by a lack of literature, but rather by a lack of workers. However, the lack of full-time agents for each ward is perhaps a symptom of cost-cutting attributable to a poor financial situation, as well as an ideological decision made by the leadership, who were determined to restrict challenges to their autonomy from outsiders.

3.4 Campaigning strategy

Finally, we can consider the Association's approach to campaigns through a study of two key by-elections — that of West Derby in 1954 and Garston in 1957 — alongside a brief consideration of the by-election in the Scotland division in 1964.

The evidence from the West Derby by-election shows how the Association preferred to handle its own affairs, fiercely resisting outside influence from Central Office. Banks' report on the by-election outlines how there was "some resistance on the part of the City of Liverpool Office to the Central Office Agent and his staff taking part in the Bye-Election Campaign [*sic*]... Neither the A.P.O. nor I were consulted" on a range of strategic decisions. Despite this, Banks was able to get "the control I needed and [bring] all necessary influence to bear upon the campaign", through "the exercise of much patience and by being as helpful as we possibly could" (CPA 1954a).

Furthermore, isolationism had led to a lack of awareness of best practice or increasing efficiency of techniques, with the "Liverpool methods of Committee Room procedure on Polling Day" being "quite peculiar and in my view hopelessly inefficient". However, the workers who were involved showed a dogged determination which, despite "the worst weather conditions" Banks had seen "on any previous polling day, house to house calling was continued throughout the day and undoubtedly contributed to the splendid result" (CPA 1954a). Overall, this suggests a stubborn association with outdated and inefficient methods but an effective and determined base of workers able to mobilise the vote and produce a canvass that counted (albeit with outside help).

Turning to the Garston by-election three years later, we see similar organisational problems. Firstly, Banks found that the "local organisation in Garston was very poor and in some polling districts almost non-existent. In spite of advice given... very inadequate preparations had been made". Secondly,

> [t]he response for help from the other constituencies in the City of Liverpool was quite inadequate and it was only when a crisis arose in

> getting out the election address on time that it was possible to get help. Even then the whole of the paid staff from the City Office had to be brought in to complete the filling of envelopes in time. (CPA 1957d)

Banks placed further blame at the feet of the divisional chair, Councillor Bidson, who "seemed concerned to assert his authority during the campaign but his knowledge of electioneering was very limited". Banks recounted how, despite the strategy of concentrating efforts in Conservative wards to counter the Liberal threat, Bidson "diverted ten experienced workers from Conservative wards to the hopeless Socialist Ward of Speke" on the evening of polling day. This is further evidence that petty personal conflicts and poor leadership hampered the by-election effort. Interestingly, Banks noted how "[t]he Socialist organisation in Liverpool is, fortunately, worse than ours" and that the regional Labour Party faced similar problems in securing help from the Liverpool Labour Party (CPA 1957d).

An interesting development arising from the Garston by-election was the fact the Liberals were contesting it, and that Banks made recommendations of how to deal with this new threat. Following a recognition that

> many disgruntled Conservatives and floating voters might be tempted to vote Liberal... It was therefore decided to pay special attention to possible Liberal voters and to persuade them that a vote for the Liberal Candidate would only help the Labour candidate. Two leaflets — one produced locally and the other from the Central Office — were distributed selectively to "Doubtfuls" and possible Liberal voters. Reports from canvassers proved that these tactics were worthwhile. (CPA 1957d)

The Liverpool Liberals followed their old tactic of being "purely opportunist and exploited every possible grievance", but "it was obvious that the electorate of Garston were not interested in the by-election and all three candidates found it extremely difficult to make any impression". As with the Labour Party, the Liberals "depended upon a circus of outside people and there was literally no local organisation in the wards". The Liberals' lack of experience was on show, exemplified by the fact that they were relying on children to act as tellers at most of the polling stations, "mostly school boys who were being paid 15/- for the whole day"; however, party officials had not been collecting numbers from them all day and "[t]owards the end of the day the boys were getting rather frustrated and anxious about the payment for their services" (CPA 1957d).

The result of the Garston by-election is shown in Table 3.4, below, and was a decent Conservative victory. Interestingly, the fact the Labour vote share remained fairly constant between the two elections suggests that it was indeed the Conservatives from whom the Liberals took votes.

Table 3.4: Voting in Liverpool Garston in the 1955 general election and 1957 by-election (CPA 1957d)

	1955		*1957*		
	Votes	*Share (%)*	*Votes*	*Share (%)*	*Change (%)*
Conservative	28,130	63.5	15,521	49.2	−14.3
Labour	16,161	36.5	11,217	35.6	−0.9
Liberal	N/A	N/A	4,807	15.2	+15.2
Majority	11,969		4,304		

For Banks, the campaign showed that "[i]t is no longer good policy to ignore the Liberal candidate" and the claim that there was little difference between Conservative and Liberal policy should be counted on the doorstep. Furthermore, the claim that a vote for the Liberals is 'wasted' "is untrue and only offends". However, it was "generally true to say that a vote for the Liberal helps the Socialist". Banks also noted how

> [t]he Liberals in Garston were very worried by our tactics and Jeremy Thorpe came personally to our Central Committee room to ask for a copy of our leaflet entitled "The Liberal Tradition". The Liberal candidate protested to the Press about the leaflet and the local papers very obligingly published our leaflet in full. (CPA 1957d)

Finally, in the 1964 Liverpool Scotland by-election, an old problem resurfaced, namely the Association's avoidance of outside help. Although there was no post-election analysis by the party the *Daily Mail* reported that the swing to Labour in the Scotland constituency — at 12.5 per cent, extending the Labour majority from 23.6 per cent to 48.6 per cent — was due to "a mishandled campaign" by the Conservatives which could lead "to moves to give less freedom to local organisations". The paper also reported that there had been "[s]uggestions of an autocratic Liverpool organisation wanting to go-it-alone, without outside aid", but that these were refuted by Alderman Hughes, the deputy chairman of Liverpool's Parliamentary party organisation, who claimed that "Mr Richard Webster, the Central Office agent for the North-west, came to Liverpool, and there were full discussions on tactics for the campaign. There was no disagreement" (CPA 1964a). This claim was itself challenged by Webster in a letter to the general director: "I must admit I did not know there was a full discussion on the Campaign, and I would really not be prepared to say that there was 'no disagreement'!" (CPA 1964b).

Thus, we can see that, a decade on from the West Derby by-election, there had been little change to the 'isolationist' and 'dictatorial' tendencies in the party hierarchy, which was detrimental to the party's cause. Organisationally, the party was not in touch with other associations in any meaningful way, to allow for the spreading of best practices, but rather maintained an aloof stance which led to the continuation of outdated or inefficient practices. Again, however, we can see that, although the Conservatives may have been poorly organised in their by-election campaigns, they still performed well in most cases — Scotland excluded, but that had been a marginal seat at no point since its creation in 1885 — and that poor strategy does seem to have been countered by effective workers on the ground.

3.5 Conclusion

Overall, this analysis has outlined the consistent, structural weaknesses in the Liverpool Conservative Association. The party suffered from clashes of personality and stubbornness which stymied or delayed necessary reforms, organisational weaknesses which were magnified by a lack of talented personnel, a poor financial outlook which resulted in the Association enacting reforms that eventually worked to its benefit, and a campaigning strategy which was cut off from best practice and suffered from the effects of egotism and arrogance. For Ramsden, the failure "to modernise the Party in a city that at that time still had six Conservative MPs (one of them Maxwell Fyfe) in turn sheds much light on the spectacular collapse of Liverpool Conservatism in the 1960s" (Ramsden 1995, 115).

However, organisation did not seem to matter. As has been identified throughout this chapter, there seems to have been a very limited relationship between the quality of the organisation and Conservative fortunes in elections, which provides support for Ball's argument that "superior organization was probably worth a few hundred votes at the most; it could add to the scale of victory, but was unable to prevent the party's defeats" (Ball 2013, 193). There is no evidence that the huge decline in the number of constituencies held by the Conservatives in Liverpool in 1964 was attributable to some sudden organisational failure, nor indeed does it support the idea that there was a lagged effect of organisational weaknesses on the electoral success of the Liverpool Conservatives. After all, the organisational reforms of the 1950s preceded strong performances (measured by Conservative vote share) in the 1959, 1960, and 1961 local elections, weak performances in the 1962, 1963, and 1964 local elections, and then the party's best post-war performance in 1968 and 1969. Instead, as will be shown in Chapter 7, swings to and from the Conservatives are better attributed to evaluations of the party in government nationally, rather than the effectiveness of the party on the ground.

There is, however, some evidence that the Liberals were able to capitalise on poor organisation to win some wards in the 1962 municipal election, but again the scope of this was limited and there is no explanation why other wards with similarly run-down organisations did not fall to the Liberals, nor why this did not happen earlier.

Ultimately, there is scant evidence for the idea that the sub-par quality of the Liverpool Conservative Association's organisation was to blame for Tory decline. Instead, we see that organisation generally meant relatively little to the party's fortunes.

4 Electoral biases in Liverpool's municipal elections

The previous chapter showed how the Liverpool Conservative Association's own organisational weaknesses were unlikely to be the main cause of Conservative decline in Liverpool. However, the Association did not act in a vacuum: the electoral system acted as the main method to "translate votes in the ballot box into seats in the legislature" (Rallings, Thrasher, and Gunt 2000, 218). Thus, it is important to examine how the electoral system influenced Conservative fortunes during the period in question.

The theoretical link between electoral biases and electoral support for the Conservatives is worth stating. If the Conservatives faced, or if over time they increasingly faced, a high level of electoral bias which meant that votes cast for them were not being effectively or efficiently transferred into seats, then voters might be less willing to bother voting for them at all since the likelihood of the candidate winning is reduced. This would clearly result in the Conservative share of the vote declining on a local level, which is what this study is primarily concerned with. Hence electoral bias can influence the extent to which voting for a party is perceived to be worthwhile — the higher the level of electoral bias against a party, all other things being equal, the lower the incentive to vote for that party.

There is also the question of ordering: which comes first, electoral bias or voting behaviour? Obviously, for electoral bias in a given year to be examined, votes must have been cast. However, those votes are cast in the broader context of the previous year's elections — and hence in the context of existing bias. Thus, it is something of a chicken and egg situation. For the purposes of this chapter, the role of electoral biases is presented as prior to the analysis of actual voting behaviour since biases set the broader context within which the actual votes are cast and how they translate into seats.

This avenue of research is warranted by the limited existing literature. Davies notes how, during the interwar period, Labour's seat share was always worse than its electoral support warranted, whereas the reverse was true for the Conservatives. He finds that minor parties were also overrepresented in the 1930s (Davies 1996, 93–94). Further, Baxter notes how the 1953 boundary reform was good for Labour's electoral fortunes (Baxter 1969, 110) and in 1955 the *Liverpool Daily Post* commented on how discrepancies in ward boundary sizes were helpful to Labour (*Liverpool Daily Post* 1955, i). Thus, it is worth examining the hypothesis that, after the Second World War, Conservative decline was hastened by an unfavourable electoral system.

To explore the effects of electoral structures this study adopts the work of Brookes (1959) and Johnston, Rossiter, and Pattie (1999) to undertake a quantitative analysis of components of electoral bias in Liverpool. The findings show that there were systematic biases against the Conservatives across the period of study but that for the most part these did not hinder the Conservatives in any meaningful sense when translating votes to seats.

Generally, the main driver of Conservative bias *vis-à-vis* Labour was the distribution of the Conservative vote — which the party could have taken steps to address — rather than structural influences, such as differential electoral sizes between wards or rates of turnout. The main exception to this was between 1963 and 1968, when these latter two factors were important. Despite this, the Conservatives performed phenomenally well from 1965 to 1970, achieving around 59 per cent of the vote in 1967. Contrastingly, the party faced some of the lowest levels of bias against them during their period of decline. It seems that the Conservatives could do well despite electoral bias and this chapter does not find that biases had an impact on Conservative electoral success.

4.1 Disproportionality in Liverpool's municipal electoral system

Rallings et al. define an electoral system as disproportionate when the share of seats a party wins differs from the share of votes it received (Rallings, Thrasher, and Gunt 2000, 218). We can construct a Gallagher index to measure the level of disproportionality in an electoral system, by "squaring the vote–seat difference for each party; adding these values; dividing the sum by 2; and taking its square root" (Gallagher 1991, 40). This can be shown as:

$$\sqrt{\frac{1}{2}\sum_{i=1}^{n}(Vi - Si)^2}$$

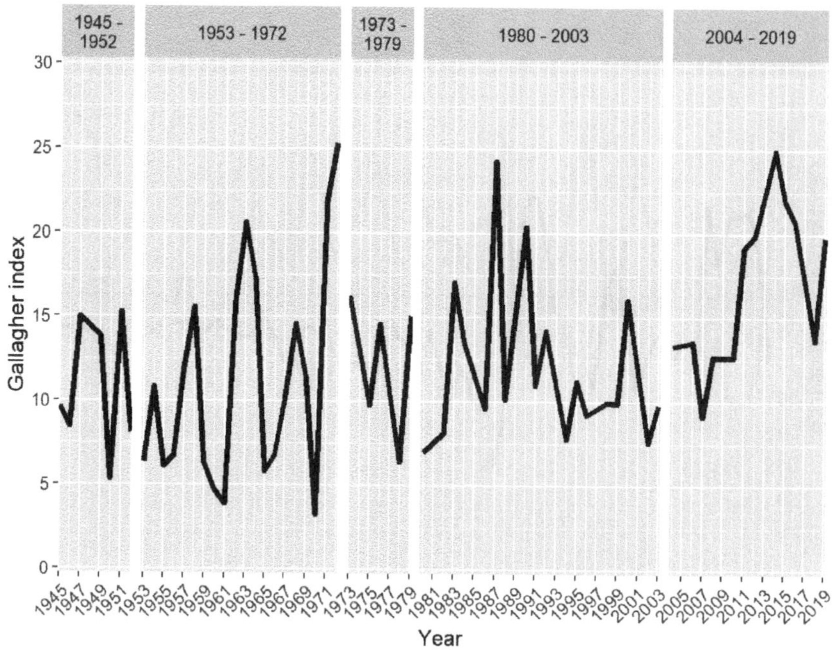

Figure 4.1: Gallagher index for Liverpool's municipal elections, 1945–2019, by ward boundary system

The index produces a range of values from 0–100, in which 0 shows perfect proportion and 100 perfect disproportion. Since municipal elections are conducted under a first-past-the-post system, where a simple plurality of votes is required to win a seat, we can expect a high level of disproportion in the system. This is shown in Figure 4.1.

The proportionality of Liverpool's municipal elections varies wildly, often with violent swings between years. For example, in 1970 the index of proportionality was 3.3, but in 1971 it was 21.9, the fifth-highest value out of the whole period. It is also clear that disproportion owed more to year-on-year changes than to boundary reforms.

However, the Gallagher index does not tell us much about the fates of individual parties nor how these changed over time. It could be, for example, that each boundary configuration saw a different party suffer from disproportion. We can explore the effects of disproportion on the three main parties by subtracting their share of the vote from seat share. A positive result means that a party gained a greater proportion of seats than their share of the votes would warrant in a purely proportional system, meaning they were

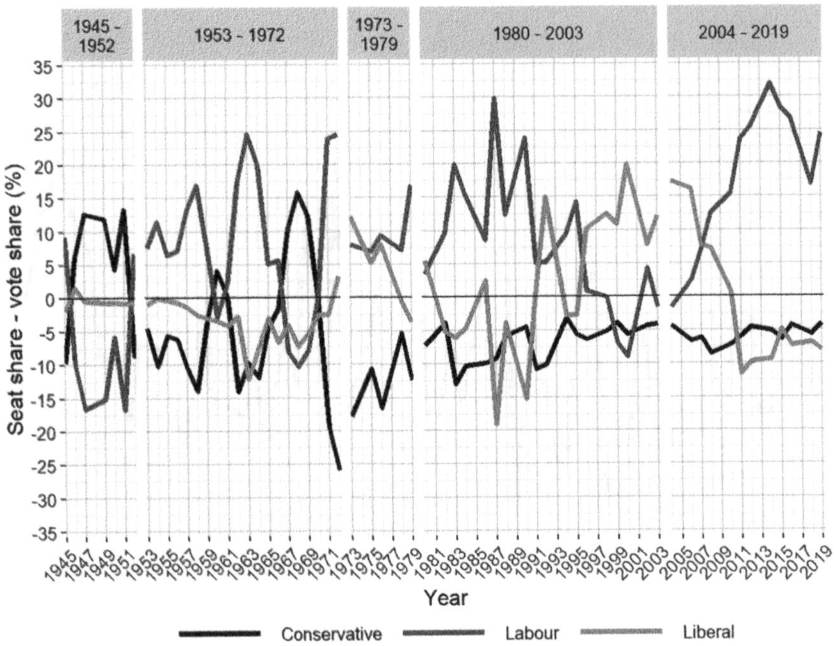

Figure 4.2: Difference between seat and vote share for Liverpool's municipal elections, 1945–2019, by ward boundary system

Note: The data controls for multi-ward elections by considering just the first-placed candidate for each party. Aldermanic seats are not included.

overrepresented in the council. A negative number shows that they would be underrepresented. This is shown for Liverpool's local elections in Figure 4.2.

Firstly, we can see that until 1953 — when the first post-war boundary reform took place — the Conservatives were often overrepresented in the council chamber, with their seat share around 10 percentage points greater than their vote share. Conversely, Labour were consistently underrepresented in the council chamber. The Liberals won very few seats but also a very low share of the vote, and hence achieved fairly proportionate representation. The position between the Conservatives and Labour was reversed in 1952, the year before the first boundary reform, and hence this could not be the key factor behind this disproportion.

Between 1953 and 1972 Labour consistently enjoyed overrepresentation. This was even picked up by the local media, with the *Liverpool Daily Post* noting how, in 1955

> The remarkable position whereby the Socialists have won the citadel with a poll 20,810 below that of the anti-Socialists... [is due to] the curious way in which the Boundary Commission, two years ago, rearranged the forty wards of the city on a supposed basis of equality... Many of the old, inner Socialist wards have little more than half the electorates of the outer Conservative one. (*Liverpool Daily Post* 1955, i)

In this period the Liberals began to suffer greater disproportion, owing to gaining votes in the city but nowhere near enough to win in most wards. In 1972, the last year of this boundary system, they managed to achieve overrepresentation for the first time since 1946, whilst the Conservatives suffered their greatest level of disproportion, with their seat share being 25.9 percentage points lower than their vote share.

The next boundary reform, in 1973, did not fix the issue of Labour overrepresentation. The number of wards was reduced from 40 to 33, and aldermen were abolished. However, these wards were not redrawn, but rather smaller wards were amalgamated to produce 33 'new' wards. Seven wards were unchanged, but the rest were described as a "hotch-potch which has not been improved" by Stanley Airey, leader of the Conservative Group, in the late 1970s (Local Government Boundary Commission for England 1978).

The Conservatives continued to be underrepresented in the council chamber throughout the rest of the period, whilst Labour was consistently overrepresented until 1998. The picture for the main liberal parties was mixed. Between 1973 and 1980 they tended to be overrepresented, whilst during the 1980s they were underrepresented before reversing this trend in the 1990s. Again, however, these periods of over- and underrepresentation do not chime with boundary reforms.

This brief analysis supports the argument that the Conservatives would have done worse in the council than they deserved if the seats had been allocated proportionately. However, it is not convincing as a cause of decline since the Conservatives had consistently suffered from disproportion, from the start of the 1950s onwards, and still managed to achieve electoral successes.

4.2 The role of aldermen

Until 1973 Liverpool's municipal government operated under an aldermanic system, in which one-quarter of the council — 40 aldermen — were elected by a simple majority of the 120 councillors. Half of the aldermanic body was elected every three years and thus each alderman served a total term of six years. Apart from being unable to elect their aldermanic colleagues they had the same powers as elected councillors. As they were (usually) elected the week following municipal elections, at the first meeting of the new full council, it was expected that they would serve to entrench/create biases towards the party in power. Thus, it is important to examine the impact they had on disproportion.

Disproportion is not the same thing as having an effect on the makeup of the council or on who holds political control, which was explored in Chapter 1. It could be that the aldermanic system itself allowed the Conservatives to prevent Labour taking power (as it did between 1953 and the aldermanic election in 1955) without changing the fact that the Conservatives were electorally disadvantaged by biases in the electoral system.

The aldermanic influence on proportion is measured by subtracting the three-year average vote share from the party's seat share in the council following that year's local election. This has been done because, when including aldermen, we are taking a council-wide view of the election rather than simply looking at the outcome of that year's elections. Figure 4.3 shows the difference between seat share and vote share for the elected councillors (solid line) and the whole council (that is, elected councillors and aldermen — dashed line), with the vertical lines denoting years where aldermanic elections took place.

Figure 4.3 shows that until 1952 Conservative overrepresentation was increased slightly by the presence of the aldermen. In 1953 and 1954 this was reversed, and it was only the presence of the aldermen that meant the Conservatives continued to get a higher overall seat share than their vote share warranted; for example, in 1954 the Conservative share of elected council seats was 4.5 percentage points lower than their share of the vote, but their total presence on the council was 2.4 points higher than their vote share.

The 1955 aldermanic election occurred when Labour had a majority of councillors and thus were able to elect 18 aldermen and take control of the council. The reduced strength of Tory aldermen meant that the Conservatives faced greater disproportion in the council as a whole. This trend continued following the 1958 aldermanic election.

Happily for the Conservatives, they managed to regain control of the council for one year in 1961, which coincided with aldermanic elections. The Conservatives used this to their advantage to boost their tally of aldermen from 8 to 26, and to reduce Labour's from 32 to 14. However this did not boost Conservative overrepresentation and their new seat share was

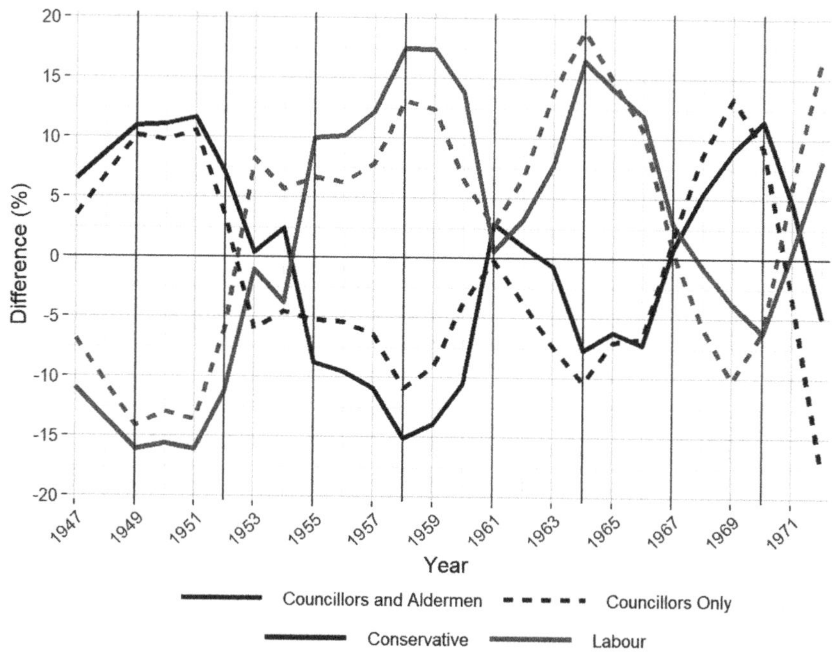

Figure 4.3: Difference between total elected councillors and averaged vote share alongside difference between total council makeup and averaged vote share, 1947–1972

just 3 percentage points higher than their vote share, compared to Labour's advantage of 17.5 points two years previously. The Conservative share of elected councillors was proportional to their three-year average vote share.

Between 1961 and 1967 the Conservatives suffered from underrepresentation in elected councillors and after 1962 their share of aldermen was insufficient to do any more than reduce their underrepresentation. However, the 1964 aldermanic election saw Labour take nine seats from the Conservatives which greatly reduced the aldermanic boost the Conservatives enjoyed. As a result, although the aldermanic system still reduced the level of Conservative underrepresentation, the extent to which it did so was lessened.

Conservative resurgence after 1964 meant that they were able to take control of the council in 1967, again a year of aldermanic elections. The Conservatives took four seats from Labour and the only Liberal seat, to give them 52 per cent of the aldermanic seats, a total of 21. This, however, was less than their share of elected councillors (which stood at 56 per cent), and the remaining Labour aldermanic seats reduced the level of overrepresentation the Conservatives enjoyed until 1970.

Although 1969 was the high-point of Conservative municipal electoral success in Liverpool, with the party having 72 per cent of elected councillors, the party still held 66 per cent of elected councillors in 1970, an aldermanic election year. The Conservatives used this to increase their seat share further, taking 8 seats from Labour to bring their total to 30, or 75 per cent of the seats. This allowed the Conservatives to boost their overrepresentation in 1970, and in 1971 when they were underrepresented in terms of elected councillors, the aldermanic bench allowed the party to maintain its overrepresentation. However, in 1972 the massive aldermanic bonus was insufficient to correct for the even greater level of underrepresentation in elected councillors, with the party underrepresented by 17.5 percentage points in terms of elected councillors, and 5 percentage points across the council as a whole.

The 1973 boundary reforms saw the aldermanic system abolished. This brief analysis has shown that whilst the aldermanic system could often exacerbate the level of disproportion — 1954 and 1972 being prime examples — generally the effect was muted. Nor does it seem the case that one party systematically benefited more than the other from the aldermanic system.

Similarly, only between 1953 and 1954, 1961 and 1962, and in 1971 did the aldermanic system mean that the Conservatives were overrepresented on the council when their elected councillor share would have left them underrepresented, whilst for Labour this never occurred. At no point did the aldermanic system make the overall seat share negatively disproportionate when elected councillors alone would have made it advantageous to the Conservatives, but this was the case for Labour in 1953 and 1954. The fact that only one-quarter of the council was composed of aldermen meant that any effects they did have tended to be muted.

This analysis, coupled with the description in Chapter 1 of the impact of aldermen on the strength of parties in the council chamber, shows that aldermen have only a marginal role to play in the story of Conservative decline in Liverpool. Broadly speaking, they did not give the Conservatives (or Labour) significantly more strength in the council chamber, nor did they allow any party to enjoy substantial overrepresentation compared to their share of votes.

Furthermore, although not shown here, smaller parties were not really impacted by the system. Until 1955, the Liberals had a small advantage owing to the aldermanic system but this largely disappeared after 1955, whilst the Protestant Party neither benefited nor suffered from the aldermanic system in any meaningful way. Overall then, the aldermanic system had a limited effect on proportionality in the council chamber.

4.3 Electoral bias in Liverpool's municipal elections

Thrasher et al. argue that bias occurs "when disproportionality does not apply equally to all of the parties; for example, one party experiences greater overrepresentation than another with the same vote share" (Thrasher, Johnston, and Rallings 2004, 70). This requires a more nuanced analysis than that presented above, since it could be argued that Labour may have enjoyed the benefits of disproportionality but not of bias.

Thrasher et al. identify three sources of electoral bias in their study of Birmingham City Council:

1. Wasted votes: "those cast in a constituency where a party's candidate loses, thus bringing no electoral returns";
2. Surplus votes: "garnered where a party's winning candidate receives more votes than are strictly necessary to defeat the nearest challenger" (that is, anything greater than the vote share of the second-placed candidate plus one);
3. Effective votes: the number of votes required to win (the number of votes for the second-placed candidate plus one).

These sources are influenced by ward boundaries, the size of ward electorates, ward turnout, the presence of a third (and fourth, and fifth, etc.) party, and the distribution of party support (Thrasher, Johnston, and Rallings 2004, 70–71). In order to assess whether municipal elections were biased — rather than just disproportionate — we can plot the seat-to-vote ratio against the percentage vote for each party. This will allow us to see whether Labour benefited from a higher seat-to-vote ratio on a given percentage of the vote than the Conservatives did. This is shown in Figure 4.4.

Figure 4.4 shows that there was indeed a bias towards Labour in the municipal electoral system. As previously mentioned, a seat-to-vote ratio greater than one means a party gained disproportionately more seats than their vote share. The chart shows that, on average, Labour needed to win around 35 per cent of the vote to have a seat-to-vote ratio greater than one, whilst the Conservatives needed just over 50 per cent. This shows a significant bias towards Labour. However, this graph encompasses all five boundary systems and as such may hide changes between boundaries and the effects of boundary reforms. To examine this, Figure 4.5 breaks down Figure 4.4 into periods when different boundaries applied.

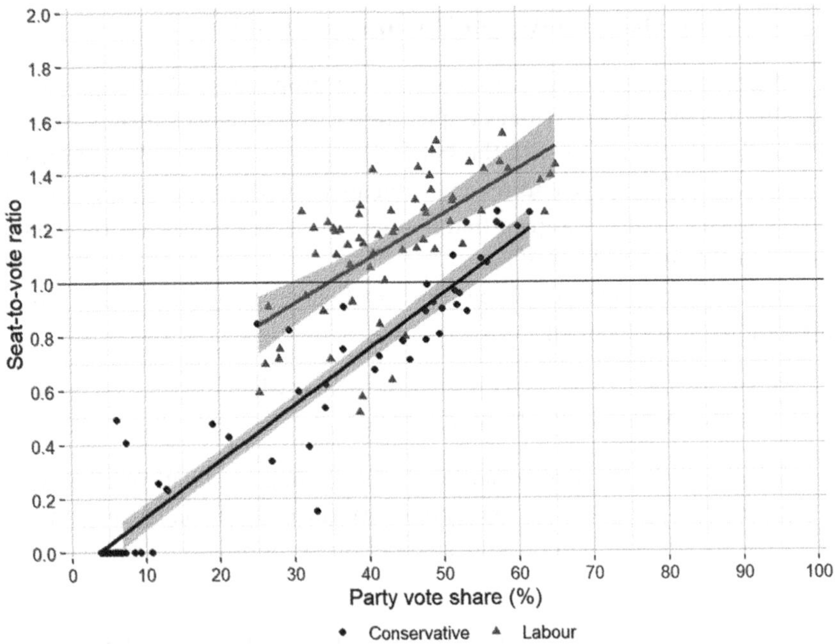

Figure 4.4: Seat-to-vote ratio compared to party vote share, 1945–2019

Note: The data controls for multi-ward elections by considering just the first-placed candidate for each party.

It shows a clear pattern of Labour benefiting from bias in all five systems, although to differeing extents. In the first boundary system Labour managed to generate overrepresentation on around 47 per cent of the vote, compared to about 50 per cent for the Conservatives. The effect of this was somewhat mitigated by the fact that the Conservatives outperformed Labour in raw vote share during this period.

Under the second boundary system, between 1953 and 1972, we can see a consistent pro-Labour bias, where the party started to benefit from overrepresentation after passing the 38 per cent mark, while the Conservatives required 53 per cent. This difference became even more marked in the third boundary system, when Labour was never underrepresented. Indeed, on a vote share of 30 per cent, the Conservatives' seat-to-vote share was about 0.5, compared to over 1.2 for Labour. The Liberals were only underrepresented when they dropped below 30 per cent of the vote. Finally, between 1980 and 1996, any bias worked against both Conservatives and Liberals, whilst Labour continued to be overrepresented by the electoral system.

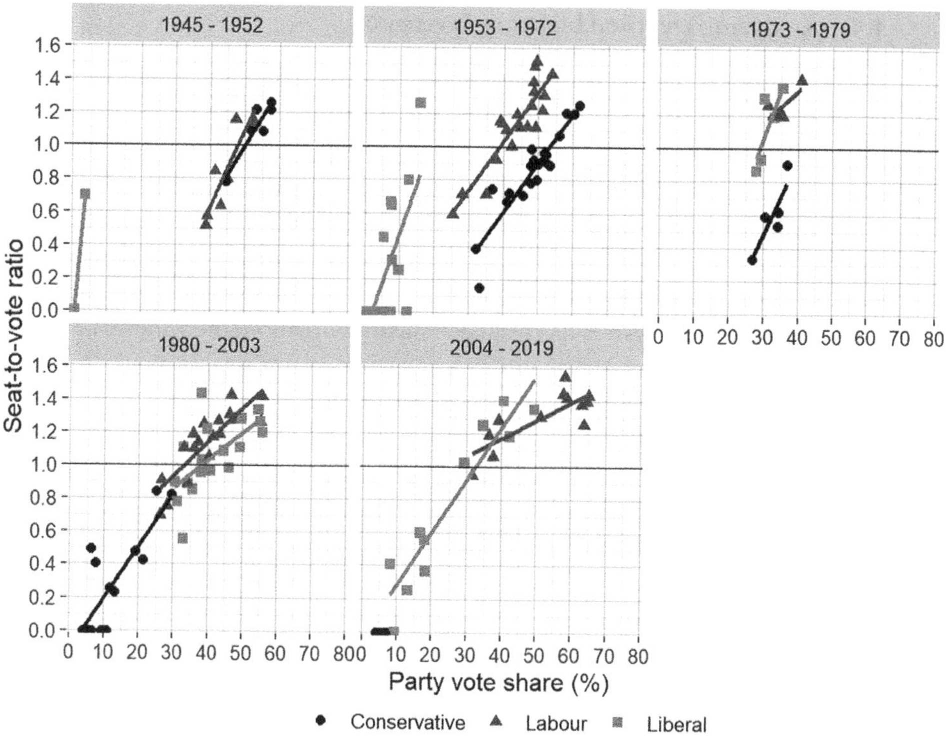

Figure 4.5: Seat-to-vote ratio compared to party vote share, 1945–2019, by ward boundary system

Note: The data controls for multi-ward elections by considering just the first-placed candidate for each party. The 1945 figure for the Liberal Party has been excluded owing to the very high seat-to-vote ratio: the party stood in three seats, winning one (2.6 per cent of the total) on a city-wide vote share of 0.9 per cent. This gives a seat-to-vote ratio of 2.9.

Thus, a more detailed analysis has shown that the bias to Labour was not corrected by any of the boundary reforms. Instead, the Conservatives faced a more hostile electoral system which coincided with their electoral decline. The 1973 boundary reform meant that it was not enough for them to win a decent share of the vote: when they won 37 per cent of the vote in this period they managed a 0.9 seat-to-vote ratio, compared to Labour's 1.2 ratio on 35 per cent of the vote. Bias could therefore be a factor in Conservative electoral decline. This analysis, however, does not identify the source of bias afflicting the Conservatives in Liverpool.

4.4 Analysing electoral biases in Liverpool

In 1959 Brookes presented a method of defining and measuring bias in electoral systems, based on the idea that "the difference in the number of seats two parties would gain in an election if they achieved the same percentage of the votes cast… is thus a measure of the effectiveness of the geography of each party's vote distribution across the constituencies" (described in Johnston, Rossiter, and Pattie 1999, 368). The formulae can be found in Johnston et al. (1999) and will not be repeated here. Whilst the existence of bias in Liverpool's electoral system has been demonstrated, this method allows us to break down the sources of bias into five categories: ward size, turnout, third party vote, third party victory, and the distribution of votes effect.

The method used below is based on what Johnston et al. term "the reverse vote shares situation" in which the two parties' electoral outcomes are reversed: if the Conservatives won 55 per cent of the vote against Labour's 45 per cent, that situation is reversed, i.e. the Conservatives get 45 per cent of the vote and Labour 55. This change is achieved via a uniform swing across all wards, although this means including in the analysis for a given year only wards where both parties of interest stood (Johnston, Rossiter, and Pattie 1999, 369).

There are, however, some restrictions which means that we cannot solely rely on Brookes. The fact that the formulae require there to be only one winner means that we would usually have to discount elections which had more than one vacancy available. We can get round this problem by treating multi-vacancy elections as single vacancy elections, through ranking candidates based on their placement within their party in terms of votes won, and then taking the best performing candidate from each party and treating that person as the sole candidate. Of course, there is a risk of generating misleading results (for example, there could be a situation in which a ward with two vacancies returns both a Labour and a Tory candidate, and with this methodology only the highest polling of the two would be treated as the 'winner'). However this is minimised by the fact that the overwhelming majority of multi-vacancy elections in Liverpool saw all winners come from the same party — which also shows the extent to which party labels, rather than individuals, shape local elections. Further, when the algebra requires a total number of votes for a party, we use a 'standardised vote': the total number of votes the party achieved in a ward, divided by the number of vacancies. As this allows us to include seats with multiple vacancies the benefits of this methodological change far outweigh the minimal downsides.

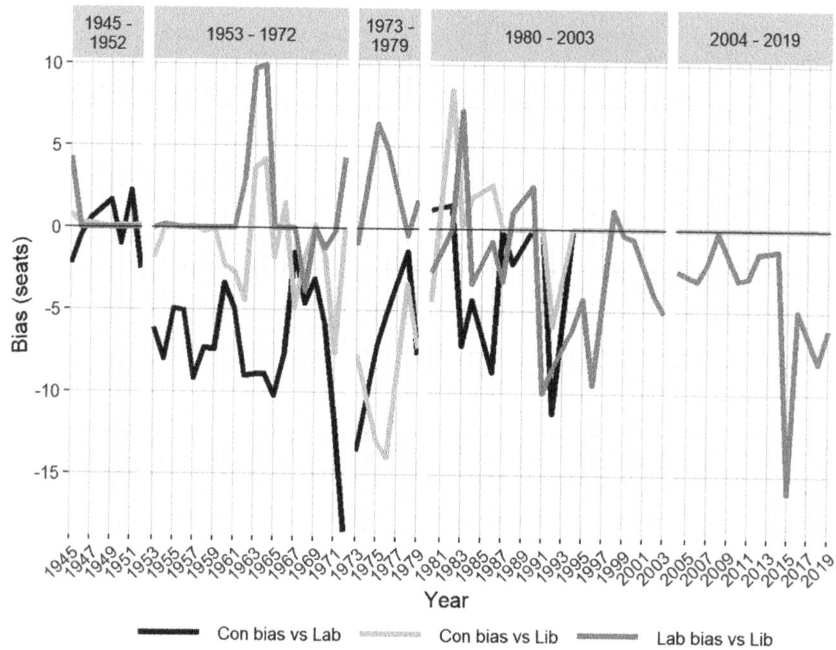

Figure 4.6: Net bias in seat allocation for Liverpool's municipal elections, 1945–2019

Furthermore, due to the scale of the Conservative decline by the late 1980s, the size of the swing from Labour/the Liberals to the Conservatives means that the non-Conservative parties receive no hypothetical seats and thus renders the model useless. As a result, the Conservative model will run only until 1986, but the Labour-Liberal model will be presented until 2019. Additionally, Brookes' method focuses on a two-party contest. This will inevitably throw up problems regarding the rise of the Liberals and the fact that the Conservatives became Liverpool's third party by the 1980s. However, with these caveats in mind, there is still analytical worth in using Brookes' method.

Figure 4.6 shows that through most of the post-war period, the Conservatives suffered from biases in the electoral system *vis-à-vis* Labour. This was most extreme in the early 1970s, when they faced a 21-seat bias against them in 1972. Interestingly, even when the Conservatives were doing well — for example in 1969, when they won 29 of the 40 seats available — they still faced a bias of five seats compared to Labour. This suggests that the Conservatives did well in this period despite the electoral system, rather than because of it.

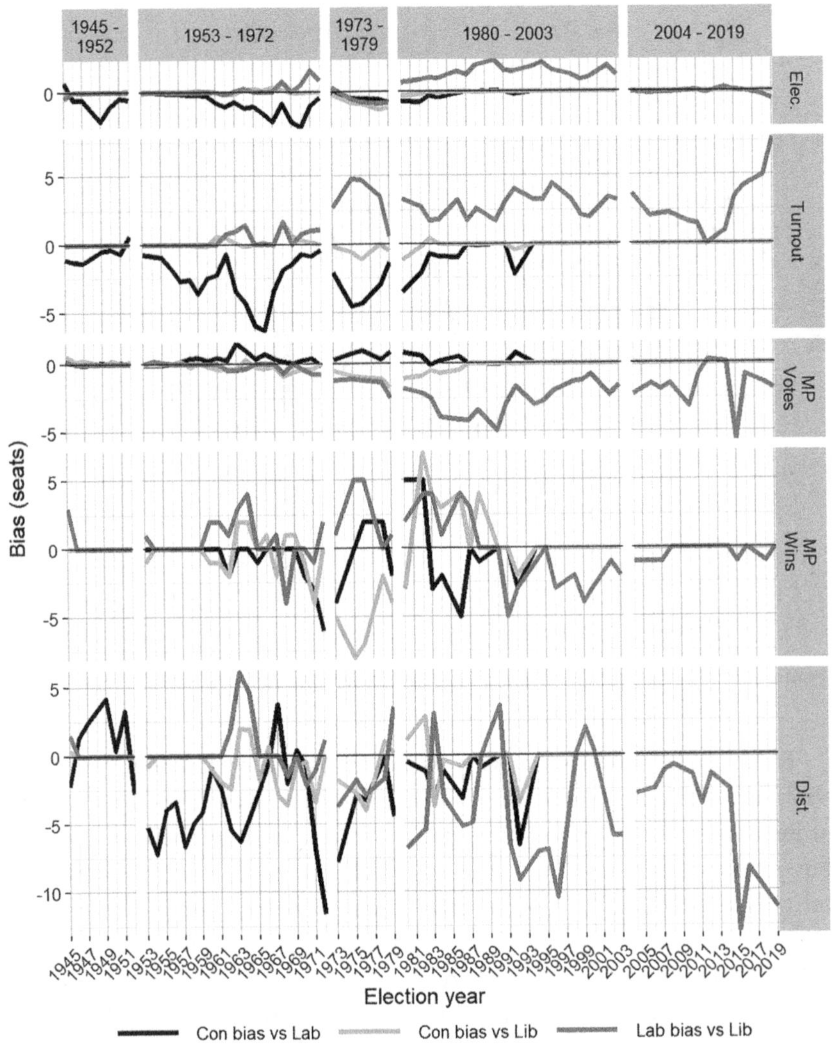

Figure 4.7: Sources of bias in seat allocation for Liverpool's municipal elections, 1945–2019

Following the 1973 boundary reforms, the Conservatives again suffered from both pro-Labour and pro-Liberal bias. However, across the period we do see the bias against the Conservatives decline in both models. After the 1980 boundary reform, the Conservatives tended to benefit from bias against the Liberal Party, but this was usually mitigated by pro-Labour bias in the Conservative–Labour model. We also see that at the start of the period of

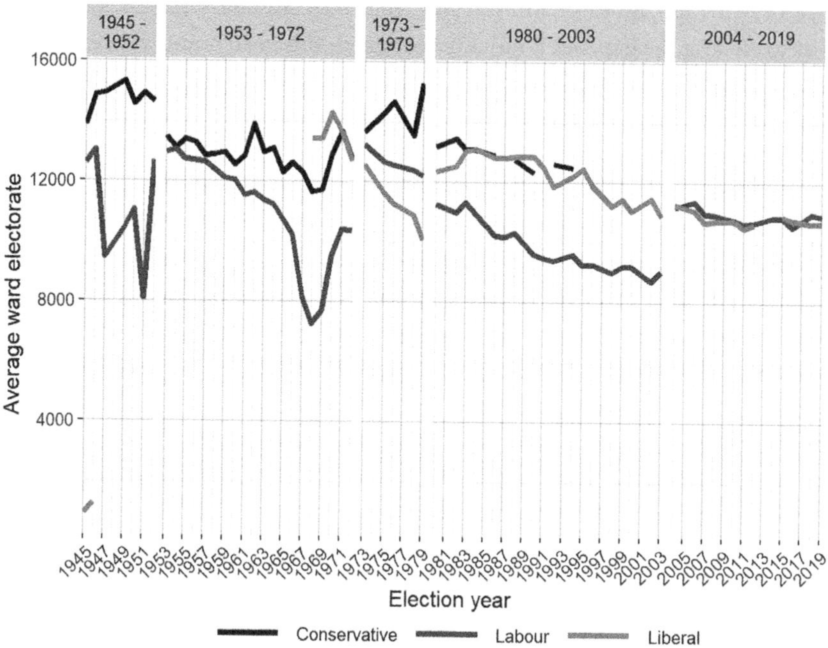

Figure 4.8: Average ward electorate by winning party, 1945–2019

rapid Conservative decline in the city, during the mid-1980s, there was bias against the Conservatives *vis-à-vis* both Labour and the Liberals.

To further develop this analysis, Figure 4.7 breaks down the bias into its five constituent parts for all three models, which are explored in greater detail below.

4.4.1 *Size of electorate*

The size of a ward's electorate is important because if a party has concentrated support in large wards then, all other things being equal, it will need a higher absolute number of votes to win a seat than parties with concentrated support in smaller wards. We can examine whether the Conservatives tended to do well in larger wards by plotting the average electorate size in wards where the Conservatives won against wards where Labour won, shown in Figure 4.8.

In all cases, Conservative wards had a higher average electorate than wards where Labour won. After 1945, the gap between Conservative and Labour wards grew from just over 1,000 electors in 1945 to 7,000 electors in 1951. The gap was reduced significantly by the 1953 boundary reform, but by the time of the 1973 reform it had opened again, peaking at over 4,000 electors during Labour's nadir in 1968. The 1973 boundary review went some way to closing the gap, but it quickly reopened; the 1980 boundary review did nothing to close the gap, but rather reduced the average size of wards won by both parties. Thus, we can expect to identify ward size as another source of bias against the Conservatives.

Looking back, Figure 4.7 shows that the size of the electorate was not a significant source of bias against the Conservatives after 1945. The largest source of bias came in 1970, when the party faced a 5.3 seat bias against Labour, out of a total of 40 seats up for election. It is also worth noting that Conservatives still won this election, with 19 seats to Labour's 17 (and seat share reflecting vote share fairly well). Further, the limited bias seems to have been corrected for in the 1973 boundary reform. Turning to the Conservative–Liberal model, the Conservatives consistently faced a small bias against the Liberals, and that electorate size was not a driver of this bias: at most it accounted for no more than three seats.

Thus the electorate size component of bias was a problem for the Conservatives, but only a minor one. Indeed, it could not be a significant factor in Conservative decline because, when the bias was at its greatest in the mid- to late-1960s the Conservatives did phenomenally well in Liverpool. Further, when the Conservatives actually faced decline, from 1973 to the late 1980s, the electorate component of bias was minimal.

4.4.2 *Turnout/abstention*

Related to the size of a ward's electorate is the level of turnout. Clearly, the lower the turnout, the fewer votes required to win a ward. For example, if 20 wards had an electorate of 1,000 and Labour won 50 per cent of the votes (plus one) in 10 wards on a turnout of 10 per cent, whilst the Tories won the other 10 wards with 50 per cent of the votes (plus one) on a turnout of 50 per cent, then Labour would require 510 votes to win 10 seats while the Conservatives would require 2,510 votes to win the same number of seats.

Figure 4.9 shows the average turnout in wards won by the three main parties. In every year the seats won by the Conservatives saw a higher turnout than those won by Labour. After the 1973 boundary reform, we see that generally the Conservatives won in wards with the highest level of turnout, followed closely by the Liberals, and then Labour. This again feeds into our understanding of why the Conservatives suffered from a lower seat-to-vote ratio: because by winning seats in wards with higher turnouts, all other things being equal, the party secured more votes per seat won than Labour or the Liberals.

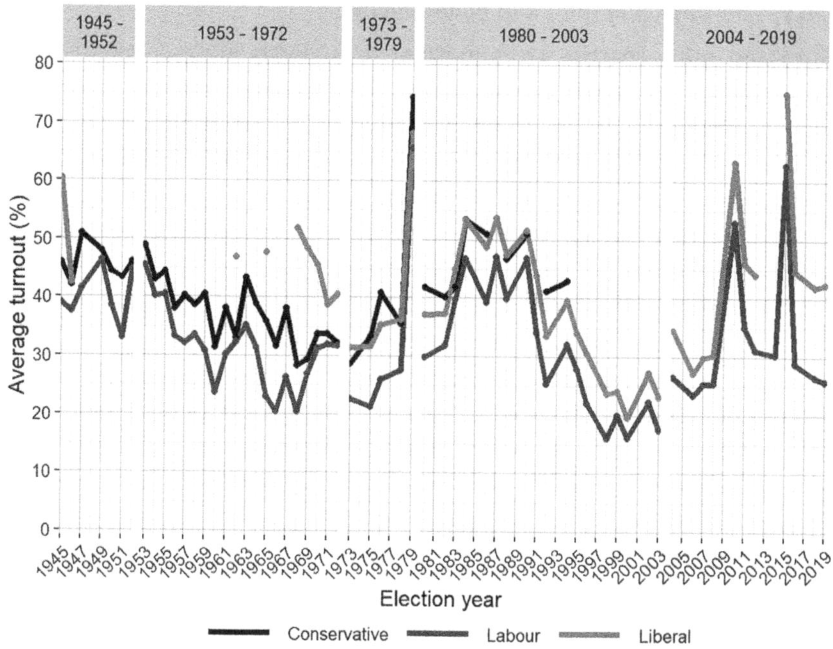

Figure 4.9: Average ward turnout by winning party, 1945–2019

Figure 4.7 shows that differential turnout levels almost always cost the Conservatives seats, to both Labour and the Liberals, but it did so most severely in the mid-1960s, costing them around six seats in the 1962 and 1963 local elections. These were years when, nationally, the Conservative Party was coming to the end of its 13 years in government and local election results were poor. Thus, the Conservatives were losing seats they would previously have won and dissatisfaction with the national Conservative government depressed Conservative turnout somewhat. For the rest of the period the size of the bias was not particularly large, apart from a couple of elections in the mid-1970s when the Conservatives faced roughly a five-seat bias *vis-à-vis* Labour. However, due to the decline in Conservative seat share at that time, addressing this five-seat bias against Labour would have put the Conservatives in a stronger position and helped to challenge the claim that they were increasingly irrelevant to Liverpudlian politics.

The Conservative–Liberal model shows little in the way of bias, reflecting the fact that the levels of turnout in wards won by the Conservatives and the Liberals was broadly equal.

4.4.3 *The impact of third and minor parties*

Third and minor parties are important in understanding components of electoral bias. As the number of parties increases, fewer votes are needed to win. Clearly, this is a tricky component to assess in the case of the Liverpool Conservatives as from 1973 they themselves became the third party. Thus, the results after 1973 should be treated with some caution, especially considering that Labour would be the third party in the Conservative–Liberal model.

The impact of third and minor parties is two-fold: the impact of third- and minor-party votes and the impact of third- and minor-party victories.

Generally, the role of third- and minor-party *votes* was extremely limited in terms of producing biases within the electoral system, in both the Labour and the Liberal models. However, third- and minor-party victories had more of an influence in terms of biases within the system. We can see that in the Conservative–Labour model generally there was a very limited effect up until the early 1970s, when the Conservatives suffered from bias presumably attributable to the rise of the Liberals in this period. However, this largely disappeared after the 1973 local elections, most likely due to the fact that the Liberals' success was more widespread.

The Conservative–Liberal model shows that, from 1973 to 1980, the Conservatives suffered from a bias against the Liberals driven by 'third party' successes, but this reversed during the 1980s. Overall, however, the bias against the Conservatives attributable to third parties was neither large in magnitude, nor consistently against the party, hence it cannot be the cause of decline.

4.4.4 *The distribution of votes*

The distribution of votes component of bias shown in Figure 4.7 is generated by

> evaluating the relative proportion of a party's votes which are effective (i.e. help it to win a seat) rather than either wasted (are cast in seats that the party does not win) or surplus (are additional to requirement in seats where it does win). The greater the ratio of effective to (wasted plus surplus) votes, the better the distribution of the party's votes. (Johnston, Rossiter, and Pattie 1999, 368)

The distribution of votes is a comparatively strong driver of bias. In the first boundary period, the distribution effect tended to benefit the Conservatives, but after 1951 this changed, with the party facing a less efficient distribution of votes than Labour in every year except 1967. The bias was greatest in 1972, when the effect of the Liberal Party was to increase the number of wasted Conservative votes. This cost the party 12 seats *vis-à-vis* Labour. Similarly, in 1973 when the whole council was up for election and the Conservatives were relegated to third place, they suffered from a bias towards Labour, costing them nine seats. During the 1973–1980 boundary system the Conservatives faced both a pro-Labour and pro-Liberal bias, but this varied from election to election in severity. A more efficient distribution of votes would have kept the Conservatives in the game for longer than was actually the case. This also shows that biased boundaries were not the reason for the poor distribution of Conservative votes. Indeed, the fact this source of bias declined massively in the next election suggests that this was more of an electoral or campaigning problem.

4.5 Discussion

Brookes' method has allowed us to identify the sources of anti-Conservative bias in the electoral system. The Conservative–Labour model shows the Conservatives did suffer from bias against them and in favour of Labour, which was most extreme in the distribution of votes component. Contrastingly, the Conservative–Liberal model shows a mixed pattern: the Conservatives suffered from pro-Liberal bias between 1973 and 1980, but afterwards they tended to benefit from any biases. Across the whole period since 1945, most of the bias in the Conservative–Liberal model was driven by third party victories, which in this case was almost always the Labour Party.

This study has shown that the Conservatives were systematically disadvantaged by the electoral system throughout most of the period of study. However, through use of Brookes' method, we have been able to analyse the individual effects of turnout, distribution of votes, size of electorate and third- and minor-party votes and victories.

In the Conservative–Labour model the distribution-of-votes effect was the most important source bias, followed by turnout. Electorate sizes and third- or minor-party victories were also occasionally relevant but generally did not make much of a difference to the magnitude of bias. Interestingly, the two major drivers of bias within the system (which was usually anti-Conservative bias) were not features that could be fixed by boundary change: the Conservatives simply failed to win votes where they needed them. Hence, this bias was not just a result of boundaries, but rather poor electioneering.

Again, it is important to remember that a bias might not lead to a loss. The Conservatives faced large biases in their most successful years during the late 1960s. However, bias does work to reduce the number of seats a party can win, and thus makes the job of forming an administration more difficult. This analysis has shown that a significant proportion of bias in both the Conservative–Labour and the Conservative–Liberal models — that arising from the distribution and abstention elements — could have been addressed through a better electoral strategy.

If we look at the period when Conservative decline began in earnest — in terms of seat share in 1971, and vote share in the early 1980s — we can see that the Conservatives did face biases in the municipal electoral system. Whilst the party was indeed outpolled by Labour and the Liberals it was not receiving a proportionate level of representation at any time in the two boundary systems that operated during this period. The long-term effect was to squeeze the Conservatives out of local electoral politics, with voters wondering what the point of voting for the Tories was when they would never win. Thus, it is fair to claim that, to some extent, Conservative decline was hastened by biases in the municipal electoral system. For example, as shown above in Figure 4.6, overall biases in 1973 cost the Conservatives 14 seats *vis-à-vis* Labour, and around 7 seats *vis-à-vis* the Liberals. Addressing these biases would have resulted in a true three-way polity compared to the two-and-a-half party system which it had become.

It is interesting to consider how history might have played out, especially in the 1970s and 1980s, had the biases in the electoral system not been present. With a greater number of seats, it is possible the Conservatives might have taken more of a lead in municipal politics during these vital periods. Indeed, with greater numbers they could have entered a coalition with the Liberals as equal partners.

4.6 Conclusion

This chapter has argued that we must look beyond unfavourable electoral systems to fully explain Conservative decline in Liverpool. Throughout most of the period the Conservatives did indeed suffer from systemic biases against them within the electoral system. Against Labour the Conservatives faced an average bias of 7.3 seats during the era when the 1953–1972 boundaries applied, whilst in the 1973–1980 boundary era they faced a bias of 7 seats against Labour and of 9 seats against the Liberals.

However, during the period of rapid Conservative decline in the 1980s, the biases faced by the party were not large by historical standards — on average 1.7 seats against Labour and a net positive bias against the Liberals of 0.4 seats. Thus the idea that biases in the ward boundary system were the cause of the Conservative Party's poor position in the council chamber is not borne out by this analysis.

5 Demographic changes and bases of party support in Liverpool

As outlined in Chapter 2, there has been a tendency in the literature to highlight demographic change as a cause of Conservative decline in Liverpool. The classic argument runs as follows: the Conservatives found themselves in a city that was increasingly demographically hostile to them, especially because of increased poverty. The party then slowly retreated into a few safe, affluent, wards in the south of the city (see Kilfoyle (2000, 36–37) and Frost and North (2013)).

This chapter rejects that argument. If anything, between 1945 and 2019 the demographic profile of Liverpool became *more* middle class and overall *more* favourable to the Conservatives than it had been in the past. Although the party was increasingly unable to reach out from its typical demographic base of support, this base was not so narrow that it drove electoral decline. Ultimately, this chapter concludes that it is not enough to base our analysis on objective categories such as class, wealth, and employment. Rather, we should look at subjective characteristics and how people describe themselves in terms of their own identity.

This chapter proceeds by using census data to examine the effects that changing ward demographics had on Conservative support in local elections. Firstly, it outlines the demographics of support for the three main parties in Liverpool, before moving to an examination of the determinants of party support in local elections based on regression analysis. This allows a better understanding of changing patterns of party support in the city.

5.1 Key periods in the history of the Liverpool Conservative Party

For this analysis, we split the 1945–2019 era into five periods, based on the electoral performance of the Conservative Party. These are shown in Table 5.1.

Table 5.1: Key periods in the history of the Liverpool Conservative Party

Years covered	*Period description*	*Av. Con. vote share*	*Av. Con. first place share*
1945–1952	Not analysed	52.0	56.3
1953–1970	Success	50.0	47.2
1971–1986	Decline	27.9	15.3
1987–2003	Irrelevance	7.2	0.9
2004–2019	Irrelevance	5.7	0.0

The first period is 1945–1952, which is not covered in this analysis because census data is unavailable. The second period is 1953–1970, a period of Conservative success when the party achieved an average of 50 per cent of the vote (not including the votes of their Protestant Party allies) compared to Labour's 43 per cent, winning 47 per cent of seats (51 per cent of the seats it contested), compared to Labour's 49 per cent.

The third period (second period of study) is 1971–1986, when we see the decline of the Conservative Party take place. During this period, the Conservatives won an average of 28 per cent of the vote, compared to Labour's 41 per cent and the Liberals' 30 per cent, but just 15 per cent of the seats (53 per cent for Labour, 32 per cent for the Liberals).

The final two periods cover eras of Conservative irrelevance: 1987–2003 saw the Conservatives win just 1 per cent of seats, on a vote share of 7 per cent, while the 2004–2019 period saw the Conservatives win just 6 per cent of the vote on average and fail to gain a single seat. These periods will form the basis of the following demographic analyses.

5.2 Demographics of party support

An individual-level analysis of voting behaviour in Liverpool is impossible with the available ward-level census and electoral data, but we can examine which ward-level structural factors were conducive to increased or decreased party support in Liverpool. Six key social variables will be explored in our analysis of party support in Liverpool: gender, overcrowding, unemployment, class, housing tenure, and age. Where possible, the base unit of these variables is people, rather than households, as it is people who vote.

The first part of this chapter is based on census data, starting from the 1951 census and continuing until the 2011 census. Data for the 1951 census was gathered from the relevant published county reports (General Register

Office 1954). The 1961, and 1981–2011 censuses, are available via Nomis (Office for National Statistics 2021). The 1971 census data was taken from the Casweb service (UK Data Service 2013) and the dataset for the 1966 mini-census was accessed via the UK Data Service (Office of Population Censuses and Surveys and General Register Office (Scotland) 1981). Before examining the demographics of party support it is worth outlining the rationale for the variables used.

Regarding gender, in their 1968 analysis of working-class Conservatism McKenzie and Silver argued that older women tended to be more Conservative than older men, but this difference decreased among younger people (McKenzie and Silver 1968, 86). However, upon completion of their analysis, they found that gender was unrelated to voting choice among the working class specifically (McKenzie and Silver 1968, 187).

This finding is somewhat contradicted by Ball's history of the Conservative Party, in which he argues that the Conservatives benefited from "the tone as well as the content of the Conservative appeal, and the result was a gender gap in voting which benefited the party from 1918 until the 1980s" (Ball 2013, 84). He cites the experiences of Vivian Henderson, who fought elections in Glasgow and Liverpool in the 1920s and claimed "I have found working-class women far more Conservative than their husbands or brothers", which, combined with the fact that "Conservatives polled better where women were more numerous", led Ball to argue that "the party had some success in projecting an appeal to them across class boundaries" (Ball 2013, 117). For the purposes of this study, gender will be measured simply by the percentage of men in the total ward population. The above generates the following hypothesis:

> H1: Conservative vote share was negatively correlated with the proportion of men in a ward.

It is often claimed that age is positively correlated with voting Conservative, usually followed by a reference to a maxim falsely attributed to Churchill: "If you're not a liberal when you're 25, you have no heart. If you're not a Conservative by the time you're 35, you have no brain" (The Churchill Centre 2016).[1] Goerres finds that, although age and generational effects — what he terms the 'grey vote' — were much more important in the early post-war

1 John Adams is generally credited with the first approximate use of this statement, saying "A boy of 15 who is not a democrat is good for nothing, and he is no better who is a democrat at 20" (Founders Online 2002).

period, a gap between older and younger voters persisted (Goerres 2008, 299). This suggests that wards with a greater number of older people would be more likely to vote Conservative. Age is operationalised as the percentage of people over the age of 45, expressed as a proportion of the total population of those aged 15 or over in a ward. These ages were chosen because they were the only ones for which suitable data could be taken from all censuses consistently.

> H2: Conservative vote share was positively correlated with the proportion of older people in a ward.

Owens and Wade argue that, theoretically, areas with higher incomes should generate greater support for the Conservatives than areas with lower incomes (Owens and Wade 1988, 41). Similarly, areas with higher levels of unemployment are expected to produce greater support for the Labour Party. The reasons for this do not have to be theoretically complex, and have been stated clearly by Runciman:

> There is nothing, in a sense, that needs to be explained about a South Wales miner voting Labour or an executive of General Motors voting Republican. The simplest model of rational self-interest is enough to explain these cases. (Runciman 1963, 94)

Although Owens and Wade's study focused on the constituency level there is no reason to suggest that this logic should not hold true on the ward level too. Their study finds that changes in unemployment and income levels both play an important role in determining shares of the constituency vote (Owens and Wade 1988, 43).

Directly measuring wealth is impossible using census data, since wealth is not requested in any census. As a proxy the measure "overcrowding" will be used, based on the assumption that the wealthier a family is the less likely that they would live in an overcrowded home. Here overcrowding is defined as the number of people who live in a dwelling with over 1.5 people per room, as a percentage of the total ward population. However, the 2001 census only gives the measure as the number of households, not persons. This is not an insurmountable problem, and so 2001 household data is included in this study.

> H3: Conservative vote share was negatively correlated with higher levels of overcrowding in a ward.

Unemployment is measured by taking the number of economically active men seeking employment and representing this as a percentage of economically active men in employment. The male population has been used, rather than the total economically active one, because it is all that is provided by earlier censuses, so using it allows for continuity.

> H4: Conservative vote share was positively correlated with lower levels of unemployment in a ward.

The literature on class and voting is extensive. The traditional argument is that those identified as working class, variously defined, tend to vote Labour, whilst the middle classes tend to vote Conservative. For Heath et al., this was tied into the economic interests of the classes: "wage labourers have different interests from those of the self-employed or from those of salaried managers and professionals" (Heath, Jowell, and Curtice 1985, 14). Even when this approach was criticised for being overly structural it was still believed to be the case that the working class have a much higher propensity to vote Labour than Conservative. Despite talk of class dealignment, work by Johnston and Pattie shows that dealignment was more strongly linked to the south of Britain (Johnston and Pattie 1992, 85). This being the case, a measure of class strength in wards will be included to examine whether there was indeed a measure of class-based voting in Liverpool.

The class composition of a ward has been operationalised as the number of men over the age of 16 who were in working-class occupations, expressed as a percentage of the total number of men in employment. For the purposes of this study, working-class occupations are those classified in socio-economic groups 7–12 and 14–16 (Benson and Payne 1997, 106) until the 2001 census, from when this measure is no longer used. For 2001 onward NS-SEC classes 5–7 are used (K. Roberts 2011, 24). Using male employment as the datum ensured consistency across measures, since female employment was not included in earlier censuses. It is expected that the higher the percentage of working-class people in a ward, the lower the Conservative vote would be — although this comes with the caveat that the Conservatives were, nationally, still able to appeal to between "a third and a half of the working class on a regular basis" (Ball 1995, 120).

> H5: Conservative vote share was negatively correlated with the proportion of working-class people in a ward.

Heath et al. put forward two arguments for the way housing tenure is transmitted into voting behaviour. The first is that housing is "an extension of the influence of the workplace… one's politics are influenced not only by one's own class position but by the class position of those around one", whilst the second is that "an individual's housing tenure will structure his or her individual interests in just the same way that position in the labour market structures class interests" (Heath, Jowell, and Curtice 1985, 46). If housing tenure does have an effect on voting behaviour, and if it operates through the first mechanism, we can expect this relationship to disappear when we control for class. If, however, the causal mechanism matches the second explanation, it should remain even when controlling for other factors.

Housing tenure is measured by the number of people classed as owner occupiers (that is, who own their home outright or via a mortgage), as a percentage of the total number of people in permanent dwellings.

> H6: Conservative vote share was positively correlated with higher levels of home ownership in a ward.

Covering all the relevant council boundaries presents a problem. Between 1945 and 2021 Liverpool underwent four boundary reforms (1953, 1973, 1980, 2004). As a result, neither the 1971 census nor the 1981 census covers the period between 1973 and 1980.

However, we can largely get round this issue. As noted in Chapter 4, the 1973 boundary reform was rather lazy. It reduced Liverpool's 40 wards to 33 by merging 15 of them together to create 7 new ones.[2] To analyse these we can sum the census figures for each 1971 ward to arrive at an estimate for the 1973 wards. The final change was that Woolton ward was split into Woolton East and Woolton West. Since we only have census data for the ward as a whole, Woolton will be excluded for the period between 1973 and 1980.

Table 5.2 below shows the years for which data from each census was applied. Generally, census data is used to cover a period of ten years, typically the four years before the census and the five years after. However, exceptions have been made where boundary changes prevent the use of other census data, or where that data is unavailable. This is not ideal, but extending the relevance of census data is necessary to maximise the number of cases available for analysis.

The following sections of this chapter explore the relationship between party support and the demographic ward-level characteristics behind hypotheses 1–6, which allows us to trace trends over time.

The first of each pair of figures is a set of scatterplots. The darker circles

2 The new wards did not have the most imaginative names: Abercromby and St James, Breckfield and St Domingo, Central, Everton and Netherfield, Granby and Princes Park, Low Hill and Smithdown, Melrose and Westminster, and Sandhills and Vauxhall.

Table 5.2: Summary of census coverage periods

Census year	*Years covered*
1961	1953–1963
1966	1964–1967
1971	1968–1972
1971[a]	1973–1979
1981	1980–1986
1991	1987–1996
2001	1997–2003
2001[b]	2004–2007
2011	2011 onwards

[a] 1971 census wards were merged into the 1973 wards as described in the text, with the except of Woolton East and Woolton West, which have been omitted from the analysis.

[b] 2001 census data was taken at the LSOA (lower-layer super output areas) level, from which we could reconstruct the 2004 wards.

represent the Conservative vote share in all wards where a Conservative candidate stood, whilst the lighter circles represent only the wards where the Conservatives won, and in both cases a line of best fit is plotted. These charts also include the Pearson's r value, a measure of the correlation between two variables, in this case the demographic variable being examined and Conservative vote share. A value of −1 means there is a total negative correlation between the two variables (as one increases, the other decreases); a value of +1 means there is a total positive correlation and a value of 0 means there is no correlation between the two variables. This measure will be used to test hypotheses 1–6. The second of each pair of figures is a line graph, which shows the average vote share in wards where each party was victorious, by census period.

5.2.1 *Gender*

Figure 5.1 shows a clear and consistent pattern across all four periods, in which the Conservatives tend to achieve a higher share of the vote in wards with lower proportions of men. The Pearson's r values confirm that this is indeed the case — the correlation between the percentage of men in a ward and Conservative vote share is consistently negative across all four groups, and all relationships are statistically significant.

Figure 5.2 shows that, on average across wards won by the Conservatives, men remained around 47 per cent of the population for all three periods in

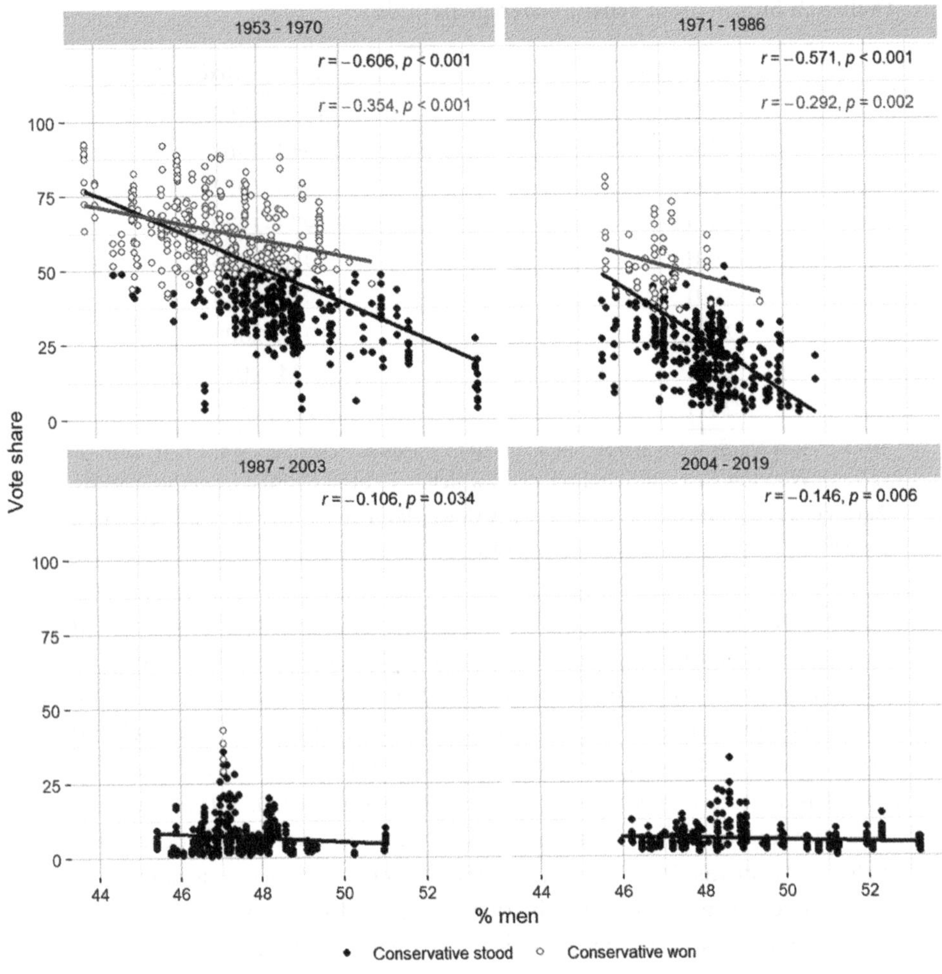

Figure 5.1: Conservative vote share against the percentage of men in each ward, with Pearson's r value

which it won seats. The Liberals' situation reversed from underperforming among men in the first period to overperforming in the final period. Relative to Labour, however, the Conservatives did tend to do better in wards with more women than men. Taken together, we have evidence that supports H1: Conservative vote share was negatively correlated with the proportion of men in a ward.

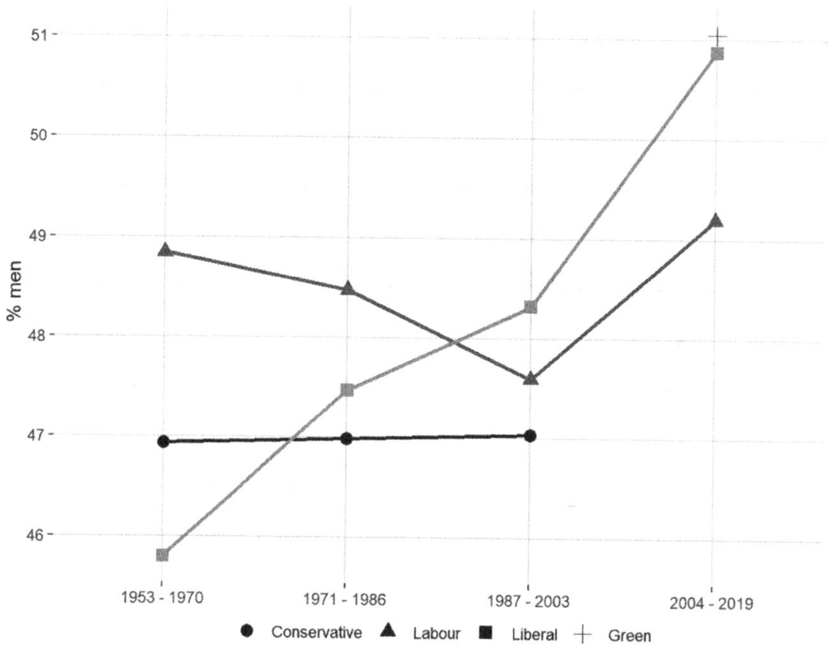

Figure 5.2: Average percentage of men in wards won by each party

5.2.2 Age

Figure 5.3 shows a positive correlation between Conservative vote share and the proportion of the population aged over 45 in a ward. In all four periods, the Conservatives consistently tended to do better in wards with higher proportions of those over 45. However, in the first period the Conservatives were winning both seats and vote share across the whole range of wards, but this range shrank in the second period. In the third and fourth periods vote share shrank considerably although, ironically, the seats they won were in wards containing both high and low levels of over 45s (particularly in the most recent period). All these relationships were statistically significant.

Moving to Figure 5.4, which shows the average percentage of the ward population aged over 45 in seats won by each party, we can see that the Conservatives' victories were in wards where, on average, there was a higher share of over 45s than in wards won by Labour. We also see the common pattern emerge of areas of Liberal support in the early periods looking similar to areas of Conservative support, but over time looking more similar to Labour areas of support — in this case for the first two census periods the

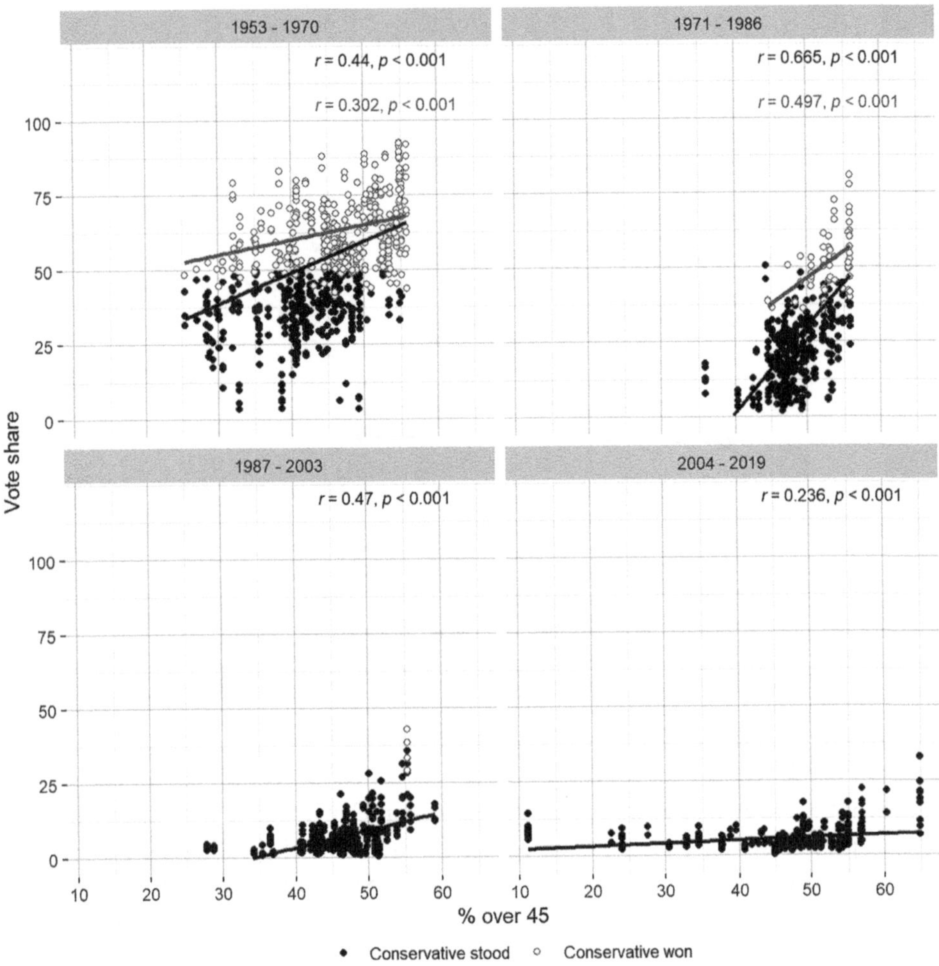

Figure 5.3: Conservative vote share against the percentage aged over 45 in each ward, with Pearson's r value

Liberals won in wards with a higher proportion of over 45s than Labour, but in the two most recent periods, on average, they were winning wards with very similar proportions of over 45s.

Thus, there is evidence here that supports H2: Conservative vote share was positively correlated with the proportion of older people in a ward.

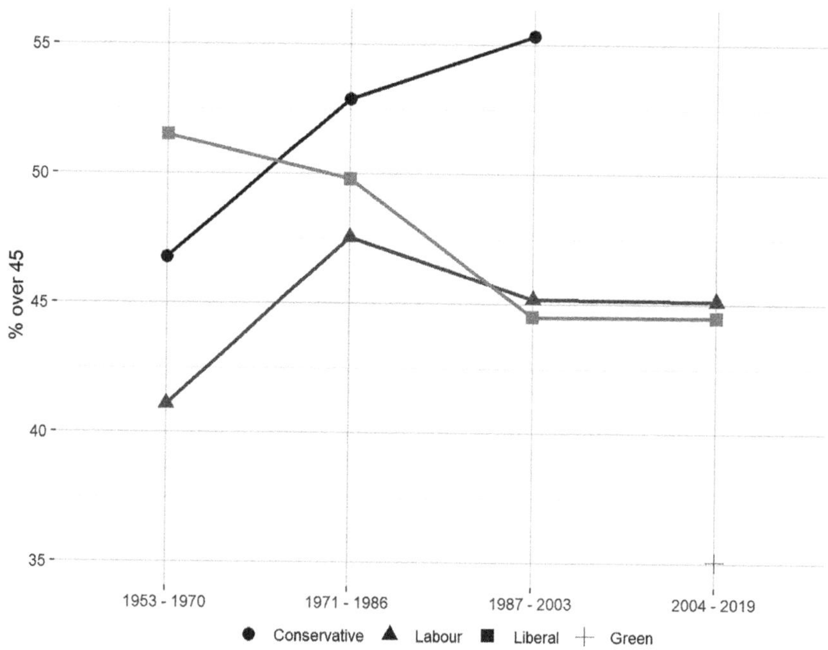

Figure 5.4: Average percentage aged over 45 in wards won by each party

5.2.3 *Overcrowding*

There is a striking difference between periods in the range shown by the independent variable "overcrowding" — in the 1961 census Central ward reported that 38.1 per cent of people were in overcrowded homes, compared to just 1.1 per cent in Aigburth ward. By the 1971 census the highest rate of overcrowding was roughly one-third lower — again, Central ward at 25.8 per cent. By the 1981 census the highest level of overcrowding was just 6.8 per cent, this time in Abercromby ward. This presumably reflects the success of Liverpool City Council's attempts at slum clearance.

Unsurprisingly, in Figure 5.5 we see a clear negative correlation between Conservative vote share and levels of overcrowding. However, there were still instances where the Conservatives managed to win relatively overcrowded wards. This can be seen in the 1953–1970 period when the Conservatives were able to win in one of the most overcrowded wards (Abercromby). However, this was an exception rather than the rule: Conservative support was heavily concentrated in wards with less than 10 per cent overcrowding. In the later periods, Conservative success was

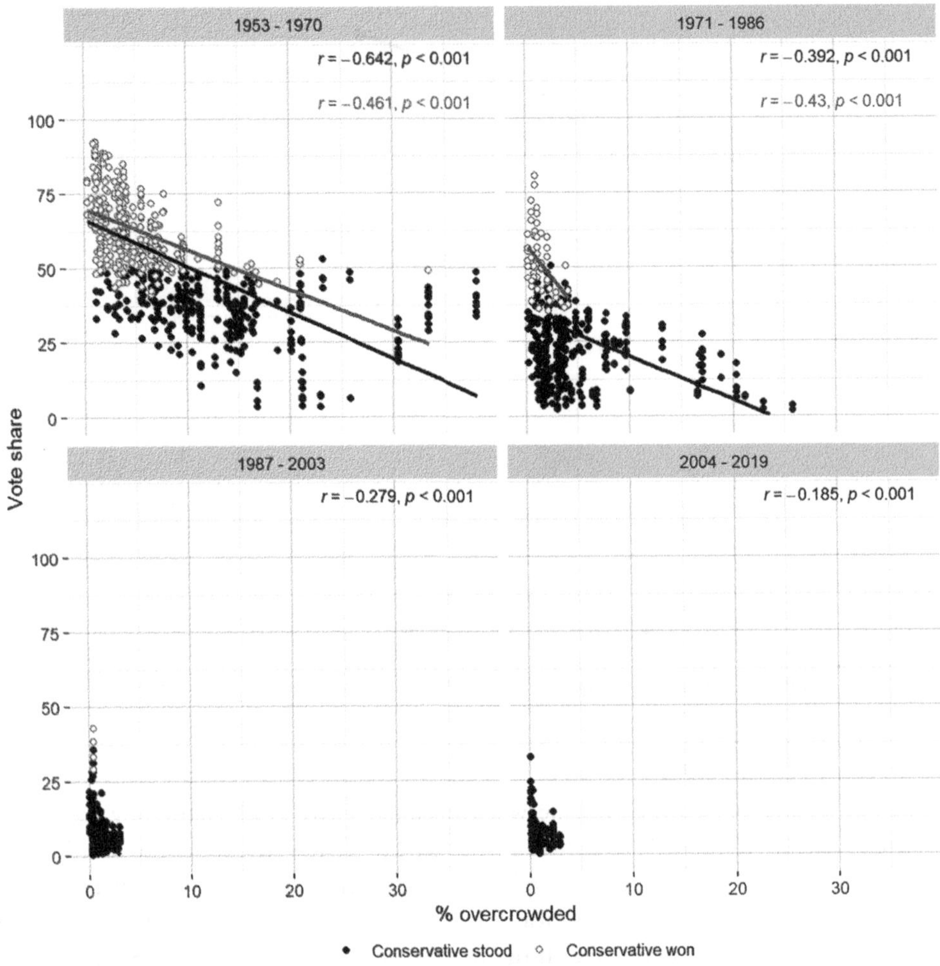

Figure 5.5: Conservative vote share against the percentage of those living in overcrowded conditions in each ward, with Pearson's r value

restricted to areas with the least overcrowding in the city. This is reflected in the Pearson r values, which are all negative, and all relationships are statistically significant.

Moving to Figure 5.6, we can see that the average percentage of overcrowding in wards won by the Conservatives was consistently lower than that in wards won by Labour. Again, this is unsurprising. Hence, there is support for H3, as the Conservatives do indeed seem to do better in wards with lower levels of overcrowding.

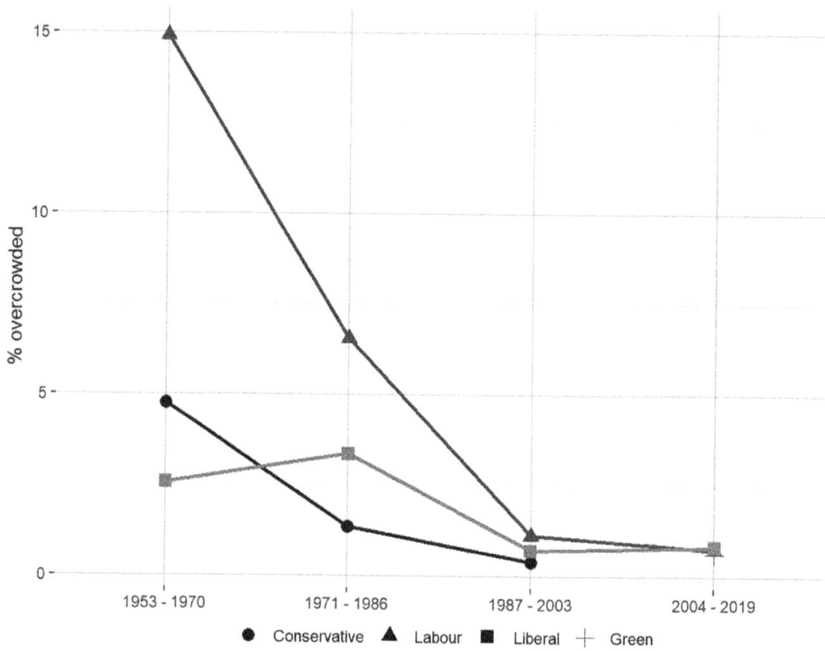

Figure 5.6: Average percentage living in overcrowded conditions in wards won by each party

5.2.4 *Unemployment*

When we look at unemployment we see the opposite pattern to that for overcrowding: the range of values for unemployment increases massively from the first period to the third period, before reducing slightly in the fourth period. The early period saw no more than roughly one in four men in a ward unemployed, and in most unemployment did not pass 10 per cent. By the second period, however, it could reach over 40 per cent of men in a ward, and by the third over 50 per cent. However, even when this was the case the Conservatives occasionally won seats.

The expected relationship — a negative correlation between Conservative vote share and levels of male unemployment — holds true overall and so we find support for the hypothesis.

Figure 5.8 shows a similar relationship to that which we have seen with previous variables, with the average level of unemployment being lower in wards won by the Conservatives than in wards won by Labour. However, by the third census period, the gap between wards in which the Conservatives and Labour won had grown massively. Moving to the Liberals, we see that in

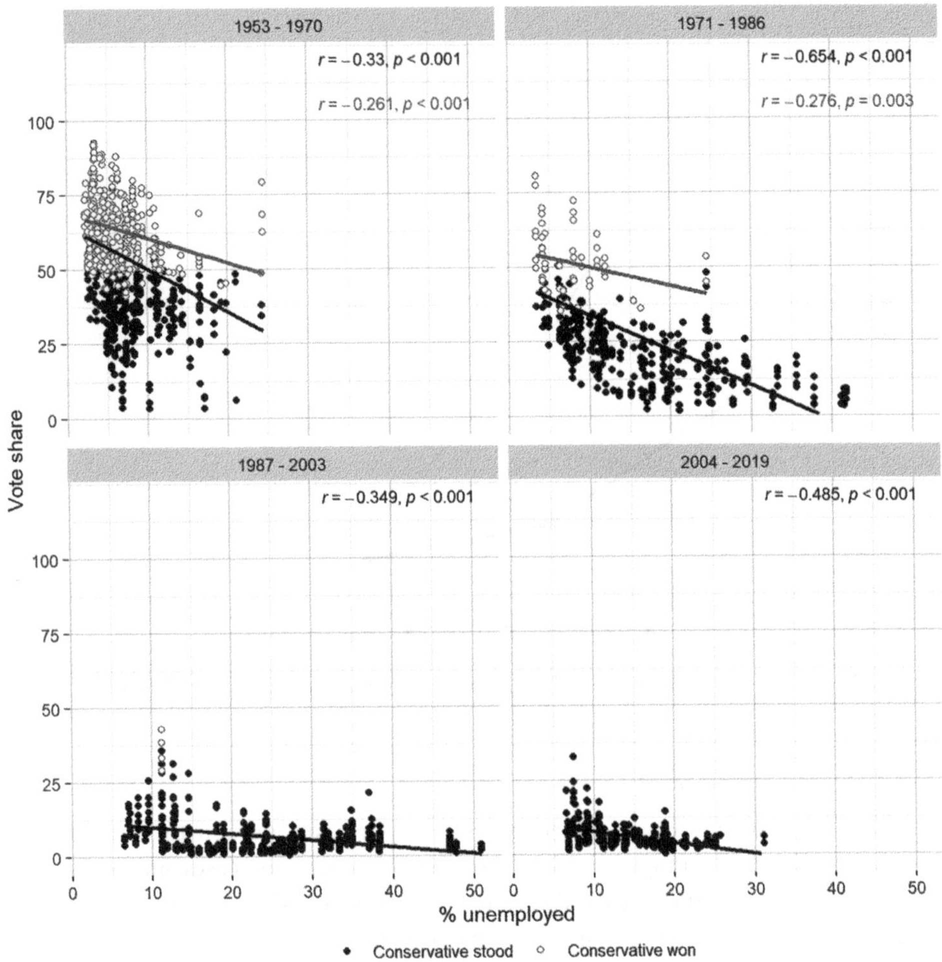

Figure 5.7: Conservative vote share against the percentage unemployed in each ward, with Pearson's r value

the first two census periods there was little difference between unemployment in Liberal and Conservative wards, but by the third census period this gap had grown, with the Liberals' share close to equidistant between the two other parties. During the fourth period the Liberals were winning in wards with a higher average unemployment level than Labour. Thus, we find support for H4: Conservative vote share was positively correlated with lower levels of unemployment in a ward.

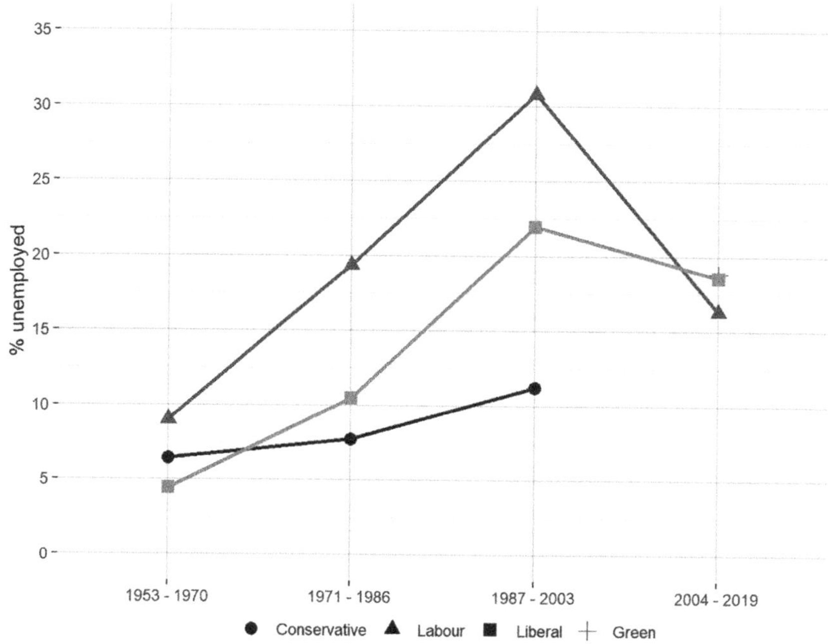

Figure 5.8: Average percentage unemployed in wards won by each party

5.2.5 *Class*

Figure 5.9 shows a clear negative correlation between the percentage of working-class men in a ward and Conservative vote share. Whilst the Conservatives were still able to consistently win in some of the most working-class wards during the 1953–1970 period, this ability diminished somewhat in the 1971–1986 period, and after this they only won in Woolton ward — not a bastion of working-class strength.

As with the previous measures, we can see a similar pattern play out in the line graphs in Figure 5.10. The average percentage of working-class voters was lower in Conservative wards than in Labour wards. On average, in the first period the Liberals won in wards that were even less working-class than those the Conservatives won in, but by the second period Liberal wards looked more like Labour wards. Interestingly, as with unemployment, in the fourth period wards won by the Liberals were actually more working class than wards won by Labour, on average. However, also as with unemployment, this probably reflects Labour's ability to appeal to a wider range of types of ward than the Liberals — especially since this era covers the Liberal Democrats'

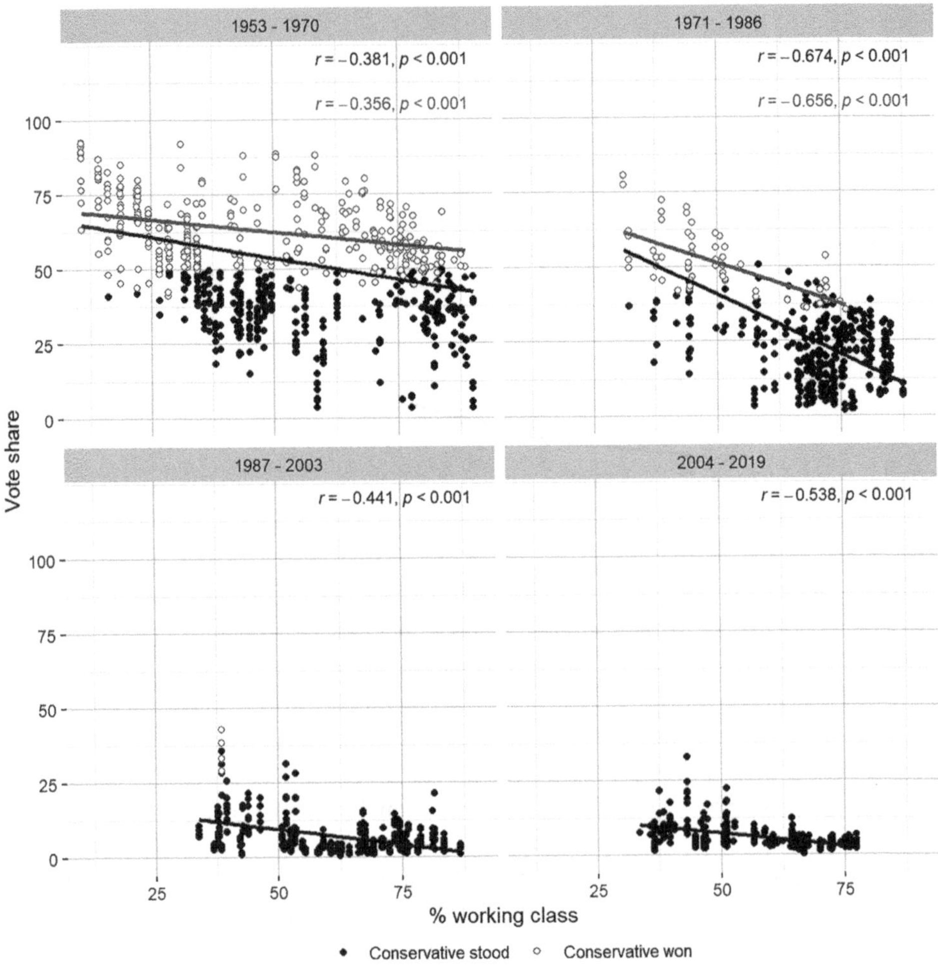

Figure 5.9: Conservative vote share against the percentage of working-class men in each ward, with Pearson's r value

post-coalition drop in support in Liverpool. Thus, we have evidence to support H5: Conservative vote share was negatively correlated with the proportion of working-class people in a ward.

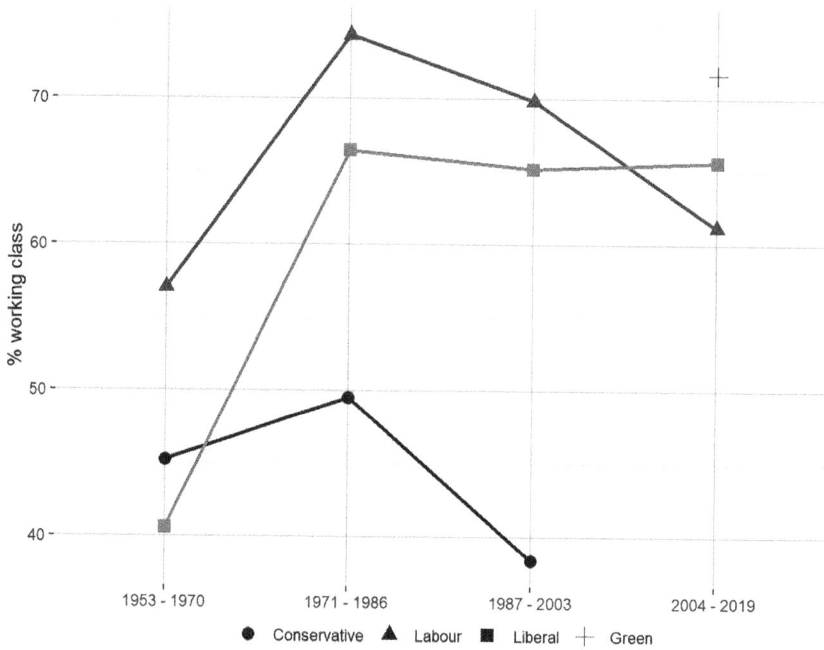

Figure 5.10: Average percentage of working-class men in wards won by each party

5.2.6 *Housing tenure*

Finally, we see the expected relationship between Conservative vote shares and housing tenure. As the proportion of people owning their own home increased, Conservative vote share tended to rise. This is a strong positive correlation, especially in the first two periods, and all results are statistically significant. Thus, we find evidence to support H6, that Conservative vote share was positively correlated with higher levels of home ownership in a ward.

Furthermore, as with the previous variables, housing tenure cannot tell the whole story. In the early period the Conservatives did well in wards with both high and low levels of private home ownership, and yet they also managed to lose in some wards where over 50 per cent of homes were privately owned. In the second period we can see that the Conservatives only won in wards with a high proportion of home ownership, but there were lots of wards meeting this criterion where the Conservatives did not win, including the ward with the highest level of private home ownership. Hence, home ownership levels cannot be the only factor in explaining Conservative voting.

Despite this, comparing the average level of private home ownership in wards won by each party — Figure 5.12 — shows that the wards the

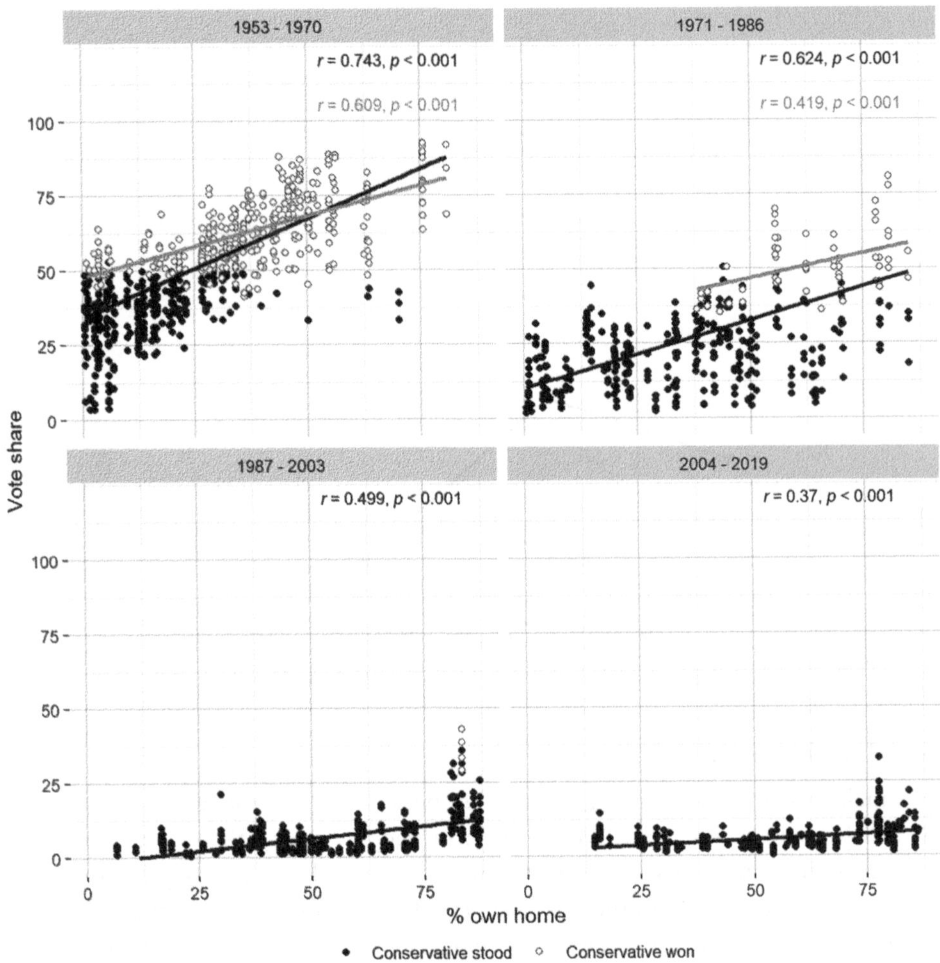

Figure 5.11: Conservative vote share against the percentage of homeowners in each ward, with Pearson's r value

Conservatives won consistently had a higher average amount of owner-occupied housing than was the case in wards won by Labour. Indeed, the gap between the average share of home ownership in Conservative-won and Labour-won wards never dropped below 20 percentage points. For the Liberals we see the same pattern as in the other demographic measures, with the Liberals 'out-Torying' the Tories over the first period (the demographics of the wards in which they were successful were closer to what we would expect in a Conservative ward than a Labour ward), but in the second, third

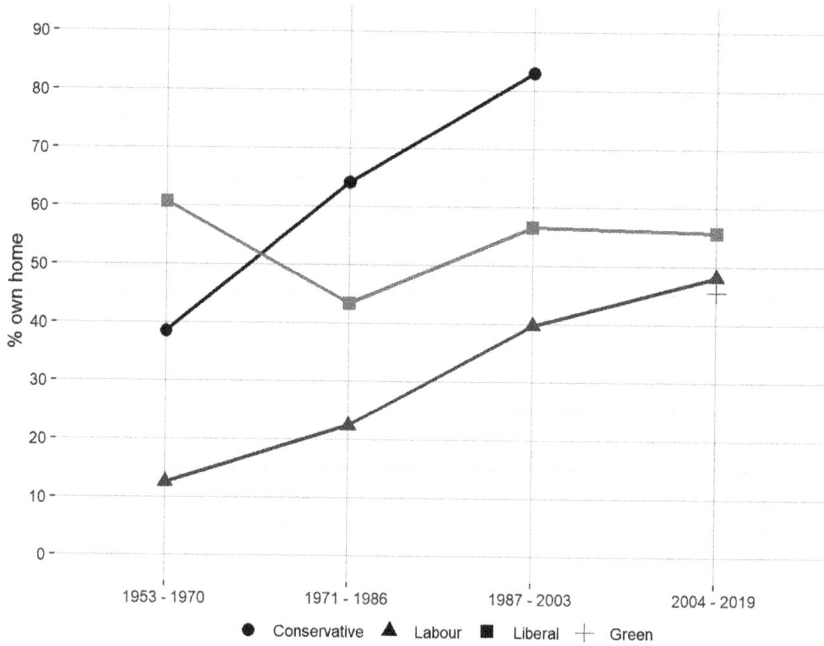

Figure 5.12: Average percentage of homeowners in wards won by each party

and fourth period the Liberals' ward profiles looked closer to Labour's than the Conservatives'. Overall, there is broad support for H6: generally the Conservatives did tend to do better in wards with higher levels of home ownership, most of the time.

This analysis has been brief and descriptive. However, some tentative findings may help us begin to explain Conservative decline in Liverpool. Firstly, the analysis shows that the Conservatives did best in wards with more people aged over 45, with a higher proportion of women, of home ownership, with a lower proportion of unemployment, of overcrowding, and with fewer working-class residents. This analysis has also found that, whilst Conservative vote share was generally correlated with demographic variables in the way we would expect, the party was by no means incapable of winning other wards too; they did have the ability to win support outside what might be seen as their core demographics.

We also see an interesting pattern *vis-à-vis* the Liberals: demographically, in the first period the wards they won in were *more* typically Conservative than the wards the Conservatives won in, but by the fourth period the Liberals' ward profile was more Labour than Labour's own profile! The fact that the Liberals tended to be 'more Tory than the Tories' in the wards they won is largely due to the Liberals only winning in eight seats between 1953 and the all-out boundary reforms in 1973 — and winning in just three seats during the first period of interest (1953–1970). As shown in Figure 5.15 later in this chapter, these seats were mainly won from the Conservatives.

One limitation of the approach followed here is that we are not able to separate cross-over effects. For example, did wards with a higher proportion of female residents produce higher Conservative vote shares, or is it because they also tended to be wards with higher levels of middle-class voters, or older voters? Section 5.3 will address these questions.

5.3 Bases of party support

In addition to the demographic variables examined in section 5.2, the regression analysis presented in section 5.3.1 will also include electoral variables, namely the year of the election, the level of turnout, whether the incumbent national government was Labour- or Conservative-led, and whether a Liberal was standing in the election. Furthermore, to explore the role of religion in party support, a variable to measure the historic Catholic strength of the area will be included. These will be explored in more detail below.

Firstly, the ward-level election data are taken from the Merseyside Local Election Results project, maintained by the author (Jeffery 2021), which builds upon and extends the British Local Election Database, 1889–2003 (Rallings, Thrasher, and Ware 2006). The data has been tidied up where necessary.[3]

The dependent variable for this study is the vote share received by the official Conservative, Labour, and Liberal/Liberal Democrat candidates. Splinter parties, such as Ward Labour or the post-1989 Liberal Party (as opposed to the Liberal Democrats), or parties which ran in alliance with one of these, such as the Protestant Party, have been excluded from the analysis.

The year of each election has been included to control for the gradual, secular decline the Conservatives experienced and the slow rise which benefited the Liberals. Without this control, the regression model would pick up changes in ward demographics (e.g. reduced overcrowding) which links to

3 This mainly involves calculating turnout where this is missing from the dataset (explained below) or estimating the size of ward electorates where necessary (based on the electorate in the previous year and cross-checked for face validity with the following year). Multi-vacancy elections also generate problems for this analysis, so only the highest-ranking candidates in each party are considered in these cases.

the long-term trend of Conservative decline. Specifically controlling for year removes this potential source of bias in the model.

The first electoral variable to be considered is turnout. Focusing specifically on Liverpool, local media and party leaders attached special prominence to the role of turnout in local elections, linking lower turnout to better Conservative performances in the 1960s (*Liverpool Daily Post* 1969, 8). The 1965 local election is a prime example, where although the Conservatives saw a swing towards them in terms of vote share, the *Liverpool Daily Post* noted that "the uncomfortable fact remains that hardly anywhere have the Conservatives actually increased their total poll… it is abstentions rather than actual desertions that are troubling the Labour Party — and to a lesser extent the Liberals too" (*Liverpool Daily Post* 1965b, 6). This leads to the first electoral hypothesis:

> H7: Conservative vote share increases when turnout is lower.

Turnout is given as the percentage of votes cast as a total of the electorate. In elections with more than one seat available, turnout has been manually calculated by summing the votes cast for each nth candidate, where n is equal to the number of vacancies in a ward.

The next variable to be included is a dummy variable that controls for whether a Conservative government was in power or not. The rationale behind this is that local elections are "second-order elections" and are often used to punish incumbent governments (Reif and Schmitt 1980, 9–10). This generates the following hypothesis:

> H8: Conservative vote share is lower when the Conservatives are in national government.

An important element in this analysis is whether a Liberal was standing in the ward. The reason for this is that it seems to be 'common knowledge' that, in Liverpool, the Liberal Party harmed the Conservatives to a far greater extent than it did the Labour Party. For Frost and North, this was because the Liberals were closer ideologically to the Conservatives (Frost and North 2013, 43). Kilfoyle argues that the Liberal Party took votes from

> disillusioned Tories, in part delivered by a residual Protestant logic that equated the Liverpool Labour Party with the Vatican, and they also appealed to a fledgling constituency of owner-occupiers, potential owner-occupiers and private-sector tenants, many of whom had been 'brought up' Labour but had since begun to see little in the party to keep them loyal. (Kilfoyle 2000, 29–30)

Unsurprisingly, Kilfoyle does not attempt to quantify the ratio of support each party lost to the Liberals. This model will attempt to go some way to increasing our understanding of just how the Liberals affected their rivals' shares of the total vote, as well as unpicking the 'Liberal effect' working in the demographics outlined in section 5.2. This is important. For example, imagine that the Liberals stood against the Conservatives only in seats with a high proportion of people under 45. The Conservative vote share would be lowered in seats contested by the Liberals, and this would be reflected in the analysis above as the Conservatives being weaker in these wards. However, this would ignore the fact that we are not comparing like with like. Multi-variate regression analysis allows us to overcome this problem.

To this end a dummy variable was created for each election, with the value 1 if a Liberal candidate was contesting the election. It is also important to be clear about who counts as a Liberal for the purposes of this study. This is outlined in Table 5.3.

Table 5.3: Candidates treated as 'Liberal'

Period	*Party*
Until 1980	Liberal Party candidates
1982–1987	Liberal, Liberal/Social Democratic Party, and SDP/Lib. candidates
1988–1990	Social and Liberal Democrats candidates
1991 onwards	Liberal Democrat candidates

As previously mentioned, this does not include the Liberal Party (not part of the Liberal Democrats) that also put up, and indeed still puts up, candidates in Liverpool.

H9a: Conservative vote share would be higher when there was no Liberal candidate standing.

H9b: A Liberal candidate would reduce the Conservative vote share more than the Labour vote share in a ward.

Finally, this analysis controls for the legacy of Catholicism. The effect of religion on voting behaviour is typically linked to pre-war politics with class generally seen as eclipsing religion by 1945 as the main social determinant of voting behaviour, reflecting a process that began following the First World War (Butler and Stokes 1974, 409–10; Wald 1983, 250). However, Liverpool offers something of an exception (Jeffery 2017). This is recognised by Butler and Stokes in their ground-breaking study of voting behaviour in Britain. They argue that the 'Irish Question' — the issue of Irish home rule, which was tied up in Protestant and Catholic identities — was historically an important factor in determining voting behaviour, and that even at the time they were writing in the early 1970s "it leaves a major mark on the politics of Clydeside and Merseyside" (Butler and Stokes 1974, 120).

The argument that religion no longer has an important effect on voting behaviour has been challenged by Tilley, who claims that religion constitutes "a stronger, more resilient cleavage because it is not about contemporary politics and contemporary party policy, but because it is rooted in… socialization processes" (Tilley 2015, 18). He argues that between 1996 and 2010 we can see Catholics tending to support Labour, Nonconformists supporting the Liberals, and practising Anglicans tending to vote for the Conservatives (Tilley 2015, 15). Hence, despite early claims that religion no longer affected voting behaviour this debate is far from settled, and thus it is important that some measure of the religious makeup of a ward is considered where possible.

This study uses a measure of Catholic strength in the 1920s to operationalise religion. This measure was developed by Davies and is based on an average of the percentage of school places in a ward that were provided by Catholic institutions and the proportion of church services taking place in Catholic churches in a ward. Wards were then classified as having a 'weak', 'moderate', or 'strong' Catholic presence (Davies 1996, 202–3). Davies has plotted this onto a map of the wards of Liverpool, which has then been imposed onto subsequent ward boundary systems to see which wards correspond to areas of 'strong' Catholic presence. This is operationalised as a dummy variable, which has been coded as 0 for 'weak' or 'moderate' Catholic areas and 1 for 'strong' Catholic areas.

This is undoubtedly a rough measure of Catholicism in wards, but since the religious demographics of a ward is a key explanatory variable *vis-à-vis* Conservative support in Liverpool (as shown in the specific literature on Liverpool, but also more generally in British elections) it is important to at least attempt to include it in this analysis. Furthermore, we would expect there to be no relationship between this dummy variable and vote share if it was not useful, or for the relationship to disappear when controlling for other factors if it is simply a result of correlating with another demographic variable. This leads to our tenth — and final — hypothesis:

> H10: Conservative vote share would be unaffected by a historical Catholic presence.

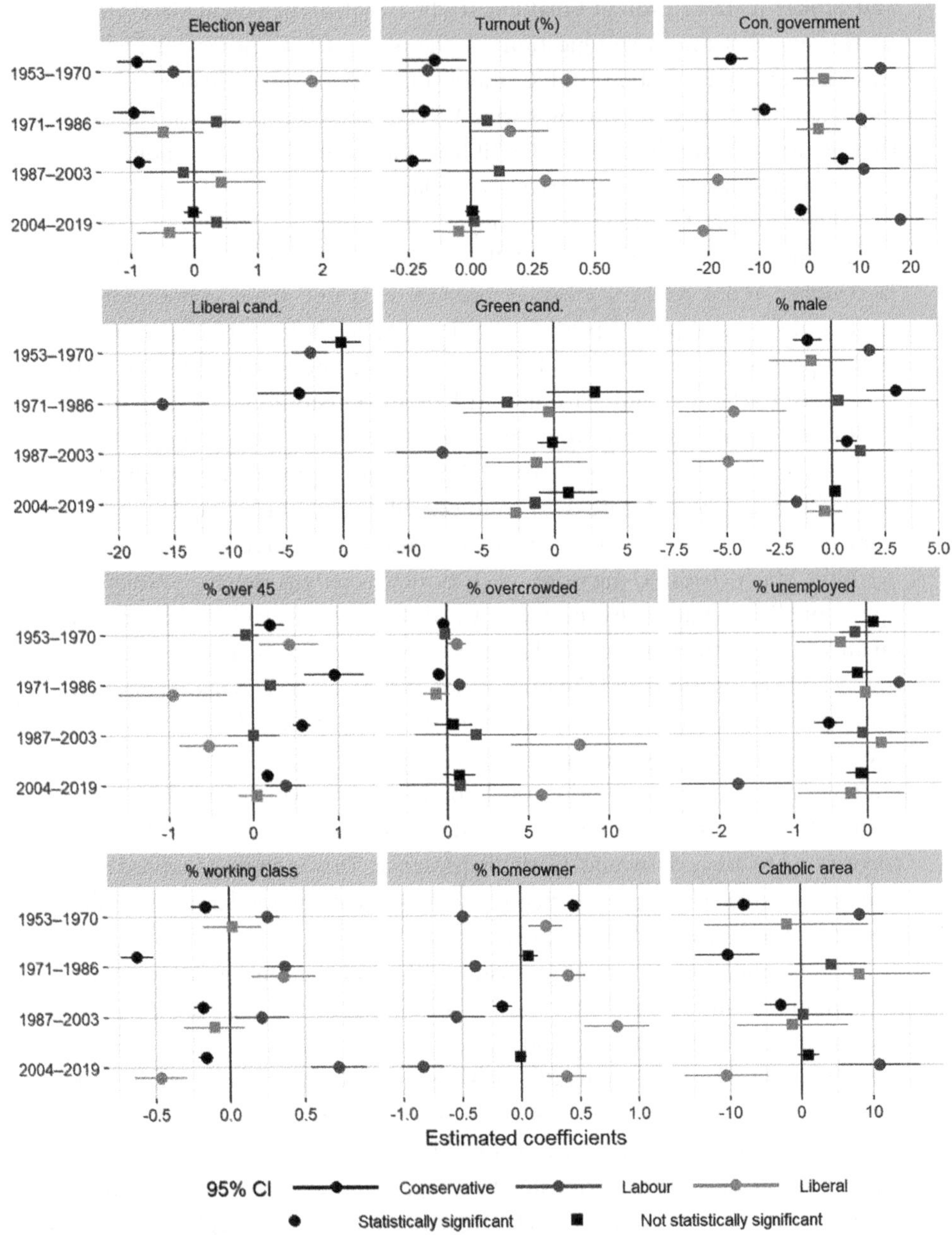

Figure 5.13: Regression analysis output for each census period

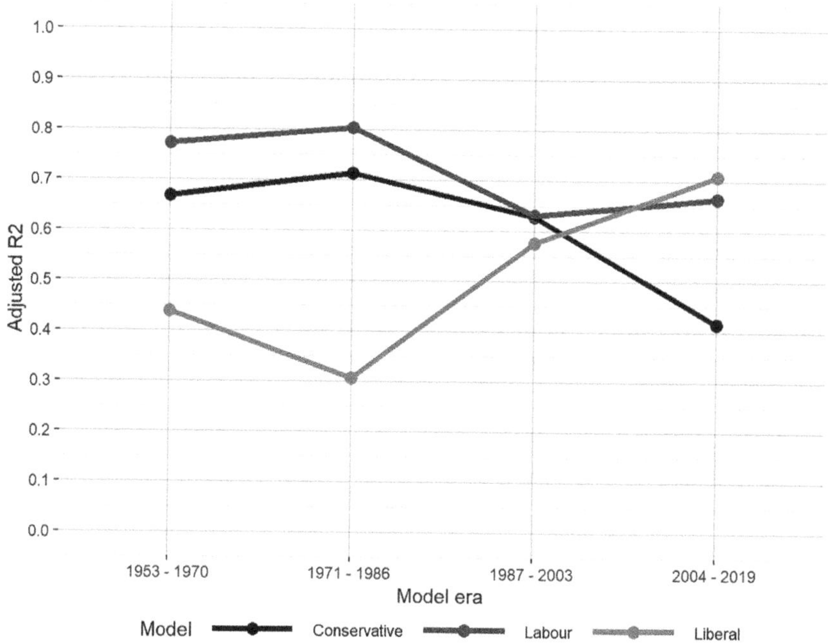

Figure 5.14: Performance of regression analysis model

5.3.1 *Analysis*

Figure 5.13 presents a graphic representation of the regression model for each party. The coefficients represent the impact of a one-unit change in each variable on a party's vote share for a given period, with the lines showing a 95% confidence interval. Statistically significant relationships are denoted by a circle, non-statistically significant results with a square. The full tables can be found in Appendix 1 (tables 10.1 to 10.4). It is worth noting that the x axis is not fixed — it varies for each variable for reasons of presentation.

Before we move to an analysis of the findings, Figure 5.14 shows the adjusted r^2 value, which measures how well our models fit the data, controlling for the number of variables used. We can see quite clearly that the models covering the 1953–1970 and 1971–1986 have very good fits for both the Conservatives and Labour, suggesting that both parties' vote shares can be largely predicted by our electoral and socio-demographic variables. The same cannot be said for the Liberals in this period, with an adjusted r^2 value of around 0.45 in the first period and just 0.3 in the second. However, for the 1987–2003 period the model is just as good for the Liberals as the other two parties, and by the final period the model actually explains vote share better for the Liberal Democrats than for any other party. Indeed, as the Liberals began to develop their own socio-demographic base they began to look more like the Conservatives they once displaced, as we shall see below.

5.3.1.1 *Election year*

Starting with year, we see the expected results for the Conservatives — during the first three periods studied they see a year-on-year decline of around 0.9 percentage points, controlling for all other factors. By the fourth period this relationship is no longer statistically significant — the party had hit its rock bottom.

Interestingly, the Labour Party also saw a year-on-year decline during the first period, although at 0.3 percentage points it was one-third of that experienced by the Conservatives. The Liberals, on the other hand, enjoyed a 1.8 percentage point increase during this period even though this was before their sudden rise in vote share, which took place in the 1973 local election (achieving 35.4 per cent of the vote, compared to a previous post-war high of 15.8 per cent in 1972). There was no statistically significant relationship between year and Labour or Liberal vote share in later periods.

5.3.1.2 *Turnout*

We find that for the first three periods increased turnout was associated with a decrease in Conservative vote share and an increase in Liberal vote share. There was no statistically significant relationship in the fourth period, and for Labour there is only a negative relationship in the first period. Thus, we find evidence to support H7 in this period: Conservative vote shares did increase when turnout was lower.

In the 1953–1970 period we find that for every percentage point increase in turnout Conservative and Labour vote shares decreased by 0.14 and 0.17 percentage points respectively, while the Liberals saw an increase in their vote share of 0.39 percentage points for every percentage point increase in turnout. This should not be too surprising, since a Liberal candidate standing could have the dual effect of convincing L/liberal voters — who might not otherwise turn out to vote — to cast their ballot since they had a candidate from a party that appealed to them, as well as perhaps encouraging Conservative and Labour voters to turn out to make sure the Liberals did not prevent their preferred candidate from winning. Similarly, a Liberal candidate standing might make the main two political parties worry about their position and campaign more, which would then feed into higher turnout.

The relationship between turnout and vote share in the 1971–1986 and the 1987–2003 periods can be explained by differential turnout. For the Conservatives, we can imagine that their supporters turned out to vote regardless of other circumstances, so the number of Conservatives voting was relatively static. Liberal voters, on the other hand, might have felt less party loyalty and so required convincing via campaigning to turn out and to vote Liberal. As a result, when turnout increased the number of Liberal voters might have been disproportionately high, and thus higher turnout would become associated with an increased Liberal vote share.

5.3.1.3 *Conservative government*

As expected, an incumbent Conservative government typically dampened the vote share of Conservatives in local elections and boosted Labour's vote. The relationship between a Conservative government and voting for the Liberals is more nuanced, however.

In the first period, we see that a Conservative government led to a reduced vote share of 15.4 percentage points for the Conservatives and an increase of 14.2 percentage points for Labour. The magnitude of the effect in the second period is slightly less, at a decrease of 8.9 percentage points for the Conservatives and an increase of 10.3 percentage points for Labour. In neither period was the relationship between party support and Conservative government statistically significant for the Liberals.

This gives some weight to the oft-made claim in local media that dissatisfaction with the current government led to Conservative losses, for example in 1971 (*Liverpool Echo* 1971, 15) and 1972 elections (*Liverpool Echo* 1972, 8). So far, these results are to be expected.

However, things get interesting in the third period, from 1987–2003. The effect is as expected for Labour: a Conservative government in office is associated with a 10.7 per cent increase in vote share. However, a Conservative government is also associated with a 6.6 percentage point increase in *Conservative* vote share and an 18 percentage point decrease in Liberal vote share. In the fourth period, this decline is even greater, at 21.1 percentage points in Liberal vote share.

What to make of this? The Conservative result can be explained by comparing the Conservative Party in government and in opposition, insofar as the party appeared more competent when in government than it did in opposition. During this period, the Conservatives were in power until 1997. There is no denying that the Major government struggled: Black Wednesday and Britain's forced exit from the Exchange Rate Mechanism destroyed the Conservatives' reputation for economic competence, while the ongoing Tory civil war over Europe, and multiple financial and personal scandals made the party a byword for disunity and "sleaze" (Bale 2010, 68). This is reflected in the findings of Rallings et al., that "[v]irtually throughout the Party's 18-year tenure of national government its presence in local government was diminishing. On its exit from office the Conservative Party had fewer than 4,500 councillors and majority control of barely one in 20 local authorities" (Rallings, Thrasher, and Johnston 2002, 272).

So diminished was the party's reputation that, if we contrast the Conservatives in government with the Conservatives in opposition after 1997, it is no surprise they did not benefit from the usual opposition boost we would expect to see. Under leaders William Hague and Iain Duncan Smith the party focused on issues that were, at least at that point in time, far removed from the interests of the electorate, especially Europe and the euro (e.g. the Keep the Pound campaign, when nobody was seriously trying to take the pound), and did very little to counter the general decline of the Conservative brand in the north of England (Bale 2010, 129–30). Furthermore, New Labour were still electorally popular in this period of analysis, and in places where they were not the Liberal Democrats were an attractive protest vote, meaning that the Conservatives did not benefit from the expected opposition bounce. Finally, as discussed in Chapter 8, the Conservatives did not attempt to address the shift in Scouse identity, which had by then taken on a distinctively anti-Conservative flavour.

The relationship between there being a Conservative government and a decline in Liberal vote share can be explained by the Liberals' success in positioning themselves as the opposition to Labour in the city, which first required Labour to be in government nationally — rather than being a direct effect of Conservative incumbency. An alternative explanation is that when the Conservatives were in office, Labour would represent a protest vote and, since Labour voters were more likely to turn out, this effectively would reduce Liberal vote share. However, when Labour took office in 1997 and the Conservatives became the opposition for the first time since 1979, Liverpudlian politics had moved on. The city now had a two-party system in which the Conservatives played a very minor role. Hence, the Liberal Democrats benefited from voters being dissatisfied with Labour, whether they stayed home, voted Liberal Democrat to give the government a bloody nose, or the dissatisfaction invigorated the Liberal Democrat support base to turn out.

Thus, we find support for H8: Conservative vote share is lower when the Conservatives are in government nationally, apart from the anomalous 1987–2003 period.

5.3.1.4 Liberal and Green candidates

Only during the first two periods did the Liberal Party in the historic sense put up candidates; after that 'Liberal' refers to the Social and Liberal Democrats, then the Liberal Democrats. After 1972 all contested wards had a Liberal candidate in them, which is a very good record for a former third party. Interestingly, and contrary to received wisdom, a Liberal standing in a local election tended to impact the Labour Party more than it did the Conservative Party: in the 1953–1970 period there was no statistically significant relationship between a Liberal candidate and Conservative vote share, compared to a 2.8 percentage point decrease for Labour. In the second period — 1971–1986 — a Liberal candidate reduced the Conservative vote share by 3.8 percentage points, but the Labour share by 16 percentage points.

This runs contrary to received wisdom surrounding the Liberals' place in Liverpool's party system, and does not chime with the party eventually displacing the Conservatives as Liverpool's second party. However, it could easily be the case that, since the Liberals targeted predominantly Conservative seats in these earlier periods, their presence in a ward encouraged many anti-Tory Labour voters to switch to the Liberals if that party seemed likely to beat the Tories in that ward (hence reducing Labour vote share) and also encouraged some Conservative voters to turn out because they feared their party might lose to the new challenger. It could also be the case that the Liberal focus on 'pavement politics' (see Chapter 7) also disproportionately impressed people normally voting Labour. We thus find no support for either H9a or H9b.

However, it is important to distinguish between this sterile statistical model and the messy real world in which elections actually take place. Although the model is clear that, controlling for other factors, during the first period a Liberal candidate standing in an election had a statistically significant effect on Labour candidates but not on Conservative candidates — and only a small effect on the Conservatives during the second period — in the real world control for all other factors does not happen. Had they stood

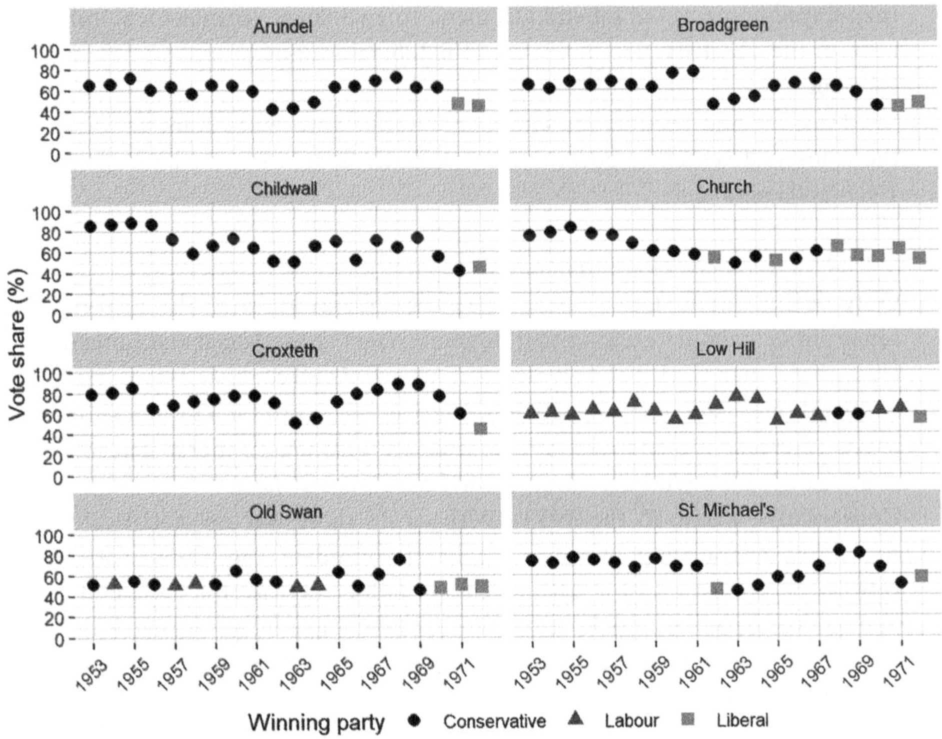

Figure 5.15: Vote share of winning party in wards where the Liberal Party ever won a seat, 1953–1972

in safe Labour seats, where they had no chance of winning, but marginal Conservative seats, where even a slight reduction in vote share could cost the Conservative candidate the seat, the Liberals could have harmed the Conservatives more than they did Labour.

Hence, when looking at the effect of a Liberal standing in this period it is important to consider *where* the Liberals chose to stand. There are two ways we can do this. The first is to consider the seats the Liberals won. Figure 5.15 shows the vote share of the first-placed candidate between 1953 and 1972 (the second boundary system) in wards where the Liberals won a seat — eight wards in total.

Only one seat could be truly described as contested: Old Swan. Low Hill ward had been held by Labour for the majority of its history, and the remaining wards were usually won by the Conservatives. This shows that in terms of seats, the Liberals did tend to do better —actually winning — in what would otherwise have been Conservative seats than they did in Labour seats.

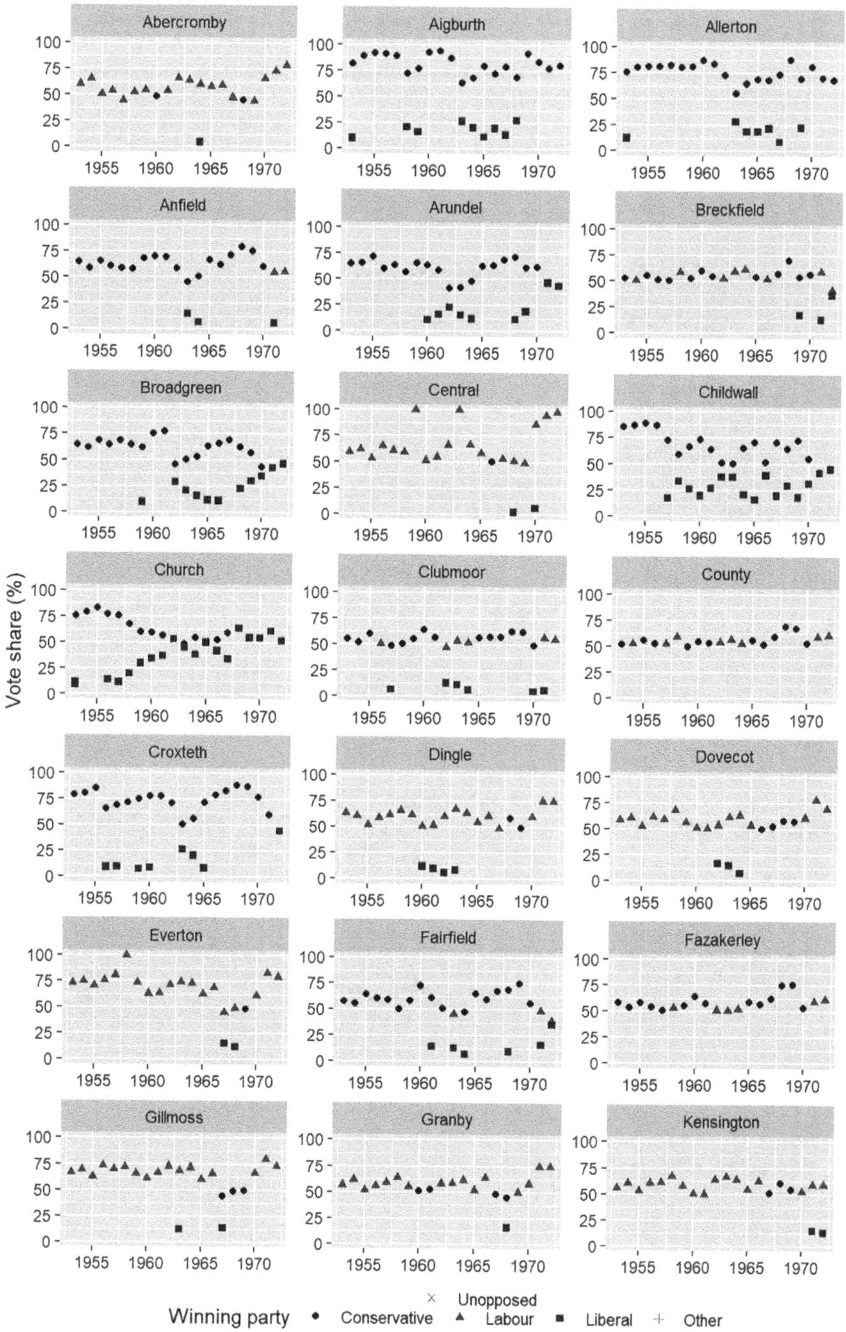

Figure 5.16: Vote share of winning party and of Liberals in all Liverpool wards (Abercromby–Kensington), 1953–1972

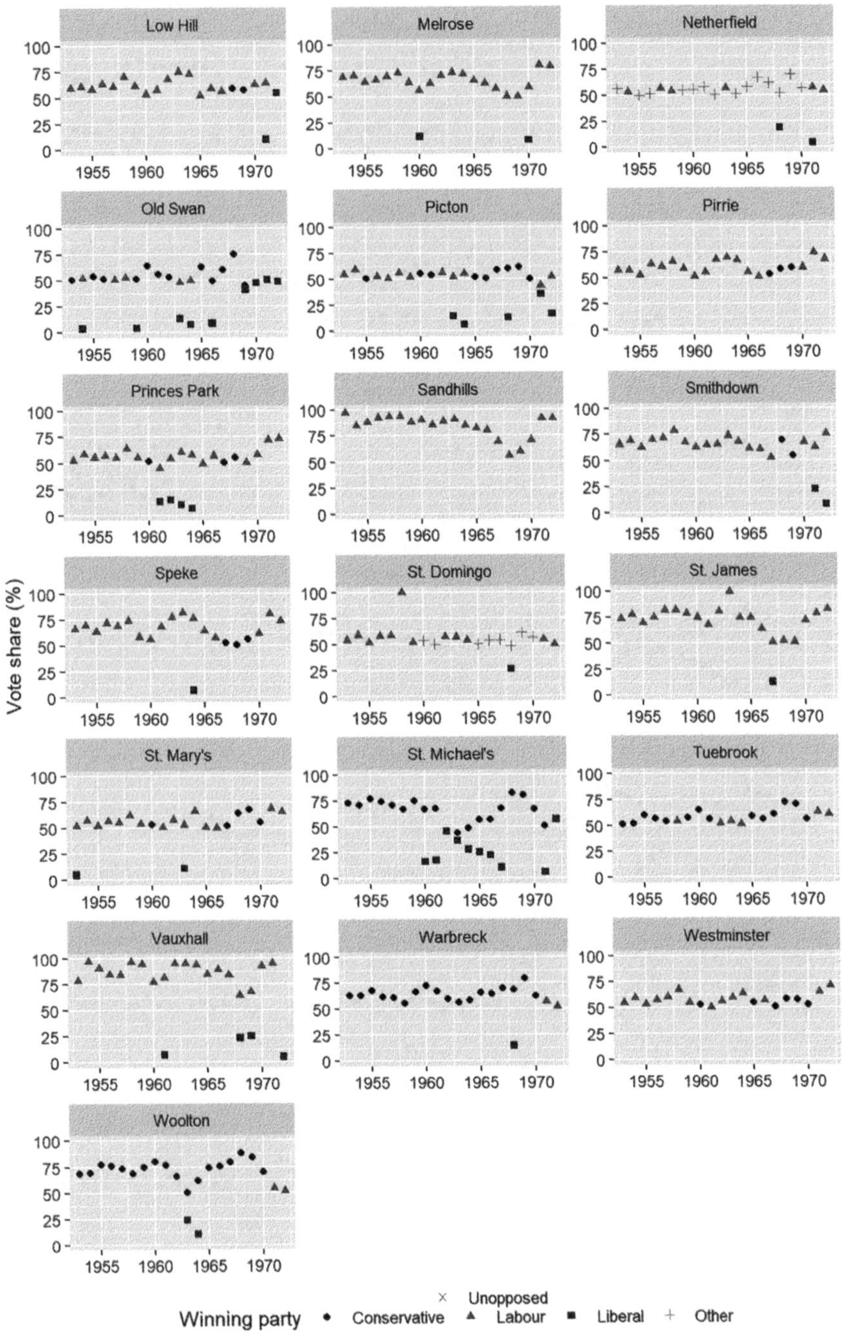

Figure 5.17: Vote share of winning party and of Liberals in all Liverpool wards (Low Hill–Woolton), 1953–1972

A second way to examine the Liberal effect is to map out the election results in each ward where the Liberals stood and see where they posed a real challenge to the dominant party. This is done in Figures 5.16 and 17, which show the first-placed party's vote share and the vote share for every election the Liberals stood in.

Again, we can see that the Liberals were much more likely to stand candidates in seats where the Conservatives were usually the victors. This suggests that there was a determined attempt to target Conservative seats and that H9a and H9b are more convincingly confirmed by reality than by the regression model.

Where a Green Party candidate stood, we see a statistically significant relationship with Labour only between 1987 and 2003, when a Green candidate would reduce Labour's vote share by 7.7 percentage points. By the 2004–2019 period a Green presence had no statistically significant impact on any party's vote share, suggesting that an element of stability had reached Liverpool's party system.

5.3.1.5 *Socio-demographic variables*

In the first period we see that all variables bar unemployment have a statistically significant impact on Conservative vote share, and all operate in the anticipated direction: the percentage of voters over 45 and the percentage of homeowners are associated with a positive increase in vote share, while higher proportions of male, working-class or overcrowded populations are associated with reduced Conservative vote share.

For Labour, only three variables are statistically significant, and all act in the expected manner: a higher percentage of men is associated with a higher Labour vote share, as is a higher proportion of working-class voters, and a lower proportion of homeowners. Interestingly, the Liberals do better in areas with higher levels of home ownership, of overcrowding, and of voters over 45 (the last two of which had no impact on the Labour vote in this period). This suggests the Liberal were carving out a socio-demographic niche for themselves within the city.

For the 1971–1986 period we see generally the same patterns, except that the Conservatives go from underperforming to overperforming in areas with a higher proportion of men, and the percentage of homeowners in a ward is no longer statistically significant. All other variables act in the same direction as during the first period. Labour perform strongly in areas with higher percentages of overcrowding, unemployment, and working-class voters and lower levels of home ownership, whilst the Liberals now underperform in wards with higher proportions of men and of older voters, but do better in areas with more working-class voters and more homeowners.

Thus, in the second period we see some differentiation between the Conservative and Liberal bases — around gender, age, and class — but also between Labour and the Liberals, around home ownership.

The most interesting aspect of the third and fourth periods is the amazing strength of the impact of overcrowding on the Liberals. For every single unit increase in overcrowding, the Liberals increased their vote share by 8 percentage points in the third period and 5.8 percentage points in the fourth period.

This finding is consistent with the literature on Liverpool in the 1980s, which emphasises the importance of housing in municipal politics. Laver finds that throughout the 1970s the Liberal vote in Liverpool could be explained by turnout, and was independent of socio-economic factors. However, by the 1980s — covered by this model — it had become related "to low amenities and private or housing association tenancies, as opposed to council tenancies". He attributes this to the 'David Alton' effect: Alton was the Liberal MP for Edge Hill (later Mossley Hill) from 1979 to 1997 and built a strong base in "those twilight areas between the inner and the outer city". Laver concludes that any area "with ageing, poor quality, private accommodation… is becoming a sort of minor Liberal heartland" (Laver 1984, 247–49).

The idea of a Liberal socio-economic base of support is backed by Lane, who claims the party performed strongly in "the wards that form the cordon between the city working class areas and the middle-class suburbs, populated in the main by higher paid manual workers, white collar workers, self-employed and young professionals", as well as help-to-buy tenants, struggling homeowners, and the aspirational (Lane 1978, 339–40). We can see evidence of this in the model, with the Liberals doing well among those in overcrowded homes and among homeowners — during both the third and fourth periods there was a positive relationship between the levels of home ownership and Liberal vote share. Parkinson claims that "the Liberals identified as their power base the private renters, and the new and would-be home owners — the skilled working classes and lower middle classes". Geographical support for Liverpool's parties could now be summarised as Labour in the inner city and in areas with a larger share of council housing, the Conservatives in the "upmarket, suburban home owners belt", and the Liberals in "the ring of Edwardian and Victorian terraced houses in the areas between those two" (Parkinson 1985, 20).

Moving on, we see a statistically significant effect of age in both the Conservative and the Liberal models in the third period, where we find an increase in the percentage of the over-45 population in a ward increases the Conservative vote share by 0.6 points and reduces the Liberal vote share by 0.5 percentage points. This could be because, despite the fact the Liberals had contested elections in Liverpool before 1945, they only became a serious party in the city's post-war politics from the early 1970s. Returning to the concept of socialisation, older voters who grew up during a time when the Liberals had a very small local presence (or sometimes no presence at all) would be less likely to have been socialised into Liberal voting, just as, until the 1950s, the Labour Party struggled to get established in the city. The reverse is true for the Conservatives. This also links to the fourth period, where there is no statistically significant relationship between age and Liberal vote share. Those who were coming of voting age during the Liberals' breakthrough were now entering the 'over 45' cohort and thus the socialisation effect was being eroded.

This analysis suggests that each party did have a socio-demographic niche in which it could appeal to voters, which will be further explored in the cluster analysis in section 5.4.

5.3.1.6 Catholicism

Finally, we can see the enduring legacy of Catholicism in the city's politics. For Labour, areas that had been strongly Catholic in the 1920s tended to produce a vote share 8.2 percentage points higher than expected, controlling for other socio-demographic and electoral factors in the model. This relationship was not statistically significant in the second and third period, but it was even stronger in the fourth period: a 10.6 percentage point increase compared to wards where Catholicism was not historically strong.

For the Conservatives, areas which historically were strongly Catholic were likely to deliver a Conservative vote share 8.1 percentage points lower in the first period, 10.3 percentage points lower in the second period, and 3.0 percentage points lower in the third period. There was no statistically significant relationship in the fourth period for the Conservatives, but the Liberals experienced a 10.6 percentage point decrease in formerly Catholic areas.

It would be surprising for Catholicism to still exert such a large effect just under a century later. It could be that wards that were strongly Catholic during the period we have studied have a high level of correlation with another variable that is positively correlated with support for Labour (e.g.

high levels of multiple deprivation, higher number of immigrants, etc.) but it does seem to be the case that in the first three periods studied the legacy of Catholicism still structured voting behaviour in Liverpool to some extent. Thus we do not find support for H10, that Conservative vote share would not be affected by a historical Catholic presence.

5.3.2 *Discussion*

Whilst it is interesting to report the impact of a percentage point increase in these socio-economic factors, comparison between these variables is limited by the contrasting ranges. For example the percentage of men in a ward usually ranges around 6 percentage points (between 46 and 52 per cent), whereas the percentage of working-class residents may range much wider, around 70 percentage points (between 20 and 90 per cent). Thus, there is simply less potential for a ten-point change in the percentage of men than there is for such a change in working-class residents, meaning it is more useful to look at the impact of a change of one standard deviation when looking at the impact of socio-economic factors on Conservative vote share.

Figure 5.18 does exactly this: it shows the impact on each party's vote share of a one standard deviation increase in a given independent variable for the census periods of interest. Since we are interested in the magnitude here, the direction of the relationship has been ignored on the x axis, but a negative magnitude is represented by a dashed line. The direction and significance of the relationships remain the same as in the regression models examined in section 5.3.1, but now it is easier to compare magnitudes. The number next to each line is the ranked magnitude of the variable for the party in question, with the largest magnitude ranked as 1. Finally, non-statistically significant variables are excluded from the figure. Full tables are presented in Appendix 1 (tables 10.5 to 10.8).

Figure 5.18 shows that in the first period — when the Conservatives experienced success — Conservative governments were the most important factor in driving support for Labour and the Conservatives, whilst for the Liberals it was the year variable (see section 5.3 for explanation). For all three parties, however, home ownership was the second most important variable, which perhaps shows the importance housing has for the city's politics. Areas that were historically Catholic deliver the third largest impact for both the Conservatives and Labour, whilst for Liberals it is the socio-economic variable overcrowding. It is worth remarking that all three factors impacted in opposite directions on Conservatives and Labour.

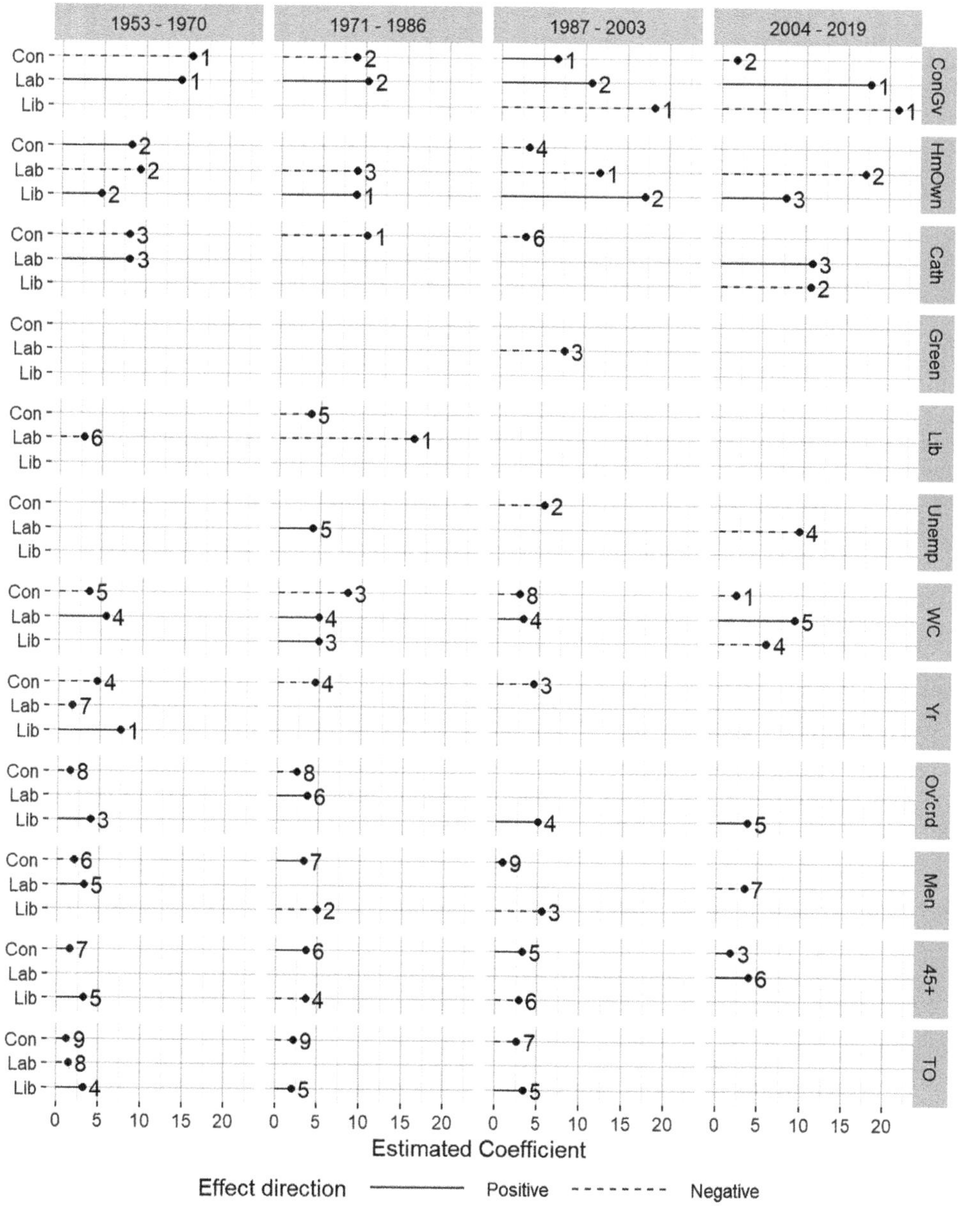

Figure 5.18: Standardised regression analysis output for each census era

The second era — of Conservative decline — sees Catholic areas having the largest impact on Conservative vote share, followed by a Conservative government and then by the percentage of working-class voters in the area. For Labour, it was whether a Liberal stood, followed by Conservative governments and then home ownership, whilst for Liberals the main driver was home ownership, followed by the percentage of male voters and then working-class communities (unlike the Conservatives, however, the relationship between working-class votes and Liberal support was positively correlated).

The third period shows Conservative government, unemployment, and year to be the most important variables for the Conservatives (followed by home ownership — now negatively correlated with Conservative vote share!). For the Liberals, home ownership is the second most important factor, after Conservative government, and this suggests the Liberals had managed to displace the Conservatives as the party of homeowners in the city.

In the final period — of Conservative irrelevance — only three variables are statistically significant in the Conservative model: the share of working-class voters (negatively correlated), having a Conservative government (likewise), and the share of over-45s (positively correlated).

What can we take from this? It is clear that the Liberals' success was based on eroding the Conservatives' typical base. In the period of Conservative decline the Liberals appealed to areas where there were more voters aged 45 or lower, but also to areas with more homeowners. By appealing to areas of traditional Conservative strength they undermined the Tories' ability to socialise new voters whom they might previously have expected to win. However, the Liberals' ability to go beyond the Conservative voter base — to appeal to areas with more working-class voters — meant they developed their own specific socio-demographic base in the city.

However, it is not enough to know that during the period of decline or irrelevance the Conservatives did better in wards with fewer working-class, fewer younger, and fewer female residents, and wards which had less overcrowding and unemployment. We should also explore whether the demographics of the city made these types of ward more or less common in the latter periods when the Conservatives did poorly.

Figure 5.19 shows the average demographic makeup of each ward in Liverpool. We see that the percentage share of men stayed broadly flat and the percentage of over-45s also remained constant after a blip in the 1966 mini-census. We can see that whilst the 1961 census reported working-class populations having a much lower share of ward populations than later censuses the overall story is a decline over time in the population

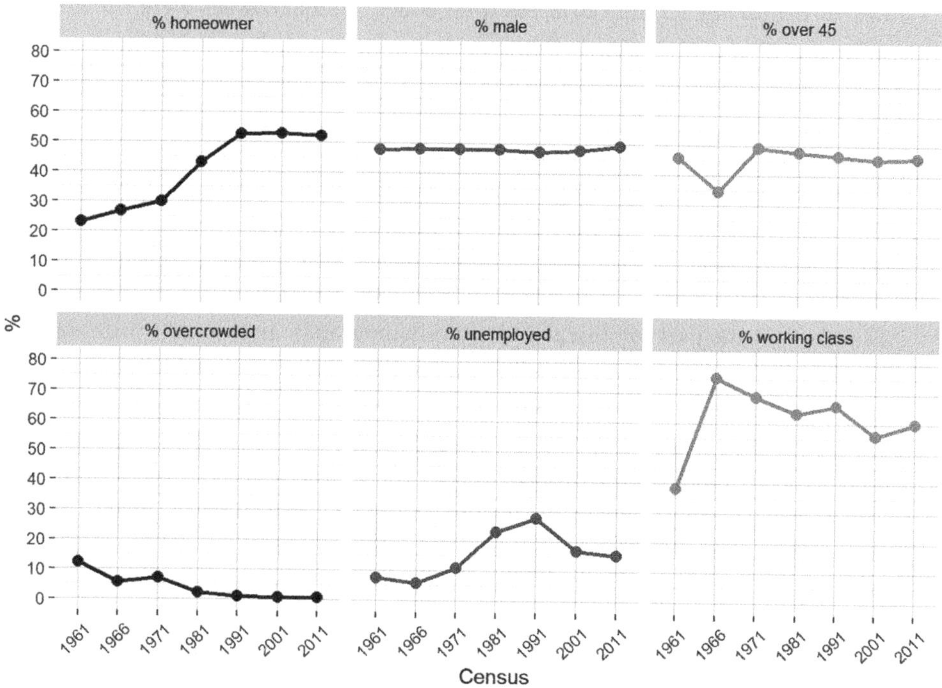

Figure 5.19: Demographic changes in Liverpool, by census (average of wards)

of working-class residents in the city. The average share of homeowners increased — quite rapidly from 1971 to 1991 — before levelling off, and the percentage of overcrowding gradually decreased throughout the period. Unemployment peaked in 1991 before beginning to reduce.

What Figure 5.19 shows us is that actually the city's demographics became more typically Conservative over the era we have surveyed. We see fewer working-class voters, fewer voters living in overcrowded homes, and more homeowners in the city too.

Thus, when we compare the actual changes in Liverpool's demographics to the regression model we see that demographics cannot wholly explain declining Conservative vote share. There must be something beyond simple demographic change to explain why the Conservatives faced the level of decline they did. This will be explored in later chapters.

Despite the focus on demographic changes within Liverpool, it is clear that national political developments were typically more important. It is worth restating that more often than not the party in government was the largest influence on voting behaviour in our model, suggesting that for all the talk of demographics and local electoral issues, national issues were the key determinant of party support. This argument is further built upon in Chapter 7.

5.4 Ward clusters

Another approach to exploring the demographics of local politics in Liverpool is via cluster analysis. Cluster analysis "comprises a large class of methods aiming at discovering a limited number of meaningful groups (or clusters) in data" (Giordani, Ferraro, and Martella 2020, 3). Cluster analysis thus allows us to look at the party-political and socio-demographic profiles of wards and simplify them down into groups. The eras and demographic variables used are the same as in the previous analysis but the variables are standardised, and we also include a first-placed party variable, measured as Conservative, Labour, Liberal, Protestant, Green, or Other.

In order to gauge how many clusters would be appropriate, we examined the average silhouette values for each era, which is a measure of how well, on average, each point fits into its cluster, for a given number of clusters. We use the partition around medoids (PAM) method and given we have a categorical variable for first-placed party, we use the Gower distance (for a more in-depth explanation of all these variables, see Giordani et al. (2020, 99)). This approach showed us that the optimum number of clusters for each period was two, three, two, and three, respectively.

The four figures included below show the output of the cluster analysis. The bar chart at the top of each figure shows the share of seats in each cluster won by each party, while the boxplots show the mean (vertical line), inter-quartile range (box), and minimum and maximum values (dark line) for each demographic variable in a given cluster.

Figure 5.20 shows the profiles of two ward clusters in the first period of study. They typically break into Labour-won wards and Conservative-won wards. There are a few interesting nuances, though. The first is that the vast majority of elections won by the Protestant Party — who were Conservative allies in the council chamber — are situated in the Labour-dominated cluster. The party won every election in Netherfield and all except the 1968, 1969, and 1970 elections in St Domingo. This shows that the sectarian element of the Protestant Party's appeal typically appealed more to otherwise Labour-looking areas and hints at a broader point covered throughout this book and widely in other literature: the historic Conservative appeal to the working class in Liverpool was aided by an appeal to Protestant working-class voters *because* of their Protestantism over and above their working-class background.

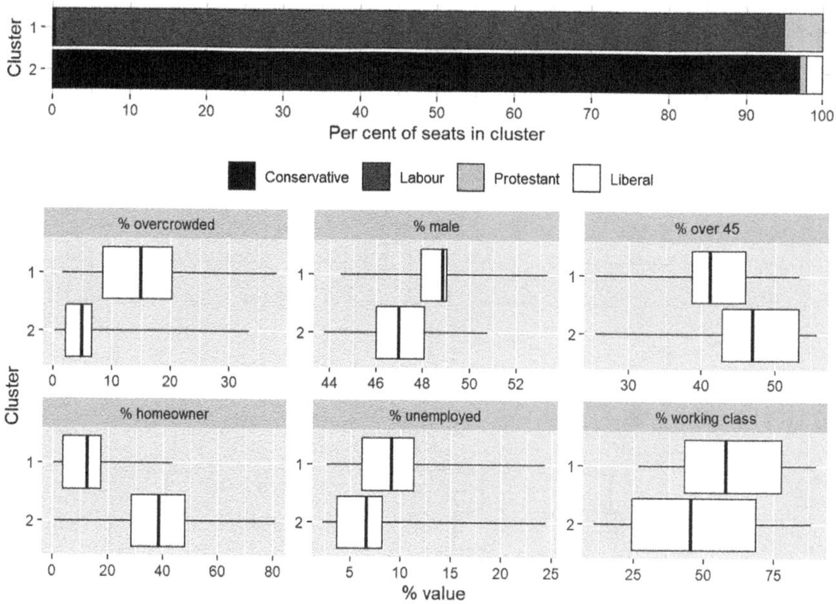

Figure 5.20: Ward clusters and characteristics, 1953–1970

Another interesting point is that all Liberal-won seats in the cluster analysis fall into the Conservative-dominated cluster, again providing evidence that the Liberals were a bigger threat to the Conservatives in terms of seats, even though in terms of vote share their impact on Labour was greater.

Figure 5.21 shows three clusters for the 1971–1986 period, each of which aligns to a given political party: cluster 1 aligns to the Labour Party, cluster 2 to the Conservative Party, and cluster 3 to the Liberals. Across all the socio-demographic variables we can see that the wards which tended to be won by the Liberals had demographic profiles which were in between those of Labour and Conservative wards.

Figure 5.22 shows two clusters, the first Labour-dominated and the other Liberal-dominated. Here, then, we see a return to the two-party system in local politics, but with the Liberals having replaced the Conservatives as the opposition to Labour.

In the Labour cluster, the relatively large 'Other' section is composed of wards won by a left-wing splinter group of Militant Labour candidates (sometimes going by the name Ward Labour). The Liberal cluster contains a handful of Conservative victories, and 13 'Other' candidates, who in this case

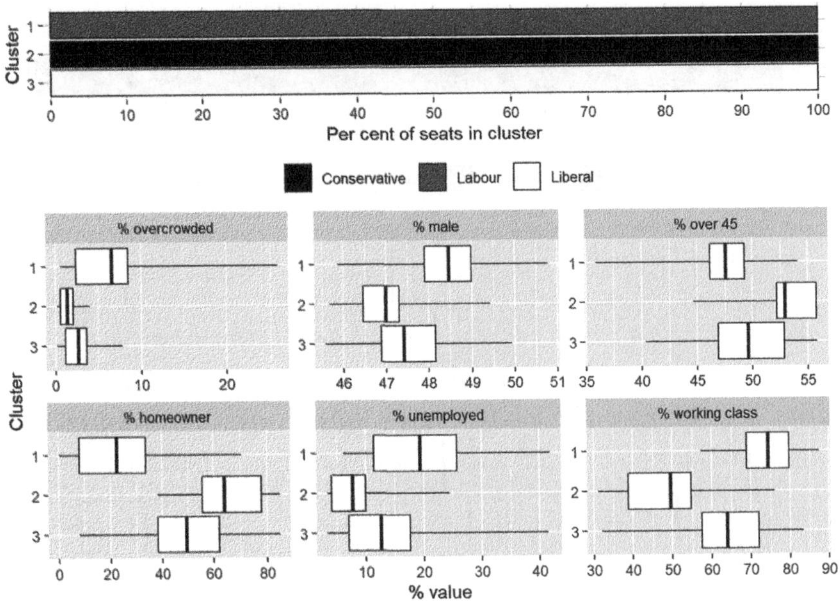

Figure 5.21: Ward clusters and characteristics, 1971–1986

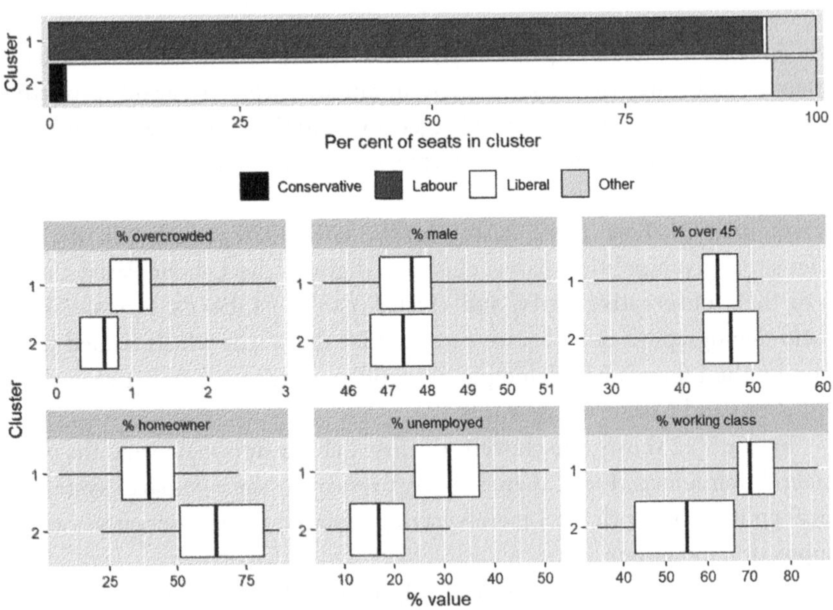

Figure 5.22: Ward clusters and characteristics, 1987–2003

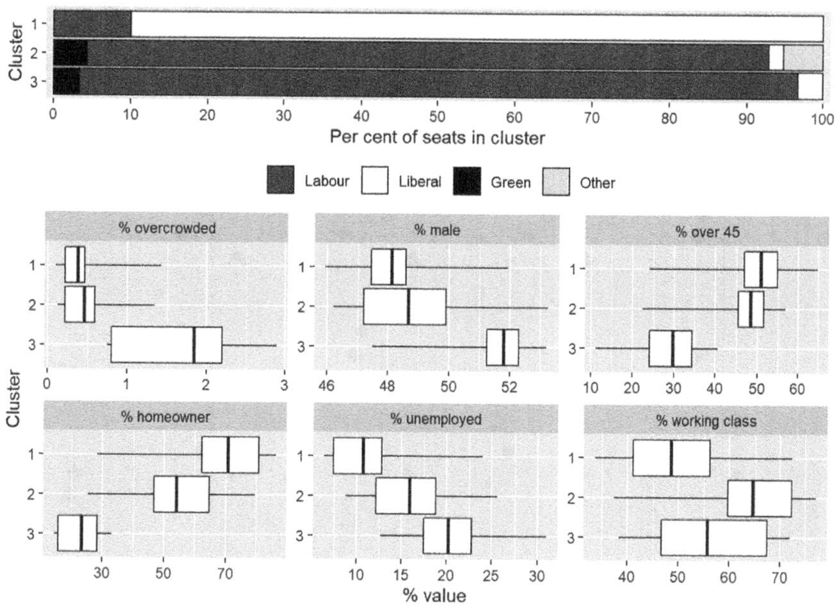

Figure 5.23: Ward clusters and characteristics, 2004–2019

came mainly from the continuity Liberal Party which refused to merge with the SDP in 1989, but include four Independent Labour councillors and one SDP candidate (interestingly, winning in Woolton ward — the ward that was the last to elect a Conservative councillor).

In the demographic profiles of the two clusters, we can see very little difference vis-à-vis gender or age, but the Labour cluster sees wards containing lower levels of home ownership and higher levels of overcrowding, unemployment and working-class populations.

Figure 5.23 shows the three ward clusters for the final period of study. The first cluster is dominated by the Liberal Democrats, the second and third by Labour. The first and second clusters show similar profiles of overcrowding, gender, and age, but the Liberal Democrat-dominated cluster has higher levels of home ownership and lower levels of unemployment and working-class populations. Similarly, the two Labour clusters are typically very different — the second is concentrated in areas with more ethnic minorities and student populations (Princes Park, Riverside, Central, Kensington and Fairfield, and Picton). This is reflected in the higher levels of overcrowding, younger age profiles, and lower levels of home ownership in these areas.

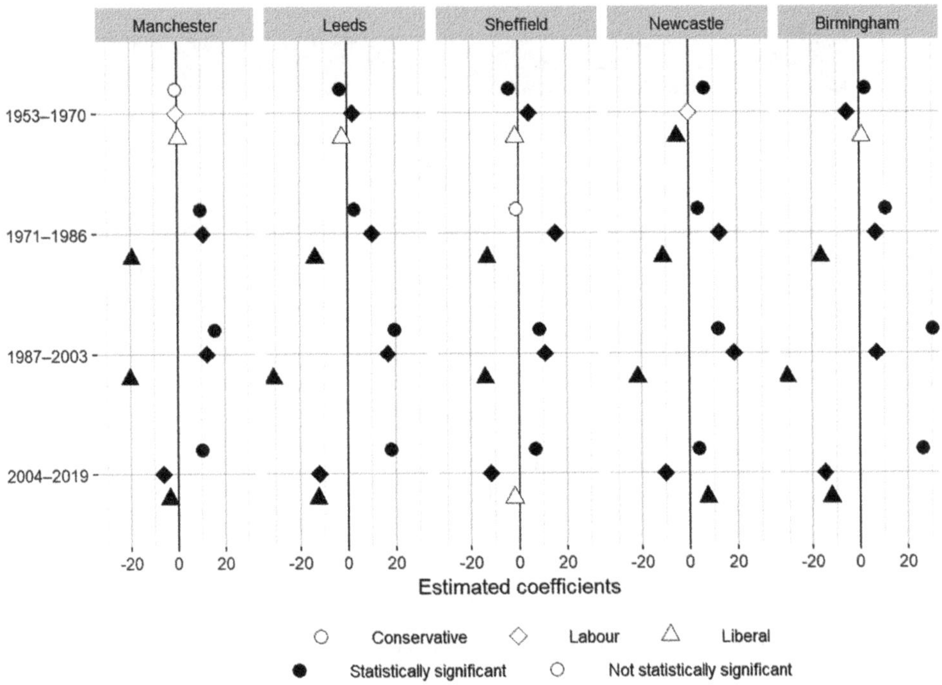

Figure 5.24: Standardised regression analysis output for each census era: comparison with five other cities

5.5 Comparative demographics

Finally, this chapter will explore the impact of demographics on Conservative vote share in local elections within Liverpool, compared to five other large cities: Manchester, Leeds, Sheffield, Newcastle, and Birmingham. Figure 5.24 represents the output for the same regression models that were run in sections 5.3 and 5.4 (the Catholic ward variable is excluded; it is not relevant to any of the other cities), and runs this analysis for each of the four periods of interest. For the purposes of space only the city variable is represented in the chart. Accordingly, each dot should be understood as representing the difference in a party's vote share in a given city, relative to Liverpool and controlling for the electoral and socio-demographic variables included in the regression models. Essentially, it answers the question how much we could expect a party's vote share to change if a given ward was taken from Liverpool and placed in the city being examined.

There is a clear pattern. In the first period, Conservative performance in other cities was mixed relative to Liverpool: there was no difference between it and Manchester, the Liverpool Conservatives outperformed compared to their partners in Leeds and Sheffield, but underperformed relative to Birmingham and Newcastle (where the Conservatives went under the label of Progressives for a large portion of this time).

By the period of decline the Liverpool Conservatives were outperformed in all cities except Sheffield, where there was no statistically significant difference. However, during the two periods of irrelevance, the Conservatives in Liverpool were consistently outperformed by their counterparts in the other cities of interest and by a much greater magnitude. For example, relative to Liverpool, a Conservative in Birmingham could expect to get a vote share 30 percentage points higher in the 1987–2003 period! It is no coincidence that from the second period the Liverpool Liberals consistently outperformed their colleagues in other cities, too.

The decline of the Conservative vote share in Liverpool relative to other northern cities over time is striking, and lends weight to the idea that Conservative decline in Liverpool occurred for reasons beyond demographic changes, which were controlled for in the model. Additionally, the fact that the Liverpool Conservatives went from generally being on par with Conservatives in other cities to massively underperforming suggests that the change in Conservative fortunes was due to local factors, rather than being solely due to a secular decline in Conservative voting across the cities covered.

What is also interesting is that, for all the mythmaking around Liverpool being a solidly Labour city and Liverpool's history being heavily pro-Labour (hopefully something this book has helped to dispel), it is only in the final period that Liverpool Labour outperformed their comrades in other cities.

5.6 Conclusion

By using census data to analyse Liverpool's local election results we have developed a nuanced understanding of just how structural demographic factors have changed since 1953.

Firstly, we have seen that the Conservatives did indeed suffer from a decline among 'secular' voters across the first three periods. By the 2004–2019 period, however, their vote could not realistically go any lower. This secular decline suggests that there was something beyond changes in demographics or electoral contexts that explained the party's performance, as does the fact that that the demographic and electoral models at no point account for more than 80 per cent of the variance in Conservative vote share. Other drivers of decline could include an eroding Protestant socialisation, the steady importing of new anti-Conservative voters, or, as is argued in Chapter 8, the adoption of an anti-Conservative, anti-Thatcher identity within the existing Scouse identity.

Secondly, we see that even until 2003 areas that were predominantly Catholic in the 1920s were still heavily biased against the Conservatives (and during the 2004–2019 period, against the Liberal Democrats), even when controlling for various socio-economic and electoral factors. Somehow, despite secularisation, religion still managed to loosely influence Liverpool's politics. Whilst the influence of Catholicism on the Conservatives was eroded by the 2004–2019 period, it was still the second most important variable in influencing Labour and Liberal vote shares in that period.

Thirdly, this analysis has shown that in the early period a Liberal presence had a great impact on Labour vote share compared to the Conservative vote share. However, because the Liberals most often stood in seats where the Conservatives, rather than Labour, tended to win, they did more damage to the Conservatives' seat share than to Labour's. This led to the myth that the Liberals took much more of a vote share from the Tories than from Labour.

There are also some consistencies between the models. The first is that, over time, the ability of the model to explain Conservative vote share declined, but its ability to explain the Liberals' vote share increased. Indeed, by the final period the model explains *more* of the variance in the Liberal vote share than in the Labour vote share, telling us that over time the Liberals became more dependent on a specific socio-demographic base, which was represented in the cluster analysis (section 5.4).

Overall, this analysis has shown that demographic changes cannot be the reason for Conservative decline: the demographic makeup of Liverpool did not change in a sufficiently drastic manner to explain such a shift in overall voting behaviour. In fact, the city's demography has become *more* conducive to Conservative support than it was in the past. Further to this, the regression models show that the Liverpool Conservatives began to do worse than the party did in other cities, even when controlling for socio-demographic variables. Thus we must look elsewhere to explain the declining electoral fortunes of the Liverpool Conservatives.

6 Migration in Liverpool

One limitation of the previous chapter is that it does not examine the *processes* of population change in Liverpool since 1945. Changes in population occur in three ways: births, deaths, and migration. As the role of births and deaths is explored in the discussion of socialisation (see Chapter 7), this chapter analyses the extent to which migration from Liverpool was a key driver of change in Conservative support, and specifically whether likely Conservative voters were leaving Liverpool whilst likely Labour voters came to the city.

Lawton and Pooley note that in Liverpool "migrational losses have offset relatively high natural growth" as the city's population "fell by over 280,000 between 1951 and 1981, mainly due to losses from inner-city wards" (Lawton and Pooley 1986, 75–77). As Ridley notes, the demographics of those who left were important:

> It was the relatively skilled, relatively young workers that went, leaving behind a disproportionate number of pensioners and those socially handicapped in one way or another, a heavy burden on local authority services, as well as groups most vulnerable to unemployment, the unskilled and the Blacks. (Ridley 1986, 129)

These remaining groups were less likely to vote Conservative, and as such this section will examine the impact of migration in Liverpool on likely Conservative voting behaviour.

Unfortunately, there are limitations on the use of migration data. The earliest digitised migration data is from the 1981 census, which is what will be used for this analysis (UK Data Service 1981b).[1] Although the migration

1 All migration data used in this section is accessed via the Flow Data website, which is a part of the UK Data Service Census Support service.

data cannot be sub-divided by the variables used in Chapter 5, and this limits the range of claims that can be made, it is still worth undertaking an analysis of migration patterns to and from Liverpool.

6.1 Migration flows from Liverpool

6.1.1 National outward migration

Our analysis of migration begins by looking at the regional destination of those leaving Liverpool. We can see in Table 6.1 that in all cases the number of men moving to each region was greater than the number of women, save for Scotland, where the figure was the same. We can also see that by far the largest migration was within the north-west. Table 6.1 does not include internal Liverpool–Liverpool flows, so the figure for the north-west represents solely those who moved out of Liverpool to other areas in the north-west. If internal flows are included, the level of migration within the north-west increases to 41,704 (20,554 men and 21,150 women).

The second largest recipient of Liverpudlian migration was the south-east, which accounts for 13.2 per cent of outward migration. No other region accounts for more than 4 per cent of the outward population flow from Liverpool. Thus, as the north-west accounts for 65 per cent of outward migration from Liverpool (rising to 90 per cent if we include intra-Liverpool flows) this region will be the focus of the next section.

Table 6.1: Outward migration from Liverpool in 1981 census by GB Standard Regions (1991) and sex, excluding internal flows

	Men	*Women*	*Total*
North-west	4,552	4,423	8,975
South-east	938	885	1,823
Yorkshire and Humberside	310	240	550
Wales	287	263	550
South-west	246	207	453
West Midlands	242	208	450
East Midlands	176	140	316
North	161	134	295
Scotland	140	140	280
East Anglia	93	78	171
Total	7,145	6,718	13,863

6.1.2 Regional outward migration

Table 6.2 shows the level of outward migration from Liverpool to each district in the north-west, again excluding intra-Liverpool flows. We can see that within the north-west there are no significant gender imbalances in terms of outward migration but people are more likely to move to areas closest to Liverpool. Knowsley, the local authority to the east of Liverpool, is the largest recipient of Liverpool's migrants, taking in 21.1 per cent, followed closely by Sefton on 20.8 per cent, then Halton and Wirral on 14.3 and 12.5 per cent respectively. It is worth noting that in many places Liverpool and Knowsley form a continuous conurbation (today it is often just the changing colour of the bins that makes one realise one has changed local authority).

Table 6.2: Outward migration from Liverpool in 1981 census by GB Districts (1991) and sex, excluding internal flows

	Men	*Women*	*Total*
Knowsley	942	959	1,901
Sefton	924	940	1,864
Halton	662	625	1,287
Wirral	580	540	1,120
West Lancashire	325	330	655
St Helens	203	232	435
Warrington	127	126	253
Wigan	104	90	194
Manchester	95	73	168
Ellesmere Port and Neston	75	79	154
Chester	55	62	117
Vale Royal	57	54	111
Other (<1% of population)[1]	403	313	716
Total	4,552	4,423	8,975

[1] "Other" includes all districts which received less than 1 per cent of the Liverpudlian migrants. In descending order of percentage, these are Chorley, Salford, Trafford, Bolton, Macclesfield, Fylde, Stockport, Preston, Tameside, Lancaster, Rochdale, Blackpool, Bury, Crewe and Nantwich, Blackburn, Wyre, South Ribble, Oldham, Congleton, Hyndburn, Burnley, Ribble Valley, Rossendale, and Pendle.

Such patterns should come as no surprise, since these are the four districts bordering Liverpool (even if the Wirral is separated from Liverpool by the River Mersey). This pattern of migration does not suggest a clear reason for outward migration; whilst Sefton and the Wirral are seen as more desirable areas, Knowsley has long suffered from deprivation and poverty. Further, there are areas of acute deprivation in Wirral — a district-wide analysis is too broad to capture the nuances in local socio-economic contexts.

After the Wirral, no district in the north-west took more than 10 per cent of Liverpool migrants, and 24 districts took fewer than 1 per cent of people moving. As a result, the next part of this analysis will focus on Merseyside alone since otherwise the number of destinations would simply be too large for a ward-level analysis.

6.1.3 Ward-level outward migration

Presenting ward-level migration data would require a large, unwieldy table showing 33 Liverpool wards against the 118 wards that make up Merseyside (including Liverpool). Including Liverpool's wards, a total of 27,520 people moved from one ward to another, 5,425 if intra-Liverpool migration is excluded. As this book focuses on Liverpool as a whole, we would not see city-wide electoral decline in Liverpool if Conservative voters moved within Liverpool, and because the intra-Liverpool migration levels are so large *vis-à-vis* the migration not within Liverpool, the next section will only consider migration to wards outside Liverpool.

As income is not recorded by the census, we must use a proxy variable. Three different variables were considered as a proxy for wealth: the percentage of unemployed men, the percentage of households without central heating, and the percentage of households without cars. Wards were ranked in terms of these measures and the Spearman rank correlation coefficient was calculated to show correlations. These are given in Table 6.3 below.

Table 6.3: Spearman rank correlation coefficient, using three proxies for ward wealth

Proxies	*Coefficient*
Unemployment–Central heating	0.81
Unemployment–No car	0.95
Central heating–No car	0.83

As we can see, the 'unemployment–no car' correlation is strongest, so we discount the use of central heating as a proxy. As there is little difference between the two that use this proxy, the percentage of homes without cars in the 1991 census will be used to rank wards by wealth.

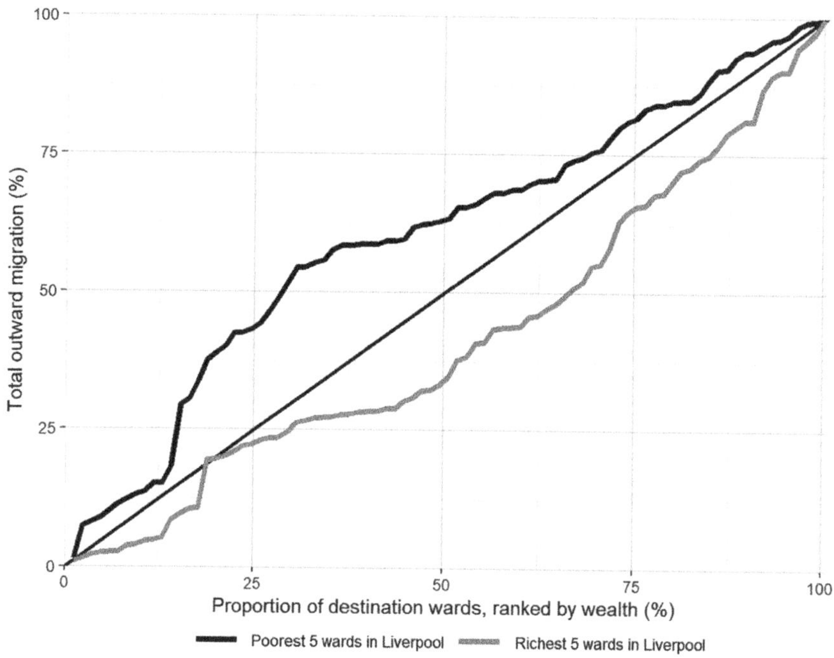

Figure 6.1: Outward migration, cumulative frequency by wealth of ward

To get an idea about the types of people who were leaving Liverpool, we can examine the wealth of the wards which they left and the wealth of the wards they went to. Figure 6.1 shows a cumulative frequency graph of outward migration from Liverpool, with the destination wards ranked in terms of wealth from poorest to wealthiest. The graph shows the total outward migration for the wealthiest five and poorest five wards in Liverpool, and the diagonal black line represents the expected outcome if outward migrants had gone to all wards in equal numbers.

Figure 6.1 shows that migration from the wealthiest five wards in Liverpool was disproportionately to wealthier wards in Merseyside, since the curve slopes below the black line. The poorest half of Merseyside's wards received just 35 per cent of the migrants from the five richest Liverpudlian wards, clearly fewer than if migration from those five wards had gone equally to all Merseyside wards. Similarly, outward migration from the poorest five wards in Liverpool disproportionately went to the poorer wards in Merseyside; this is shown by the fact that the black line is consistently above the diagonal line.

These findings suggest that people moving from richer wards in Liverpool tended to migrate to richer wards within Merseyside, whilst those from poorer wards tended to migrate to poorer wards in Merseyside. This is interesting because it suggests two dynamics at play. The first is that the richer wards — where the Conservatives were strongest — saw an exodus of well-off people, shown by the fact that they were more likely to move to wealthier wards elsewhere in Merseyside, rather than moving to poorer areas because income had fallen or they had not been able to afford the higher prices in more affluent wards. Thus, in this period the Conservatives were potentially losing elements of their affluent core vote due to outward migration. Secondly, those who left the poorer areas tended to go to poorer areas too, suggesting that we are not witnessing upward social mobility or suburbanisation, but rather other reasons for moving (perhaps such as better employment prospects).

6.2 Migration flows to Liverpool

6.2.1 *National inward migration*

It is also important to consider who was moving into Liverpool. Were the people who came into the city likely to be Conservative voters? As per the analysis above, we will begin with a look at the national flows, broken down by standard regions.

Table 6.4: Inward migration to Liverpool in 1981 census by GB Standard Regions (1991) and sex, excluding internal flows

	Men	*Women*	*Total*
North-west	3,285	3,077	6,362
South-east	463	350	813
Wales	185	178	363
West Midlands	156	128	284
Yorkshire and Humberside	149	99	248
Scotland	103	93	196
South-west	104	88	192
North	104	65	169
East Midlands	74	66	140
East Anglia	41	25	66
Total	4,664	4,169	8,833

Table 6.4 shows the migration into Liverpool from each region in Great Britain. Compared to Table 6.1 above, where showed outward migration of 13,863, we see that just 8,833 people moved to Liverpool from the rest of Great Britain. Again, movement within the north-west makes up the bulk (72 per cent) of inward migration. This is followed by the south-east, at 9 per cent of total inward migration, reflecting trends seen with outward migration. No other districts represent more than 4.1 per cent of inward migration. Due to the sheer dominance of the north-west in inward migration, that region will be the focus of the next section.

6.2.2 Regional inward migration

Table 6.5 shows the level of inward flows to Liverpool from each district in the north-west. There is a limited gender split, with 52 per cent of total inward migration being men, and 48 per cent women.

Table 6.5: Inward migration to Liverpool in 1981 census by GB Districts (1991) and sex, excluding internal flows

	Men	*Women*	*Total*
Knowsley	1,192	1,214	2,406
Sefton	721	691	1,412
Halton	271	273	544
Wirral	275	244	519
West Lancashire	148	148	296
St Helens	139	109	248
Wigan	61	52	113
Manchester	60	49	109
Warrington	60	36	96
Chester	47	32	79
Ellesmere Port and Neston	44	31	75
Other (<1% of population)[1]	267	198	465
Total	3,285	3,077	6,362

[1] "Other" includes all districts which contributed less than 1 per cent of total inward migration to Liverpool. In descending order of percentage, these are Vale Royal, Lancaster, Bolton, Blackpool, Preston, South Ribble, Trafford, Salford, Blackburn, Rochdale, Macclesfield, Hyndburn, Crewe and Nantwich, Oldham, Stockport, Rossendale, Chorley, Fylde, Bury, Pendle, Congleton, Wyre, Tameside, Burnley, and Ribble Valley.

Interestingly, we can see that the six districts at the top of Table 6.5 are the same as six at the top of Table 6.2, and in the same order. Knowsley is the only district that saw net inward migration to Liverpool, of just under 500 people (1,901 people left Liverpool for Knowsley, against 2,406 people who made the reverse journey); net total migration was outward, amounting to just over 2,600 people. As suggested above, this could be because Knowsley was perhaps a poorer district than Liverpool overall, and thus relative to Knowsley, Liverpool was a 'step up'.

Again, Merseyside provided the majority of inward migration to Liverpool: if Merseyside is compared to the GB Standard Regions in Table 6.4, it would be the largest provider of inward migration, representing 37 per cent of all inward migration to Liverpool from across Great Britain. The north-west represented 81 per cent of inward migration. Thus, it makes sense to continue the previous approach and examine which wards provided the most inward migration.

6.2.3 *Ward-level inward migration*

Akin to Figure 6.1, Figure 6.2 shows the cumulative frequency of inward migration to the five poorest and wealthiest wards in Liverpool. As in that figure, departure wards are ranked from poorest to wealthiest. Of those moving into Liverpool's richest five wards, around half came from the poorest half of all wards in Merseyside, and over one-third came from the poorest quarter of wards. On the other hand, three quarters of the inward migration to the poorest five wards came from the poorest half of Merseyside wards and around half of inward migration to the poorest five wards came from just the poorest quarter of Merseyside wards. Thus, inward migration to Liverpool tended to come disproportionately from poorer areas across Merseyside, and these voters would be unlikely to be natural Conservative supporters.

This matters when assessing any decline in Conservative support in Liverpool. Other areas of Merseyside did not have the same historic link between the working class and Conservatism via Protestantism, and so it is likely that those from lower socio-economic groups would have a smaller propensity to vote Conservative than their Liverpudlian counterparts. Accordingly, it can be hypothesised that those who came into Liverpool, especially into poorer areas, would be less likely to vote Conservative than those who left, which would clearly harm the Conservatives' chances in the long run.

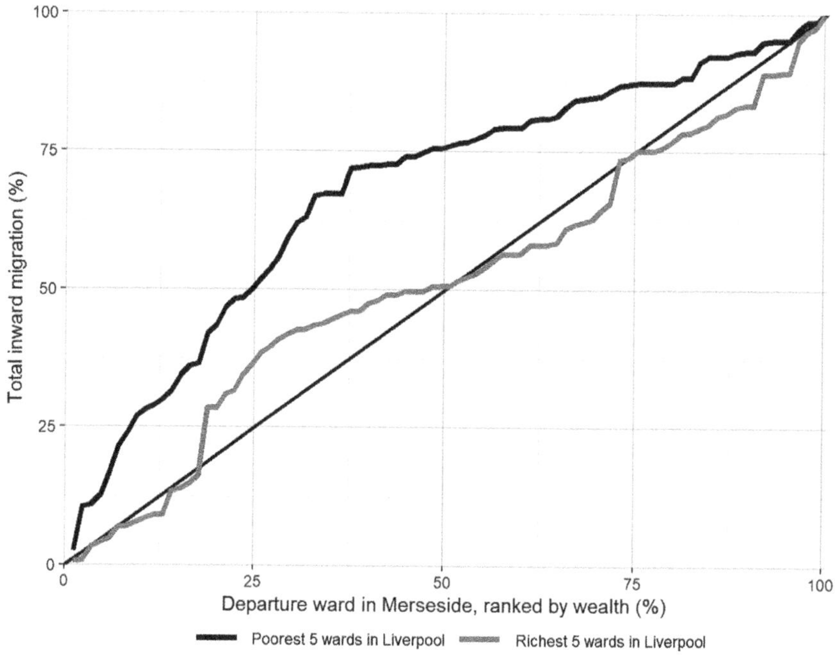

Figure 6.2: Inward migration, cumulative frequency by wealth of ward

6.3 Commuting patterns in Merseyside

The final area to examine is the idea that many of the people who had a greater propensity to support the Conservative Party were perhaps more likely to live outside the city and commute in for work, thus depriving the Liverpool Conservatives of their votes. The hypothetical assertion is that during the 1970s and 1980s Liverpool was a less attractive place to live than neighbouring boroughs or suburbs, such as the Wirral, areas of Sefton, or Cheshire; but a large number of middle-class jobs were still based in Liverpool. This section explores whether middle-class voters, who were more likely to vote Conservative, were more likely to commute into the city than working-class voters. If this were the case, the argument would be that the Conservatives were harmed electorally as the quality of the city's urban environment would have driven likely Conservative voters away to Liverpool's hinterland.

Local politicians had recognised the effect that Liverpool's poor urban environment had on encouraging people to live in the city. John Tilney, Conservative MP for Liverpool Wavertree from 1950 to February 1974, claimed in a House of Commons debate in 1967 that bosses perceived Liverpool as

> a place where there are too many slums, and a place to which their wives, on the whole, do not want to come... They see the litter in the streets. Liverpool is far less litter-conscious than probably any other city. So people think of the amenities they know in the South and which they would like to see on Merseyside and throughout the North West, but which in many cases are not there.

The poor quality of Liverpool's urban environment led to people making "their money in the North West and then retir[ing] to Bournemouth, or to the South" (HC Deb 1967, vol. 756, cc434–573, cols 535–37). In view of this, it is not unreasonable to expect that the well-to-do voter, who was more likely to vote Conservative in the first place, would choose to live outside the city.

We can test this theory using commuting data from the 1981 census (UK Data Service 1981a), which allows us to map commuter flows broken down by social grades. There are risks with this approach, as it relies on a 10 per cent sample of workers. However, by aggregating the social classes used by the census into two broad socio-economic classes, outlined below, we can mitigate some of the problems of a small sample size. This is shown in Table 6.6.

Table 6.6: Census social classes used as proxy for socio-economic class

	Group	*Class*
Social class I	Professional, etc. occupations	Middle class
Social class II	Managerial and technical	
Social class III(N)	Skilled occupations — non-manual	
Social class III(M)	Skilled occupations — manual	Working class
Social class IV	Partly skilled occupations	
Social class V	Unskilled occupations	
Social class VI	Armed forces and inadequately described	Not used

Table 6.7 shows the raw numbers of people commuting into Liverpool, broken down into census social classes, thereby our proxy classes, and then by sex. What is initially obvious is that the majority of commuters into Liverpool at the time of the 1981 Census were male (62.5 per cent) and middle class (63 per cent).

Table 6.7: Number of commuters into Liverpool from Merseyside, by class and sex

	Men	*Total*	*Women*	*Total*	*Both*	*Total*
I	373	2,804	45	2,422	418	5,226
II	1,464		659		2,123	
IIIN	967		1,718		2,685	
IIIM	1,512	2,366	182	676	1,694	3,042
IV	574		412		986	
V	280		82		362	
Total	5,170		3,098		8,268	

This does indeed lend weight to the idea that likely Conservative voters, the middle class, worked in Liverpool but lived elsewhere, thus denying the Party some potential voters.

6.4 Discussion

This analysis leads to three main conclusions. Firstly, those from wealthy wards were leaving Liverpool for other wealthy, middle-class areas in Merseyside, whilst those from poorer wards were leaving Liverpool for other less wealthy areas, suggesting that people were not moving out of Liverpool for reasons of financial necessity but rather through choice. Although this outward flow was damaging to Conservative fortune, it is unlikely that outward migration from the least wealthy wards was as damaging as migration from the wealthier wards. Those who left Liverpool from the poorer wards were more likely to go to other poorer wards in Merseyside, perhaps suggesting that they were not upwardly mobile or the typical 'aspirational working class' who would vote Conservative.

Secondly, inward migration was much lower than outward migration. As such, the chances of the Conservatives 'replenishing' their voter base from outside the city were slim. The data shows that those moving into the city tended to be from poorer wards in Merseyside, although many of them moved to the richer wards in Liverpool. Furthermore, the majority of inward migration to Liverpool from Merseyside came from the poorest third of wards in the region. Generally speaking, these people would be less likely to vote Conservative than those leaving the city.

Thirdly, an analysis of the commuting data suggests that middle-class people were more likely to commute into Liverpool for work — of those who commuted in, 63 per cent were middle class. The fact that many people seem to have chosen to live outside Liverpool and commute into the city suggests that the Conservatives were denied a segment of potential voters who might have lived in the city had it offered a better environment, as Tilney suggested.

Another important point to consider is whether the quantity of migration is sufficient to have any meaningful effect on Conservative vote share. The 1981 census puts the population of Liverpool at 503,726, so outward migration to the rest of Great Britain represents just 2.8 per cent of the city's total population, whilst inward migration represents 1.8 per cent. Thus, net migration from Liverpool to the rest of Great Britain represents just 1 per cent of Liverpool's total population. This is not a massive trend.

However, the data presented here refers to people who on 5 April 1981 were resident at a "usual residence" different to that a year previously, and as such only represents one year of outward migration. If we assume that the level of net migration remained stable at that level over the ten years since the 1971 Census, we would see a 10 per cent decrease in Liverpool's population over a decade. The census put Liverpool's 1971 population at 607,454, which means that the population declined by 103,728 over the decade, a decrease of 17.1 per cent. Thus the idea of a 10 per cent decrease attributable to net migration is clearly plausible; and this net migration would have represented 28 per cent of Liverpool's population leaving, many of whom would have a greater propensity to vote Conservative than those who came to Liverpool to replace them. This would mean that the Conservatives consistently saw the outward migration of their core vote — the middle class — an effect reinforced by mainly working-class people moving into the city. Thus, demographically, the Conservatives were engaged in a Sisyphean task: appealing to an electorate that was increasingly less likely to support them.

6.5 Conclusion

This chapter has used census data from 1981 to undertake an analysis of migration and commuter patterns in Liverpool, finding that the Conservatives suffered from an exodus of middle-class voters from wealthier wards, and an influx of working-class voters from poorer areas in Merseyside. Further, whilst the demographics of Liverpool may have become more middle class after 1945 — and thus superficially more favourable to the Conservatives — this is against an overall backdrop of population decline. Similarly, whilst the proportion of middle-class people may have increased in Liverpool, as noted in Chapter 5, the people who made up this group will have changed.

Migration patterns suggest that those who moved from middle-class wards left for other middle-class wards outside Liverpool, whilst the majority of people who moved into the top five wealthiest wards in Liverpool came from the poorest half of Merseyside's wards.

Overall, whilst both the demographic changes outlined in the previous chapter and the migration patterns outlined in this one are clearly important to help us understand voting behaviour in Liverpool they cannot fully account for Conservative electoral decline. These patterns were not sudden, but rather occurred slowly over many years, decades even, which does not chime with the rapid decline in Conservative support.

Hence, although demographic changes are important in understanding bases of party support they cannot account for the decline or continued irrelevance of the Conservative Party in Liverpool. Instead of looking at changes in how we describe people — e.g. whether they are working or middle class, old or young — we must look at how people describe themselves. That involves an examination of what constitutes a Scouse or Liverpudlian identity, and how that identity has changed since 1945.

7 The slow decline of the Liverpool Tories

It is clear from previous chapters that Conservative success, decline, and irrelevance cannot be explained by a single phenomenon. This chapter will instead focus on the first two periods of Conservative performance — success (1945–1972) and decline (1973–1986) — leaving irrelevance (1987 onwards) for Chapter 8.

This chapter will argue that the concepts of socialisation, path dependency, and critical junctures are vital in explaining the periods of Conservative success and subsequent decline. The argument runs thus:

1. Originally, Conservative support was based (broadly speaking) on the relationship between Protestantism and Conservatism. Hence Conservative support was derived directly from Protestantism.

2. After the Second World War, religion ceased to be a key driver for party support for most people and was replaced by class.

3. However, Conservative support was maintained by the socialisation of new voters by existing Conservative supporters. Now, new Conservative support was derived indirectly from Protestantism.

4. The fact that this continued for 30 years can be explained by the concept of path dependency. The relationship was challenged by the 'critical juncture' of the 1973 local boundary reform, which coincided with the rise of the Liberals, an unpopular Conservative national government, and a complacent local party to create a perfect storm which undermined Conservative support in a key election.

5. Once pushed to third place, the logic of the first-past-the-post electoral system took hold and squeezed the local Conservative Party, with the

1980 local boundary reform broadly repeating the effects of the 1973 reform.

The remainder of this chapter will flesh out this argument in greater detail.

7.1 Explaining Conservative support: Path dependency and socialisation

The concepts of path dependency and socialisation were outlined in Chapter 2, but it is worth revising the key definitions before these concepts are applied to Conservative success and decline. Path dependency is the idea of "social processes that exhibit positive feedback and thus generate branching patterns of historical development" that, once established, reinforce a certain socialising tendency and become self-perpetuating, requiring a larger exogenous shock to change course. This results in an equilibrium, which is resistant to change (Pierson 2004, 21, 44). Socialisation, in this case voter socialisation, is the process whereby an individual's beliefs, outlooks, and other, related values are shaped by the environment in which they find themselves.

These are linked to the concept of 'historical causes', the idea that "some initial event or process generates a particular outcome, which is then reproduced through time even though the original generating event or process does not recur" (Pierson 2004, 45). It is worth revisiting how sectarianism and Protestantism enabled Conservative dominance before we move on to outline Conservative decline.

7.1.1 Religion and voting in Liverpool: A (brief) pre-war history

As a result of Irish and Catholic migration, Liverpool became split geographically along national–religious lines from the mid-nineteenth century, which led to the polarisation of these communities (Baxter 1969, 1–2). Although the extent to which the Conservatives played on or fuelled sectarian divides is contested (O'Leary 2004; Davies 1996), it was shown in Chapter 2 that there is clear evidence of links — ideological, organisational, and electoral — between Protestantism and Conservatism in Liverpool (D. A. Roberts 1965).

A prime example of the interests of Protestantism and Conservatism coinciding is the issue of Ireland. One of the most politically salient issues in late-nineteenth-century Liverpool was the issue of Irish home rule, as a consequence of which those against home rule tended to vote for the Conservatives, whilst those in favour tended to vote for the Irish Nationalist Party (in its various guises). The strength of the Catholic Nationalist vote can be seen in the fact that Liverpool contained the only constituency outside Ireland to return an Irish Nationalist MP, T.P. O'Connor, who represented Liverpool Scotland from the seat's creation in 1885 until his death in 1929. As such, the potential for Labour to reach either the Protestant working class or the poorer Catholic working class was heavily restricted before the 1920s. Murden argued that, in Liverpool, Labour only started to "emerge as a significant force after it merged with the Catholic Centre Party in 1928", the consequences of which are spelt out below (Murden 2006, 448).

The final political force in the city, the Liberal Party, alienated Protestants through its support for Irish home rule whilst Catholics felt better represented by explicitly Catholic parties. As such, Liberal support was reliant upon a smaller, squeezed, electoral base of artisans and large business owners. The Liberals appeared aloof, in stark contrast to the 'man of the people' approach taken by prominent Tories. Belchem quotes the *Liverpool Daily Post* from October 1861, reporting that the Conservatives "owed their mastery in municipal matters to their ready rapport with the electorate". They were

> affable, kind and conciliating. There is about them what is called bonhommie [*sic*]. The leading Liberals, on the other hand, are somewhat imperious. They are not conciliatory; they repel rather than attract. In fact, they are far more exclusive than the Tories. (Belchem 2000, 174)

Thus, nineteenth century Toryism in Liverpool "continued to thrive in the interlocking associational network — party, popular and sectarian — which facilitated ready interaction between the classes" (Belchem 2000, 174). The Conservative political machine was complemented by the social elements of the Liverpool Working Men's Conservative Association, a Protestant-only social club which served as a political hub in wards and a source of volunteers at election times. As such, party political support in Liverpool in the nineteenth and early twentieth centuries was rooted in religious divides between Protestants and Catholics, not class. Generally, the Protestant electors lent their support to the Conservatives whilst Catholics backed the various Catholic parties and later the Labour Party (D. A. Roberts 1965).

However, the days of religion as a politically salient cleavage in Liverpudlian society were numbered. Nationally, 1918 is seen as the election when class replaced religion as the main determinant of voting behaviour, but the effects were not instantaneous (Wald 1983, 250; Butler and Stokes 1974, 409–10). Wald argues that the Elementary Education Act 1870 was key in undermining "the traditional agents of transmission" of religion, through "the adoption of a system of state-supported, nonsectarian elementary education".

This freed the voter from a religious world-view, allowing him (and, in the twentieth century, her) to "choose a party on the basis of the most salient of his remaining social characteristics — his class" (Wald 1983, 251–54).

However, the direct applicability of national-level explanations in the context of Liverpool is, as we have seen, debatable. The replacement of religion with class in a city with Liverpool's socio-economic makeup would lead one to expect a massive surge in support for Labour at the expense of the Conservatives, but this did not occur.

Jenkins points to a range of interrelated factors in Liverpool that came into effect after 1911 and served to create a "dramatic decline in large-scale sectarian violence coinciding with the erosion of the city's relative exceptionalism in terms of national political culture and identity". These factors were secularisation attributable to "uneven modernisation"; the extension of the franchise in 1918 which "channelled militant Protestant energies away from the street into political agitation"; the rise of Labour, which encouraged individuals to think along class, not religious, lines; the resolution of home rule for Ireland; and "the undermining of the local cultural and community infrastructure of sectarianism by mass interwar slum clearance" (Jenkins 2007, 177–78). Day argues that the depression of the 1930s reduced the importance of sectarianism in Liverpool "in the face of other, overwhelming problems". This trend was reinforced by the Second World War, epitomised by Liverpool electing its first Catholic Lord Mayor in 1942 (Day 2008, 275).

For Ramsden, the decline of religion was evident by the 1964 general election, which he terms a

> historically significant milestone… traditional religious cleavages broke down with remarkable suddenness; without militant Protestantism Glasgow and Liverpool soon became almost no-go areas for Conservatives, who hung on to only four of the two cities' twenty-four seats where previously they had held half of them; at Bebington, Geoffrey Howe saw a large majority shrink to marginal proportions as "people — even Irish people, on Merseyside at least — were more inclined to vote with their class than with their Church". (Ramsden 1996, 230)

As previously mentioned, to focus, like Ramsden, on general elections in Liverpool provides a unidimensional account of Conservative decline which cannot account for the highs of the 1969 municipal election or the sudden, dramatic decline in the early 1970s. It also hides the fact that the Conservatives still won over 40 per cent of the city's vote in the next two general elections. Ramsden's broader point, however, still stands: the direct link between Protestantism and Conservatism had been deteriorating.

At the municipal level, Roberts argues that by the 1950s questions of religion were important in only a few of Liverpool's wards (D. A. Roberts 1965, 151). Evidence of this can be seen in the fact that the Protestant Party continued to be successful in the wards of Netherfield and St Domingo's until it merged with the Conservatives in 1973. This success, however, comes with the caveat that the Conservatives never put a candidate up against the Protestant Party, and thus the Protestants were usually the only anti-Labour party available to voters in these wards. Simply being Tories with a different name, however, does not seem to be a suitable explanation for Protestant success in the Netherfield ward. In 1956 and 1959 a Protestant candidate stood, and in both cases was victorious; in the two years when a Protestant candidate did not stand, and a Conservative did — 1957 and 1958 — Labour won. Religious labels were important in some areas of Liverpool, even if the importance of religion was declining elsewhere in the city.

However, this history of the psephological influence of religion is only of interest insofar as it can speak to voting behaviour in the period after 1945. It has been established that there was a link between Protestant identity and Conservative voting, even if the contours of this relationship are contested, and that this relationship began to break down, even if the exact time and causes are debated. It is at this point in the analysis that Stinchcombe's (1968) concept of historical causes is useful to understand just why the Conservatives were able to continue to rely on such a large segment of working-class support in the city until the 1970s. It is the relationship between socialisation, historical causes, and path dependency in Liverpool, which will be explored in the next section.

7.2 Socialisation and the maintenance of the Conservative vote

Political socialisation is most effective during one's formative years, with parents and social milieu providing the most important cues. Thus, a Liverpudlian child born into a working-class family might have been expected to grow up supporting Labour, like their parents, but if the parents were Protestants and from an era where Irish home rule was salient, the child would be highly likely to follow its parents in supporting the Conservatives. Furthermore, if the family lived in an environment which was heavily Conservative, perhaps due to being heavily Protestant (such as the Woolton or Warbreck wards), the environmental influences would also prompt the child to support the

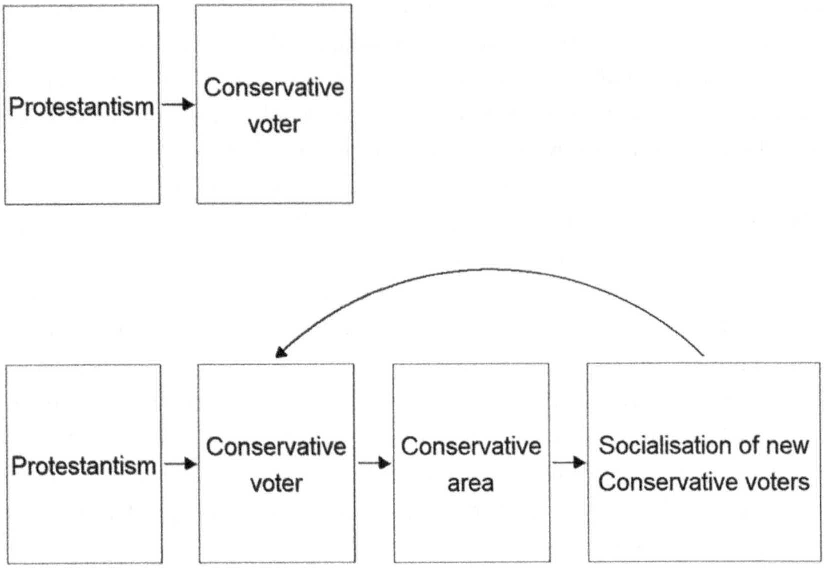

Figure 7.1: First- and second-degree electoral effects of Protestantism

Conservatives. Hence, the historical cause of Protestantism would be the reason why the child supported the Conservatives, whilst socialisation would be the mechanism by which that support was transmitted through generations. This can also be understood as a second-degree effect of religion — compared to the direct 'first-degree' effect seen before the Second World War. The difference between the two is shown in Figure 7.1.

Butler and Stokes argue that, until 1945, the socialisation of working-class Conservatives, nationally at least, was partly a result of Labour's newness in the eyes of the electorate (Butler and Stokes 1974, 185). This is supported by Ball, who states that the

> pre-1935 age group were those whose socialization was in the period when the Labour Party was either marginal, untried, and possibly alarming (before 1923), or when it was a more significant force but not yet an established or successful party of government (1924–1935) [while] only the Conservatives were credible contenders for power throughout the interwar era, a position which has always paid dividends for the party in attracting support from all social classes. (Ball 2013, 121)

This logic can be applied at the municipal level. Since the Conservatives were almost consistently in power from the mid-nineteenth century they could be portrayed as the natural party of local government in Liverpool, with Labour yet to gain the legitimacy granted in 1945, and the Liberals a declining force.

7.2.1 *The local media*

Another important factor in understanding socialisation is the role of the local media, especially the local print media. Much has been written about whether the media leads or reflects public opinion — almost certainly a mixture of both (Newton 2006) — but one can expect local newspapers to be especially reflective of local opinion, since an overtly Labour paper in a Tory stronghold is unlikely to be a commercial success. The position the local print media take is at least potentially important as it feeds into an area's political environment. However, it seems unlikely that any decline in Conservative voting can be pinned on Liverpool's newspapers.

There were two local print outlets in the area, the *Liverpool Daily Post* and its cheaper sister-paper, the *Liverpool Echo*. Both had a strong historic tradition of liberalism, but the *Liverpool Daily Post* articulated its stance as "independent of party but none the less having its own opinions" (*Liverpool Daily Post* 1959, 7). The *Daily Post* served the business sector and a more up-market, middle-class readership whilst the *Echo* offered more of a tabloid experience. Each reflected the preferences of different readerships.

While in local elections both papers generally bemoaned low turnout and the influence of national issues and party labels, before general elections they regularly endorsed parties in editorials. Tracing those endorsements suggests that the Liverpool public was not exposed to any extremely anti-Conservative message from its local media during the period of Conservative decline. Instead, the local media — to the extent that it is important at all in shaping voter preferences — would largely serve to reinforce Conservative support until at least the 1983 general election, after which there was more divergence between the two papers.

Interestingly, from 1945 to 1959 both papers endorsed the Conservatives ahead of each general election, but neither endorsed any party in 1964 or 1966. In 1970 the *Liverpool Daily Post* issued a very lukewarm endorsement of Labour under the heading "the voters' choice: Labour mediocrity or Tory uncertainty":

> The decision will not be an easy one. It involves a choice between mediocrity and uncertainty; between the minor key rule of Wilson or the uncharted seas of Heath… If Labour are given a mandate for a further term, it would appear likely that they will guide the country along a safe,

> unadventurous path. We will be neither rich nor poor. Neither great nor inglorious. In terms of Europe, a middle-aged aunt in relation to the vigorous Germans and the volatile French… We are not too happy with the unity Britain image that Mr Wilson has created. We are to be persuaded that Mr Heath offers convincing alternatives at this time.
>
> On balance, we believe that Labour will give a more stable administration. But to any voters in doubt, we advise a return to grassroots democracy; vote for the candidate, bearing in mind that the new Parliament will need more than ever men of integrity and vision. (*Liverpool Daily Post* 1970, 8)

In the February election of 1974, both papers endorsed the Conservatives and argued that a vote for the Liberal Party was "a gamble" (*Liverpool Daily Post* 1974a, 8). However, in that year's October election both papers argued that voters should look beyond party labels and to the candidate:

> If the result this time is a repeat of last February, and there is no clear majority for whatever government is formed, each back-bencher will find real power devolving upon him. So choose your MP carefully. We believe you should vote for a person you assess as likely to be moderate; a man able to understand and, where possible, accommodate the point of view of his political opponents as well as that of his political supporters. (*Liverpool Daily Post* 1974b, 6)

In the run-up to the 1979 general election, when the Conservatives were losing ground in the council and held just one constituency, both the *Echo* and the *Daily Post* endorsed the Conservatives. The *Echo* argued that "Conservative policies offer the hope of the transformation Britain needs from a nation which has lost confidence and incentive to one where industry can see its future and is ready to expand", and that this was "particularly important to Merseyside because, though our economic problems are among the worst in the country, there can be no real solution without an upswing in the national economy" (*Liverpool Echo* 1979, 6). The *Daily Post* argued that a Liberal vote was "putting their trust in a party which has not exercised meaningful power for more than half-a-century" and "in the event of a 'hung' Parliament they will enjoy the power of the nagging wife, uninhibited by her failure ever to pass a driving test, who nevertheless tells her husband how to drive the car" (*Liverpool Daily Post* 1979, 6).

Both papers again endorsed the Conservatives ahead of the 1983 general election, although begrudgingly in the case of the *Daily Post*. Both endorsements were due to the failings of Labour and the fact the (Liberal–Social Democrat) Alliance was untested, rather than any particular admiration for the Conservatives (*Liverpool Daily Post* 1983, 17; *Liverpool Echo* 1983, 6).

The 1987 election saw a divergence between the two newspapers. The *Echo* argued that Labour's policies were the best for the region but that local MPs' support for Militant was unacceptable (*Liverpool Echo* 1987, 6). On the other hand, the *Daily Post* endorsed Thatcher's Conservatives, arguing that

> despite the high price of large-scale unemployment and all the appalling misery that [Conservative policy] has brought to areas where it has hit hardest, among them Merseyside and North Wales... they still represent the best bet for Britain — seemingly in the public's view as well as in our own. (*Liverpool Daily Post* 1987, 16–17)

This pattern continued in 1992, by which time an anti-Conservative identity had firmly taken hold in Liverpool (see Chapter 8) and this was somewhat reflected by the *Echo*'s endorsement: "our belief is that it is time for a change, and time for Labour. But that is an endorsement which must be less than whole-hearted" with the editorial praising the work of the Liberal Democrat David Alton in Mossley Hill and Conservatives David Hunt in Wirral West and Lynda Chalker in Wallasey, who "have the experience and the talent to help the Tories return to its 'one nation' roots" (*Liverpool Echo* 1992, 6). The *Daily Post*, however, continued to endorse the Conservatives based on their perceived economic competence in the post-war era and Labour leader Neil Kinnock's supposed lack of it (*Liverpool Daily Post* 1992, 20).

We see the same division in endorsements before the 1997 general election. The *Echo* argued strongly that "Britain is ready for a change, and for very good reasons... The Tories have been in power for too long and have lost their discipline and, in some obvious cases, their decency" (*Liverpool Echo* 1997, 6). The *Daily Post*, however, argued

> [t]oday we believe, very strongly, that every vote cast for the Conservatives is a vote of confidence in Britain. Only by backing the party that has promised — and delivered — so much for the past 18 years can we be certain of maintaining that progress. (*Liverpool Daily Post* 1997, 6)

From this brief survey, it seems clear that the local print media in Liverpool, even presuming it possessed that kind of influence, was unlikely to have played a significant role in undermining or disrupting Conservative socialisation: after all, it was never wholly anti-Conservative at any point in this study.

7.3 The decline of Conservative socialisation

Clearly, Conservative socialisation could not continue indefinitely. Like a coasting bike on a flat road, friction will eventually slow it to a halt — and in this case the friction that slowed Tory support was provided by national-level, class-based, socialisation patterns. Roberts outlines how, as the twentieth century progressed, "people had begun to be 'steered' much more by class politics and trade union membership, as opposed to a politics based on religion" (K.D. Roberts 2015, 240). On a local level, the labour movement began "a sustained programme of education and agitation... that the way forward for working-people was Labour representation" (K.D. Roberts 2015, 244) whilst technological innovations, such as the mass media and television, "helped create a national political environment by bringing the same issues to the attention of voters everywhere, [and] at the same time accentuated potential conflict by bringing home to the disadvantaged the advantages of those elsewhere" (A.E. Green 1985, 307). In Liverpool, this would broaden the political consciousness of the electorate to beyond their city. They would now be much more aware of the lifestyles and wealth of people they would never meet. Indeed, by "World War I the scale of ideology had replaced the scale of experience as the most important structuring influence on politics" (A.E. Green 1985, 308). This view is shared by Smith, who argues that because "British society was 'local' before the First World War, local conditions could give rise to quite different patterns of organization and beliefs" (Smith 1984, 49–50).

Furthermore, as Butler and Stokes argued, in the period after the Second World War more voters were growing up in an environment where Labour was a serious contender for power, unlike those who grew up before the 1930s. As such, these new voters were being socialised into seeing Labour as a viable governing party, in ways their parents, and especially their grandparents, would not have done (Butler and Stokes 1974, 409–10). This explains why Butler and Stokes found in their study's youngest two cohorts that "no significant religious difference is associated with the incidence of working-class Conservatism. But among our oldest respondents, religion makes a vast difference to the likelihood of a working-class voter's being a Conservative" (Butler and Stokes 1974, 165). What was happening on the national level was also happening on the local level.

Butler and Stokes also noted that those who were socialised in a politically homogenous environment "almost never seem to have deserted" the party their parents supported. Crucially, however, if an individual faced no partisan lead from their parents they tended to accept "the lead that is so clearly given in Britain by a class milieu", whilst for those facing conflicting socialisation patterns (for instance when each parent votes for different parties) "the possibility of a change of preference became much greater" (Butler and Stokes 1974, 57–65).

However, over time, a voter who supported one of the two leading parties at one election was "far more likely to shift towards the other party at the next election if this shift moved him towards the dominant opinion within his local constituency rather than away from it" (Butler and Stokes 1974, 140). Pattie and Johnston (2000) also found that people are more likely to align their partisan preferences with those of people they most often speak to, especially if these are family members. MacAllister et al. (2001) and Johnston et al. (2001) also find support for a neighbourhood effect on voting.

This is perhaps to be expected, since both scenarios represent the path of least resistance. It does, however, emphasise the positive reinforcement aspect of the movement to Labour in Liverpool. Labour's increasing national dominance among the working class would serve to increase the reach and effectiveness of the socialisation of new voters, whilst those who faced competing socialisation pressures were more likely to switch towards their 'natural' party (based on class), which was usually Labour. Thus, the Conservatives were harmed twice over by this trend. Firstly, as class replaced religion and national issues trumped local issues voters would be more likely to support Labour. Secondly, those who changed their party allegiance at all would be more likely to switch to Labour.

However, religious identity mattered for Conservative socialisation in Liverpool. It provided the initial link between the working class and Conservative voting, and was the 'historical cause' for the parental and neighbourhood socialisation that sustained Conservative support after 1945. Owing to the strength of religious feeling in Liverpool, this continued longer than in other cities, and certainly longer than one would expect given the economic and demographic makeup of the city. Over time, however, the national-level socialising effects of class eroded the number of new Conservative voters, until they became concentrated in the southern, affluent wards of the city.

Both the Conservatives' long-term decline in the city, therefore, and their surprising strength before 1973, can be attributed to the socialisation patterns we have discussed here. This, however, does not explain the cyclical trends in Tory support that we identified in earlier chapters — this must be explained by national influences. Figure 7.2 shows the vote shares for

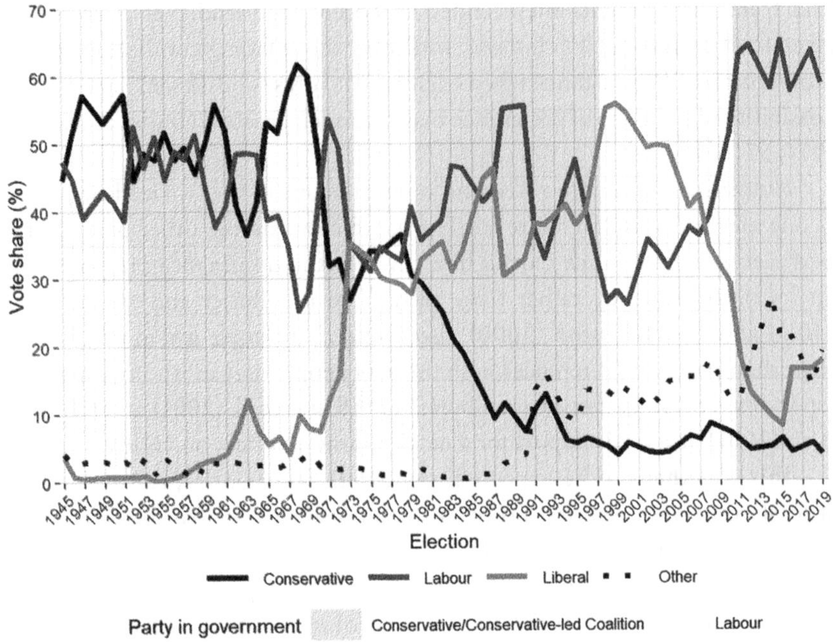

Figure 7.2: Party vote share in local elections in Liverpool, and party of government, 1945–1973

the main three parties in local elections in Liverpool, plotted against the government in power for that year (the background of the graph is shaded to show perids when the Conservative Party was in government). Broadly speaking, we can see that the Conservative vote share greatly outperformed Labour's vote share in years when Labour was in power, up to 1973.

Figure 7.3 shows the same elections, but this time gives the number of votes cast for each party rather than the party's share of the total vote. This graph reveals that the number of votes cast for the Conservatives varied much less wildly than the numbers cast for Labour and, more often than not, it was few Labour voters turning out that gained the Conservatives a larger share of the overall vote, rather than the Conservative vote rising. The election of 1960 is a prime example: the Conservatives polled 8,000 fewer votes than in 1959, but saw their vote share rise 6 percentage points, due to the fact that the Labour vote dropped by nearly 23,000. We can also see similar examples during the first Wilson government, when it was Labour's decline, rather than a Conservative ascendancy, that led to the latter's extraordinary shares of the overall vote during the period of success.

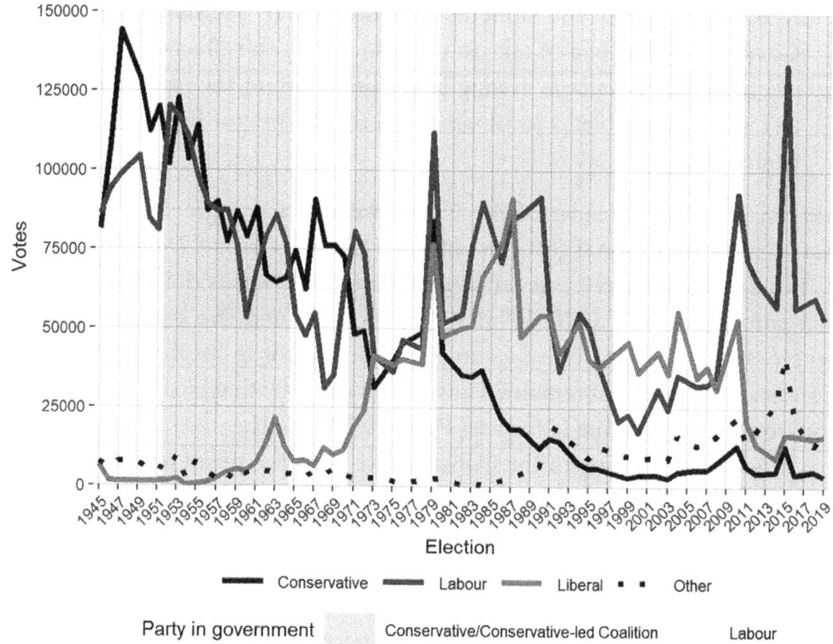

Figure 7.3: Total party vote in local elections in Liverpool, and party of government, 1945–1973

This analysis lends weight to the idea that, in order to explain the short-term swings away from a general trend of Conservative decline, we must look beyond the socialisation thesis and move to other influences on voting behaviour — the most obvious being the behaviour of politicians. Though academic work on analysing election results and political opinion in Liverpool is sparse, election coverage from Liverpool's two newspapers can help to fill the blanks. Due to constraints of space, this section will be restricted to the impressive Conservative rise and fall between 1965 and 1972. The picture painted below also chimes with evidence provided by an internal investigation into why the Liverpool Conservatives fared so poorly in the 1962 local elections, which found that in many wards national issues had overshadowed local issues (CPA 1962c).

Perhaps unsurprisingly (and not altogether unreasonably), there is a consistent pattern of each main party attributing local defeats to its national party, when in government, being unpopular, a view broadly shared by its rivals. For example, discussing Labour's 1965 defeat, Alderman Sefton, the council and Labour group leader, claimed

> It is evident that the difficult and unpopular decisions the Labour Government has had to take in order to rectify the effects of the neglect of our economic affairs arising from the failure of the last Government to tackle the problems in time has led to a feeling of frustration among some people.

Alderman Steward, leader of the Conservative Party, agreed that dissatisfaction with the national government was a factor (*Liverpool Daily Post* 1965b, i). This victory reflected a general, national trend towards the Conservatives that continued until 1970. Whilst in 1965 and 1966 the issue of comprehensive education was billed as an important factor in local politics by the Conservatives, turnout remained low, which suggests that local passions were not aroused by the issue (*Liverpool Daily Post* 1966, 1).

Whether this swing to the Conservatives was the result of Conservative popularity or a reduced turnout of Labour voters is a pertinent question. For the *Liverpool Daily Post*, the answer was clearly the latter (*Liverpool Daily Post* 1965a, 6). This is unfair. As Figure 7.3 shows, although the 1965 Labour vote did drop by 20,000, the Conservatives still enjoyed an increase of 10,000 votes. However, the broader argument — that the Conservatives were not winning, rather Labour was losing — was correct.

Regardless, in 1967 the Conservatives took control of the council and Labour's Alderman Sefton again repeated the refrain that his party's losses were a result of discontent "with the Government's economic policies" (*Liverpool Daily Post* 1967b, 1). This view is supported by the *Liverpool Echo*'s editorial, which stated "[a]s elsewhere in the country, the political change in Liverpool City Council is chiefly the product of a protest vote against Government, not local, policies" (*Liverpool Echo* 1967, 16). Meanwhile, the Liberals were floundering, their total votes falling from 8,129 in 1966 to 6,493 in 1967 despite having one more candidate — this represented a drop of 350 in the Party's average vote per candidate, from 1,161 to 811 votes (*Liverpool Daily Post* 1967a, 14).

After securing control of the council, 1968 saw a further Conservative victory with successes reported in all parts of the city, despite the fact that the Conservative vote fell by 14,000 to 76,000. According to the *Echo*, "if a General Election were held now and produced the same result, Liverpool would be an all-Conservative city" with local issues of little importance (*Liverpool Echo* 1968a, 7). Opposition to a proposed motorway was the basis of an attempt by the Liberals to whip up local fury, but "to no avail" (*Liverpool Daily Post* 1968b, 6). It was also noteworthy that the Communists put up more candidates than the Liberals in that year: 17 candidates to 14 (Tanner 1968, 9; Jeffery 2021). Furthermore, the *Echo* argued that low turnout was because "the hearts of erstwhile Labour supporters must be heavy" owing to the Conservatives' national lead in the polls (*Liverpool Echo* 1968b, 14) a view shared by the *Daily Post* (*Liverpool Daily Post* 1968a, 8).

Following the 1969 local election, Labour representation on the council numbered just 41 out of 160, which included 18 aldermen; "[n]ot since 1951, when Labour's total strength on the council was 40, has the picture looked so gloomy" (*Liverpool Echo* 1969, 7). The *Daily Post* believed that

> even the leaders of the major parties in Liverpool City Council don't see any major issues to fire the electors' enthusiasm… This must drive some to vote on national party issues, which is always a poor approach to local polls, and others to stay away altogether. (*Liverpool Daily Post* 1969, 8)

As such, we can see that informed opinion pinned the majority of the Conservatives' gain on dissatisfaction with the national government. What is important to note, however, is that the Liberals did not seem to benefit from this dissatisfaction at all. In 1969, they had just three seats. Labour voters chose to stay at home, rather than transfer allegiance to the Liberals. This can be attributed to the fact the Liberals were not yet perceived as a serious contender by many, had no distinctive policy platform, and did not stand a full slate of candidates until 1975 (and never, between 1945 and 1972, did they contest even half of the wards in the city). Hence, many voters could not vote for them even if they had wanted to.

With Heath's surprise victory in 1970, the effects of national politics on local election results began to work against the Conservatives. The year 1970 saw a swing to Labour in the local elections, and an analysis by Alderman Steward found that "[t]he outstanding feature of the election is the great increase in the Labour vote. It will be noted, however, that the Tory support is not dropping, but that discontents of the Labour movement are coming back to their support" (*Liverpool Echo* 1970, 1). The return of Labour malcontents can be seen in Figure 7.3, where the Labour vote jumped from 35,362 to 63,955 whilst the Conservative vote dipped slightly from 76,255 to 72,584. The next year, 1971, saw a further Conservative decline, with the party's council majority reduced to 25 and its vote reduced to 48,040 — a drop of around 24,000 votes — taking the party to below 35 per cent of the vote for the first time since 1945. Meanwhile Labour's vote increased by 16,806 to 80,761. For Alderman Steward, "[t]here is little doubt that once again the electors are voting against the government of the day" (*Liverpool Echo* 1971, 15).

By 1972, Labour were in control of the council on the back of a promise not to implement the Heath government's Fair Rent Bill, with Alderman Sefton arguing that this, plus dissatisfaction with the government more generally, contributed to the Conservatives' downfall (*Liverpool Echo* 1972, 8). Indeed, it is important to note that in these years of Labour victories, turnout was on average around 4 per cent higher than during the Conservative victories (6 per cent if the anomalous 1967 turnout figure is excluded), thus supporting the idea that Labour voters were more likely to turn out to register their dissatisfaction with a Conservative government.

It is also important to note the growth in the Liberal vote, from 9,974 in 1969 and 11,381 in 1970 to 18,972 in 1971, 23,514 in 1972 and 41,321 in 1973. This change suggests that many Conservative supporters felt able to do what Labour supporters in the late 1960s could not and register their dissatisfaction with the government by transferring their support to the Liberal Party rather than abstaining.

This analysis has shown the importance of taking national factors into account when explaining Conservative electoral success in Liverpool. It is clear that, more often than not, Conservative success depended upon Labour abstention rather than a surge in Conservative support. This suggests that the Conservatives had a much lower natural base of support in the city, and were lucky that Labour were less adept at mobilising their own support.

Ultimately, when after the Second World War the Conservatives were successful in Liverpool, the historical cause of Protestantism swelled the ocean upon which the Conservative ship could sail, whilst national trends provided the headwinds that could blow them off course. Sadly for the Liverpool Conservatives, regardless of their ability to navigate the national seas, their ship had sprung a leak and was slowly, but surely, sinking.

7.4 The beginning of the end: The rise of the Liberals

The rise of the Liberal Party was nothing short of astounding. In 1969 they held just three seats, but by 1973 were only two seats short of a majority in the new council with 99 members. The causes are a mix of long- and short-term factors. In the long term, weakening socialisation processes contributed to the decline of the Conservatives' electoral base whilst the closed Labour and Conservative party machines bred disaffection and a lack of engagement in local politics. In the short term, emphasis on pavement politics by the Liberals

— especially the Young Liberals — was an effective campaigning strategy that helped the party encourage voters to prioritise local over national issues in municipal elections.

7.4.1 *Party machines and pavement politics*

The problem of closed party machines had plagued Liverpool for decades. Baxter notes that:

> [i]n common with many cities in the United States of America, which have large Irish immigrant communities, Liverpool developed a political power structure that was not entirely in accordance with liberal democratic theory, and was out of line with the normal practice of British political parties. The leaders of both the Conservative and Labour Parties acquired unusual power inside their organisations. (Baxter 1969, 1)

Powerful, popular, dominating party leaders, coupled with continued electoral success on the back of working-class Protestantism, led to numerous opportunities for the exercise of the power of patronage, resulting in the emergence of 'boss politics' within the Conservative Party. Boss politics was not a problem for the Liverpool Conservatives whilst the Working Men's Conservative Clubs were active, as they provided a direct link to grassroots Conservative supporters. However, once these clubs began to decline after the Second World War, party bosses became more detached from the working classes, and ultimately this led to a Conservative Party that had very few roots in the local community.

The party recognised its lack of local roots in a confidential report written in 1956 by Mr Banks, the party's central office agent for the north-west. It noted that the party suffered from poor membership figures, weak organisation, and negligible doorstep work (CPA 1956f). Similarly, in 1962 the loss to the Liberals of the Church and St Michael's wards was attributed to weak local organisations by the party's own internal investigation (CPA 1962c), a problem which had spread across the city by 1966 (CPA 1966a). In brief, the centralisation of power by Conservative bosses had served to consistently undermine the freedoms of the various ward and constituency associations, for example in candidate selection, although there is evidence that certain ward or divisional parties could escape central control if they became sufficiently powerful (CPA 1962b).

For Labour, it was clear what had encouraged boss politics before the Second World War. The party only gained traction in the city after the Catholic Centre Party merged with the Labour Party in 1928. This came about owing to the Archbishop of Liverpool's opposition to political groupings based on religion and resulted in the absorption of Catholic councillors, who brought their own style of politics to the Liverpool Labour Party.

For Kilfoyle, after 1945 Labour councillors lacked the

> experience of local government and the mix of pragmatism and ideology common in Britain's other great cities, and influenced as it was by the more conspiratorial aspects of Irish politics, Liverpool's Labour Party was deeply affected by Tory-bequeathed boss politics. (Kilfoyle 2000, 1–2)

When Labour gained control of the council in 1955, the leader Jack Braddock continued the tradition of boss politics, leading Anthony Howard to describe Liverpool under Labour as "Cook County, UK" — a reference to the mighty Democratic Party machine, headed by a powerful political 'boss', in Cook County, Chicago, Illinois (Howard 1964, 138).

The closed nature of Liverpool Labour was evident not just in the council group, but also in the local associations. Kilfoyle recalls how he was stopped from joining his local association in the 1960s, being told that "the ward was 'full up' and that there was 'an extended process' for new members wanting to join", concluding that "in Liverpool generally, an attitude prevailed of: 'Keep it closed. Keep it tight. Keep new blood out.'" Again, this can be traced back to the Tammany Hall style of politics, where influential councillors and MPs kept membership low and exclusive to protect their "private fiefdoms" (Kilfoyle 2000, 6). As a result, "the party's organisation was virtually moribund and amounted to a collection of rotten boroughs", with the Trades' Council acting as the centre of political activity in Liverpool until the late 1970s (Kilfoyle 2000, 82).

Taaffe and Mulhearn quote Simon Fraser, a secretary for the Liverpool Trades' Council and Labour Party, who conceded that "the organisation was poor and intentionally kept poor to keep out the 'wrong sort of candidate'" (Taaffe and Mulhearn 1988, 36). Heffer agrees with this characterisation, describing how these moribund wards saw "fiddling", with many new members suddenly drafted in before a selection meeting (Heffer 1991, 94).

Actively turning away new members obviously had a knock-on effect on campaigning. Taaffe and Mulhearn argue that "[t]he right wing had taken the support of the workers for granted", recounting the story of one house in Wavertree where "a man told Derek Hatton that in 20 years of living in the area no one from the Labour Party had knocked on his door before!" (Taaffe and Mulhearn 1988, 65). Further to this, Parkinson argues that Labour's record in local government was nothing spectacular, and that by the 1960s

> Labour was a typical inner city party machine — organisationally and politically bankrupt. It was short of money, members and organisation. Many of its sitting councillors were old, patronising and out of touch with their constituents. As a former councillor admitted, the party should have got rid of many of them but didn't. So the electorate did it for them. (Parkinson 1985, 19)

Lane makes a similar argument, claiming that this was not just an issue in the historically Catholic wards. Instead,

> by the late 1960s party organisation had become so degenerate in the Catholic wards that it consisted of little more than the sitting councillors and small cliques of friends. Things were not noticeably better in the adjacent and largely non-Catholics wards that by then were reliably Labour. The political style of working brought into the Labour Party by relabelled but unreconstructed Irish Nationalists, and adopted by successive leaders, had so permeated the party that organisation almost everywhere was an empty shell. (Lane 1997, 111)

This brief outline shows the extent to which the two parties, based on the legacy of sectarianism and powerful leaders, created a local political system that excluded the public, and (in the Labour Party) actively excluded membership. It is in this context that the Liberals were able to capitalise on dissatisfaction with the two main parties, reaching out to those who did not vote and those who voted for other parties out of habit or as a 'least bad' option (Parkinson 1985, 19–20).

7.4.2 *The rise of the Liberals*

The Liberals' rise is impressive not only because they made such significant gains in such a short period, but because they did so in a city with only a patchy history of liberalism and as a party with a shoestring organisation that amounted to a single ward, a single constituency, and a city-wide party, with positions generally filled by the same people (Kilfoyle 2000, 27). Until the 1970s, Liberal success in Liverpool — in the limited cases where it occurred — typically came at the expense of the Conservatives, as it did nationally (Cook 2002, 141).

Although the groundwork was laid under Jo Grimond's leadership of the national party in the 1950s and 1960s, the turn to pavement politics by the local party came following the disappointing 1970 general election result. A successful resolution put to the party's autumn assembly that year by the Young Liberals suggested the party "focus its campaigning at the community level". The logic was that localised success, based on an effort "to help organize people in their communities to take and use power... to build a Liberal power-base in the major cities of the country... to capture people's imagination as a credible political movement, with local roots and local successes" would trickle up into success on a constituency level (Dutton 2013, 197).

Frost and North argue that the pavement politics strategy drew in "an energetic new wave of activists [to] the Liberal Party, and in particular, the Young Liberals" which "began to challenge the moribund Labour and Conservative machines". The Liberals focused "on identifying and meeting local needs, exposing the machines as complacent and out of touch at best, corrupt and authoritarian at worst" (Frost and North 2013, 42). Murden concurs, seeing pavement politics as "a reaction to the national Tory government and the failure of the LLP [Liverpool Labour Party] to provide solutions locally... providing a city under fire with an analgesic form of local politics" (Murden 2006, 452). For Kilfoyle the Liberals were able to capitalise on the fact that the council, "in the hands of either Labour or the Conservatives, was failing to deliver the most basic and vital of services, particularly street cleaning and refuse collection", whilst "both parties presided over a redevelopment process in Liverpool" that had uprooted inner-city communities and transported them to soulless housing estates on the periphery of the city. Further to this, the Labour Party was becoming "more introspective... overly concerned with the divisions within the Labour group and debates within the Trades' Council", whilst the unpopular Heath government eroded support for the local Conservative Party (Kilfoyle 2000, 27).

Housing was long a key political issue in Liverpool, and it played a role in the rise of the Liberals. Heffer attributes the party's rise to the emphasis on city planning, which saw Liverpool become "a construction site. Buildings were demolished but little was put in their place. In the end, both the Labour and Tory parties lost support due to the state of the city and the Liberals became the major party" (Heffer 1991, 105). Parkinson claims Liberal success was based partly on "their own virtues, but also on their opponents' vices", including Labour's role in presiding over a hugely unpopular slum clearance programme that had broken up working-class communities and relocated them to unpopular high-rise flats on the outskirts of the city. This was coupled with a poor repair and maintenance service and aloof Labour councillors (Parkinson 1985, 19).

As a result, as well as focusing on staples of pavement politics like lighting and potholes, the Liberals also made housing a key part of their identity, which Parkinson termed "Labour's Achilles' heel" (Parkinson 1985, 20). Using the Housing Act 1974 to prioritise the role of housing associations, he goes on to argue that

> [a]s Labour did before them, and would do after them, the Liberals used housing policy partly to meet genuine housing need and diversify the housing stock, but partly with an eye on the votes. As the in-joke went, the Liberals only had one housing strategy — to build houses for sale in Labour wards and houses for rent in Tory wards. (Parkinson 1985, 21)

Kilfoyle argues that this was at the expense of council housing, "in which the majority of Liverpool's population continued to live, and [the Liberals] continued to increase council rents at the same time as they were running down services in order to subsidise the business rate and secure the *petit-bourgeois* vote" (Kilfoyle 2000, 35).

As a strategy, pavement politics involved a number of then-novel campaigning techniques, such as the *Focus* newsletter which "became the hallmark of much local campaigning" (Stevenson 1988, 23). From the perspective of someone involved in the Labour Party, Kilfoyle derides pavement politics as "cheap confidence tricks" which deceived a "gullible and near-despairing electorate" (Kilfoyle 2000, 30). He describes *Focus* as a flexible tool used to target each ward with key, ultra-local issues:

> Typically, *Focus* would include bold headings with variations on the theme of: 'The Liberals have put the pressure on the council and the following things have been done'; whilst underneath would be the equally emphatic: 'We have asked the Labour council about the following but still nothing has been done'. Famously, Harold Wilson spoke of a party with 'a policy for every street corner' but no coherent approach to the larger issues of the day. (Kilfoyle 2000, 28)

This represented a new approach to politics in Liverpool. The fact it was not mimicked by their rivals was due to differing views on the appropriate role and aims of the local council, rather than doubts about its effectiveness as a vote-winner. Whilst the Liberals focused on issues of cracked pavements and refuse removal, opponents blasted them for not having a broader vision. Alderman Sefton's earthy observation was that "[t]hey concentrated on bloody pavements when the unemployed were walking over them!" (Kilfoyle 2000, 28). Regardless of Labour's views, as Weightman argued, "[b]y holding up a magnifying glass to the city's cracked paving stones, and offering 'community politics' to mend them, the Liberal Party clearly struck a chord more profound than mere parochialism" (Weightman 1974).

Lane criticises the Liberal approach, arguing that

> [u]nlike Labour and Tory administrations which have taken an overall view of Liverpool's problems, the Liberals have sought a base in the particular and localised fears and hopes of one section of the population. It is, of course, an opportunist politics and it is to be even money as to who hates them the most — the Labour Party, the Conservative Party or local government officers. The Liberals have no policies it is said. And that is true if you are thinking of politics for the city as a whole. The politics they do have are concerned with consolidating and developing their own narrow social base. (Lane 1978, 340)

Traces of the nascent Liberal approach can be seen in various communications with the electorate. On the eve of polling in 1967, the Liberal leader — and sole councillor — Cyril Carr focused not on ideology or policy, but rather on the claim that "[f]or years only shades of emphasis have separated the Labour and Tory Machines in Liverpool. No wonder less than one in three of the electorate bother to vote at all", and talk of a "Labour/Tory establishment... an artificial battle between the twin political juggernauts" (Carr 1967, 8). This line was repeated in 1970, almost word for word, with a nod to the rising emphasis on pavement politics by arguing "[i]t has been left to the Liberals to define and fight for the real issues. Liverpool's streets and pavements are dirty and dangerous. We have started a massive campaign to clean up the city. It's about time" (Carr 1970, 9).

Regardless of one's assessment of the Liberal approach, there is no doubt that they pursued it effectively under Trevor Jones, a key figure within the Liverpool Liberal Party, who led a team of young activists (Meadowcroft 2016). For Parkinson, the Liberals were "young, energetic, hardworking and they seemed to care about people". They pursued a focused, split-ticket strategy, persuading "many people in Liverpool who voted Labour nationally to vote Liberal locally" (Parkinson 1985, 19–20). Dutton saw the increased Liberal vote in 1970 as "testimony it seemed to the electorate's readiness to repay patient hard work carried out at a municipal level" (Dutton 2013, 196), whilst Kilfoyle goes for the more pessimistic claim that a Liberal vote was "a case of saying to the two established parties, 'a plague on both your houses'" (Kilfoyle 2000, 28). Davies agrees that the success of the Liberals was "no doubt due to voter disillusionment with the two main parties" (Davies 1999, 20).

The effectiveness of this approach, then, was broadly attributable to the failings of both Conservative- and Labour-run councils, which created the political space for a new party to fill. Hence, to some extent, the rise of the Liberals was down to luck. They were blessed with long-term social trends that undermined Conservative support and local political parties whose aloofness increased dissatisfaction amongst the electorate and who emphasised grand plans, such as the troubled, municipally owned airport or new housing estates, rather than tackling sources of local ire. On the other hand, without taking the decision to follow the pavement politics strategy, and to do so with such skill and gusto, it is unlikely the Liberals would have won the support they did. Indeed, when the Labour Party asked the local press why they gave so much attention to the Party's rivals, they were told that the Liberals "were ringing them up every day with a story" (Kilfoyle 2000, 29).

7.4.3 *Municipal boundary reforms as critical junctures*

Hogan describes critical junctures as "an event, prior to which a range of possibilities must exist, but after which these possibilities will have mostly vanished" (Hogan 2006, 664). The 1973 boundary reform can be understood as a critical juncture that significantly narrowed the possibility of a Conservative resurgence, whilst the 1980 boundary reform reinforced the new path-dependent reality in Liverpool.

7.4.3.1 *The 1973 boundary reform*

Following the Local Government Act 1972, in 1973 the number of wards in Liverpool was reduced from 40 to 33 and the aldermanic system was abolished. The whole council was up for election, with the Liberals unexpectedly winning a plurality of seats and coming just two short of a majority. Ironically the Conservatives, with just nine seats — their lowest seat share in a century — held the balance of power. Conservative failure was again blamed on classic 'mid-term blues', alongside the Liberals' effective local campaign (*Liverpool Daily Post* 1973, 1).

However, by the 1975 local election Harold Wilson was once again prime minister. In previous years, a Labour government could have been expected to provide a boost to Conservative electoral fortunes. Yet the Conservatives gained just five seats in Liverpool, compared to "substantial" gains across Merseyside, which the *Liverpool Echo* argued "will have come as a sharp warning to the Government that the electorate is far from pleased with the way things are going" (*Liverpool Echo* 1975, 9).

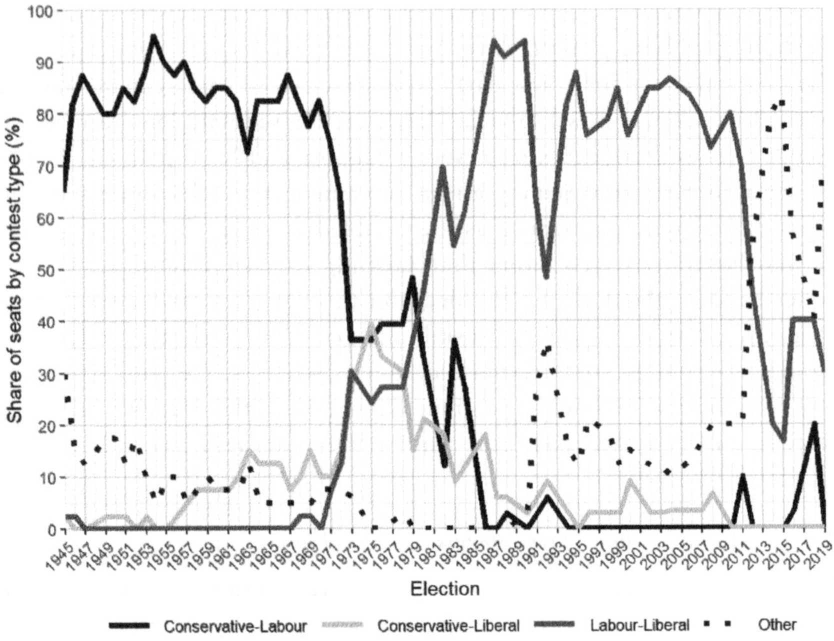

Figure 7.4: Share of wards by first- and second-placed parties

Because the Conservatives had been defeated so significantly in 1973, instead of making substantial gains in Liverpool there was a shift in both the nature and the narrative of Liverpudlian local politics. Local politics was no longer a two-party Conservative–Labour system, but now a more evenly split, three-party system, with the Conservatives usually the third-placed party and suffering under the logic of first past the post. This is shown in Figure 7.4, which outlines the sudden and dramatic decline in the number of straight Conservative–Labour contests at the ward level after 1972 and the growth in Conservative–Liberal and Liberal–Labour contests. The pattern was broadly maintained throughout the 1970s. By 1981, however, most ward elections were clearly between Labour and the Liberals. The Conservative vote became increasingly concentrated in a few safe wards, while elsewhere the Liberals became the main opposition to Labour. This can be shown in the results of the 1976 local election, where the Conservatives won 6 seats and 45,410 votes, compared to the Liberals' 13 seats on the lower tally of 40,283 votes and Labour's 15 seats for 46,321 votes; and by the Conservatives' worsening seat-to-vote ratio under the 1973–1980 boundary system.

7.4.3.2 *The 1980 boundary reform*

Liverpool's third post-war municipal boundary reform came in 1980. Unlike in 1973, when some wards were simply merged in an attempt to even out the number of electors, for the 1980 reform ward boundaries were completely redrawn (Local Government Boundary Commission for England 1978). Despite this, as shown in Chapter 4, the Liverpool Conservatives still won a lower seat share than their vote share warranted, largely as a result of building up surplus votes in their electoral strongholds.

The 1980 local election was fortuitously timed for the Liberals. Dissatisfaction with Labour's performance in national government was still fresh in the minds of voters and Liverpool Labour's local rate rise was unpopular. The Conservatives were now seen as the 'third party' and the Liberals were seen as the best placed to oppose Labour. The Liberals' pavement politics strategy had been going for over a decade by now. Even in a normal year, this would have been a good election for the Liberals but once again the boundary reform meant all of the council's 99 seats were up for election, and this "increase[d] dramatically the number of seats the Liberals won that year". Instead of Labour "losing just one councillor in each ward, in some it actually lost all three. This was an enormous piece of electoral good fortune for the Liberal Party which arrested their gradual decline and established them as a major force"; however, this masked the long-term trend in Liverpool, which Parkinson claims was "very much against the Liberals in favour of the Labour Party, which again increased the likelihood of a Labour victory in the 1984 election" (Parkinson 1985, 60–61).

The drastic effect of the logic of the first-past-the-vote system allowed the Liberals to capitalise further on the Conservatives' demise. For example, in 1982 the Conservatives won 7 seats on 25 per cent of the vote, but in 1983 they won just 3 seats on 21 per cent of the vote. We have already seen the sudden drop in the number of wards in which the Conservatives gained either first or second place between 1979 and 1982 (Figure 7.4), and the temporary rise in the number of wards where the Conservatives won either first or second place in 1983. This can be explained by the drop in support for the Liberals in that year, by 7 percentage points, rather than a rally in Conservative support.

The 1984 local election run by Militant supporter and Labour campaign organiser Mike Hogan not only doubled the vote Labour had gained in 1980, but also polarised the city's politics between Labour and the Liberals, who also saw the largest numbers voting for them that year. As a result, "the Tories completely vanished as any kind of force in the city" (Frost and North 2013, 88).

Frost and North highlight how "Liverpool Liberals were closer philosophically to the Tories and their approach was consequently not attractive to many radicals in the city" (Frost and North 2013, 43). This became more important as the 1980s rumbled on, with the key divide in Liverpool's municipal elections being whether you sided with the Militant-led council or not; those who did would vote Labour, whist those who did not would vote Liberal. There was a very limited pro-government vote, highlighted by Parkinson's findings that even amongst Conservatives in Liverpool, "who in almost every other respect took the Government's side... a substantial minority believed Labour's claim that Liverpool had had a raw deal from the Government" (Parkinson 1985, 66). Once again, the Liverpool Conservatives were at the electoral mercy of national events, and by 1987 the party dropped below 10 per cent of the city-wide vote share, failing to win a seat on the council for the first time ever.

Unlike 1973, which represented a critical juncture in the municipal politics of Liverpool, the 1980 election further perpetuated the changes which had already taken place in 1973: the Conservatives, as the third party, were squeezed out by the electoral system, seeing their image tarnished by the actions and rhetoric of the Conservative national government. In both cases, however, these all-out elections facilitated a narrative that placed the Liberals as the main anti-Labour party in the city.

7.5 Conclusion

Whilst it is undeniable that the Liverpool Conservatives experienced electoral decline under Thatcher's government, this chapter has argued that the initial causes of this decline can be attributed neither to Thatcher herself nor to her government. Instead, this analysis offers an alternative explanation of Conservative decline in Liverpool, which allows an understanding of how long-term decline coupled with short-term cyclical changes in electoral support, which the structural explanations examined in previous chapters could not convey.

Firstly, the erosion of long-term socialisation trends, which had typically sustained Conservative support despite the socio-economic structure of Liverpool, meant that people were less likely to inherit a strong Conservative identity as the second-order effects of Protestant socialisation wore off. However, this alone was not enough to guarantee continued decline. Although the Conservatives did suffer as a result of voter dissatisfaction with the Heath government, just a few years earlier the Tories had enjoyed their best post-war election result and there was nothing to suggest that the typical two-party cycle in Liverpool would not continue when Wilson was returned to Downing Street in 1974, especially since there was no alternative party to vote for in many wards.

Indeed, through most of the post-war period Conservative strength lay in low turnout when Labour voters stayed at home. This is also a reason why Labour outperformed the Conservatives in general elections from 1964 onwards, as general elections tend to have much higher turnout than local elections. The importance of differing party supporter turnout also explains how the Conservatives managed to maintain a high vote share in municipal elections despite the declining effects of socialisation.

The ability of the Liberals to provide a convincing anti-Labour alternative to the Conservatives in Liverpool put the final nail in the Tories' coffin. The rise of the Liberals and their use of pavement politics allowed them to gain legitimacy in the eyes of the public on local, although not national, issues. The Liberals' anti-socialist position meant disaffected Conservative voters could feel comfortable voting for them, especially when the national Conservative Party made voting Tory unappealing. Furthermore, those dissatisfied with the lacklustre, unresponsive local party machines could also find a home in the Liberals.

These factors led to the erosion of the Conservative vote share for two reasons. Firstly, the number of Conservative voters in the city was lower than Labour's, but could be relied upon to turn out and vote. Thus, if the Liberals took equal numbers of Conservative and Labour supporters, then the likelihood is that the Conservative vote would decline more than Labour's as the Conservative supporters taken would have a greater propensity to vote. Secondly, the sudden success of the Liberals in the 1973 local election, when the whole council was up for election, created a powerful narrative which placed the Liberals as the primary opposition to Labour in many wards, not the Conservatives. This might not have been the case had the elections continued in their traditional, gradual manner: electing just one-third of councillors each year. Indeed, without local government reform the 1974 local elections would have taken place during a Labour (minority) government, and so the Liverpool Conservatives might have experienced a stronger anti-government bounce.

This new narrative of the Liberals as the main anti-Labour party stymied the usually cyclical Tory recovery experienced in previous years, since those who voted Conservative to oppose Labour would now face greater pressure to vote Liberal. Finally, the first-past-the-post electoral system operated as one would expect, and squeezed out the third party — which was now the

Conservatives. All of these trends continued during the Thatcher era, but they had their origins well before her premiership.

As such, the twin forces of the unpopular Heath government and the rise of the Liberals as an alternative opposition to socialism, coupled with a socialisation trend that favoured the Labour Party and unresponsive party machines, meant the Conservatives were doomed. The rotting foundations of their support had collapsed beneath them, burying them so deep that they were unable to climb out.

What this chapter does not explain, however, is why the Conservatives were unable to stage a resurgence in Liverpool in the long term, either by aping the Liberals' pavement politics strategy, or by developing an approach of their own. Whilst unpopular national governments do retard their party's vote share in local elections, parties tend to bounce back when the leader and/or the government has been removed from office. Why did we not see any significant rebounding when Thatcher was replaced by Major, or Major by Blair? This question of Conservative irrelevance is addressed in Chapter 8.

8 Identity crisis

Chapter 7 outlined the reasons for the decline of the Liverpool Conservatives, but it did not explain their continued irrelevance. In fact, in a city with Liverpool's shifting demographic patterns we would expect a boost in Conservative fortunes. As shown in Figure 5.19 in Chapter 5, Liverpool had fewer working-class and unemployed residents in 2001 than in 1991, and more people who owned their own home. These factors would traditionally be good for the Liverpool Conservatives, and yet the party was unable to stage a comeback.

This irrelevance cannot be attributed to other factors, such as the logic of the first-past-the-post electoral system, as minor parties (e.g. the Communists, the Trade Union and Socialist Coalition, Socialists, Greens, etc.) continue to perform better than the Conservatives in many wards. Nor can it be due to poor organisation, as the local party has been revivified in recent years and has put up a full slate of candidates since 2007. This has been strengthened by the new federal structure of the local party, with the City of Liverpool association encompassing all five of Liverpool's constituency parties. The perceived success of this approach was shown in recent talk of expanding the federation to include the Bootle and Knowsley constituencies.

Despite this, even in wards where campaigning and organisation have been focused, and where demographics are favourable to the Conservatives, the party have still failed to shine. In the 2015 local elections — held concurrently with the general election — the Liverpool Conservatives won 21 per cent of the vote in Woolton, 14 per cent in Allerton and Hunts Cross, and 13 per cent in Cressington — some of the city wards that ought to be highly promising — as well as 15 per cent in Central ward, one of the most deprived wards in the city (Jeffery 2021). In elections for the Liverpool city mayor, first held in 2012, the party has failed to win more than 5 per cent of the vote.

This chapter will draw upon research from the field of social psychology to explain why the Conservatives were — and indeed still are — unable to stage a resurgence in the city. Drawing on a framework provided by social identity theory, it will argue that as religion became less salient the main identity in the city became 'Scouse', in place of the historic sectarian Lancastrian Protestant and Irish Catholic identities. This Scouse identity was brought to the fore in the 1960s by the city's temporary economic resurgence, the influence of Merseybeat — especially the Beatles — alongside wider cultural growth, and the city's sporting prowess. This identity became much stronger when the city was faced with economic decline in the 1970s and 1980s, and became a new source of pride and solidarity which could stand in contrast to Liverpool's economic and social failings, which were especially clear during the 1980s.

As all identities are social constructions, they are subject to change. Scouse identity was transformed politically during the Thatcher years. The use of Liverpool as an example of municipal profligacy, and of its people as feckless scroungers, by both politicians and the media, forced Liverpudlians to seek 'positive self-esteem' via a rejection of the key tenets of Thatcherism, and instead place an emphasis on concepts of solidarity, collectivism, and a reformulation of anti-establishment (read: anti-Conservative) values. This, in effect, led to the emergence of a strong anti-Conservative, and especially anti-Thatcher, element in the Scouse identity which has effectively stymied the ability of the party to enjoy electoral success. As noted by Himmelweit et al., "changes in the cultural, political or economic climate of a society as well as those generated by important national and international events" can lead to a change in the zeitgeist of a society, through a "[re]evaluation of existing institutions of a society" — of which identity is but one (Himmelweit, Humphreys, and Jaeger 1985, 49). This identity has been subsequently reinforced by socialisation, and it continues to this day.

8.1 The emergence of a Scouse identity

It is important to understand the historic role of identities within Liverpool's body politic before moving on to the Scouse identity as it stands today. Indeed, as will be shown in this chapter, the emergence of Scouse as a politically salient identity is contextually rooted in the demise of two older identities.

As was discussed in Chapter 2, in Liverpool the key identity groups historically were Lancastrian Protestants and Irish Catholics. Roberts outlines how their differences went from being antagonistic and violent, seeping into all areas of social life, to a more ritualised conflict in the mid-twentieth century, based on tradition and history rather than a deep-rooted antipathy (K.D. Roberts 2015, 321). Roberts' argument is that rather than one group being assimilated by another, the Protestant–Catholic split was superseded by a new identity: Scouse. This occurred even as the Troubles raged in Northern Ireland (K.D. Roberts 2015, 3). Ultimately, this trend was only made possible by secularisation, and a movement away from religion as a source of personal fulfilment.

Unsurprisingly, Scouse was heavily influenced by the history of the city and of the identities it engulfed. One of Roberts' interviewees, Liverpool-born Séafra Ó Cearbhail, of Cairde na hEireann Liverpool, suggests that far from being the badge of distinction it once was, Irishness became integrated as a feature of Liverpool's 'personality', and that "Irish settlement in Liverpool was so profound and so substantial in its effect on the social makeup and culture of the city that Scouseness is Irishness in its Liverpool form" (K.D. Roberts 2015, 323–24). For Greg Quiery, a Northern Ireland-born Catholic and researcher in Irish Studies, the Scouse identity was a way "to become an equal person in local society", where one's religious denomination would not matter (K.D. Roberts 2015, 324). As a result, by the time of the Troubles "Liverpool's Irish Catholic community had lost much of its earlier Irishness and was muted regarding the Northern Ireland conflict" (K.D. Roberts 2015, 315).

However, it is important not to gloss over the variations within Scouse identity. Crowley argues that "imagined communities are themselves made up of imagined communities... 'Liverpools'" (Crowley 2012, 116). He notes that localised "patterns of identification are common in Liverpool" and uses differences within the Dingle, Allerton, and Garston as case studies. For instance, in Garston identities are centred on the areas known as 'the Village' and 'under the bridge', and these are often as strongly held as a Scouse identity (Crowley 2012, 122). Crowley also describes the essentially imagined and idealised nature of these local (and Scouse) identities, by pointing out that "the Dingle was at once a 'close-knit' community and one that was riven by sectarianism and largely segregated in terms of race" (Crowley 2012, 121). As such, it is important to remember that Scouse identity is not the only identity at play in Liverpool, but there is evidence that these ultra-local identities complement, rather than eclipsing, the city-wide Scouse identity.

For scholars of Liverpool, Scouse as a salient identity — rather than as a descriptive label — came to the fore in the 1960s. As Peter Kilfoyle, Labour MP for Liverpool Walton (1991–2010) describes them, the 1960s

> brought Liverpool a respite from reality... The place buzzed with self-confidence, and few could see that Liverpool was in reality dying on its feet. Even the supposedly enlightened shared an optimism with the populace at large that everything would come up rosy in the end. Alas, it was all a mere smokescreen for a city in the wrong place at the wrong time. (Kilfoyle 2000, 3)

Despite the long-term decline of Liverpool's port, which began with the depression in the 1930s and accelerated as a result of changes in the national and international economy, Parkinson notes that "[f]or a brief period during the 1960s, government policies to strengthen its economy promised to arrest the process. But it proved to be a false dawn. Since then, decline has turned into collapse" (Parkinson 1985, 9). Frost and North present a similar analysis:

> Liverpool at the end of the 1960s was enjoying a brief Indian summer, as the success of its bands, its comedians and its football clubs masked the serious and long term decline of its industrial and commercial bases. Its city fathers were, with one or two exceptions, oblivious to these real conditions. (Frost and North 2013, 28)

As an identity, Scouse was forged in the 1960s, when the salience of religious labels began to erode; a brief respite from economic misery was seen as the start of a new dawn for the city. Section 8.2 will explore the key elements which helped to build this new identity.

8.2 Making Scouse: Ingredients

8.2.1 Linguistic and geographical

Language is important in identity formation for a range of reasons. Firstly, Scouse as an accent/dialect is important as it acts as a 'membership rule' for entry to the wider Scouse identity. Secondly, as Johnstone et al. argue, "a group of people using, or orienting to and/or talking about, a particular set of linguistic features, [is] a process that also constructs the group itself" (Johnstone, Andrus, and Danielson 2006, 79).

Regarding the impact of linguistics and geography, it is clear that these 'membership rules' are not fixed. It is not necessary to have both the accent and the birthplace to be a Scouser, but you have to meet one of the conditions. Boland noted this tension when he argued that "linguistic experts argue that Liverpool English is found in Liverpool and other areas of Merseyside... This raises important geographical issues... is Scouse identity determined by where a person is born or how they sound?" He concluded that, in terms of accent at least, "Scouse continues to retain its phonological integrity and vocal uniqueness... Scousers can come from areas of Merseyside other than Liverpool" (Boland 2010, 6–9).

Similarly, 'Scouseness' can be conferred on individuals who have come to the city and lived here for an unspecified length of time, and in a similar way removed from those who have left the city for an equally unspecified length of time. Boland outlines this point by drawing on a debate between Cilla Black and Ricky Tomlinson on their respective Scouse credentials:

> 'Well he's [Ricky Tomlinson] not even a Scouser', [Cilla] responded. 'He wasn't born in Liverpool.' [Tomlinson's] response was 'I may have been away from Liverpool for the first three days of my life, but she's been away for the last forty years'. The *Liverpool Echo* picked up on the story and went hard on the feud angle. They even offered readers the chance to vote on the person they believed to be the truest Scouser. Cilla got annihilated. (Boland 2010, 10)

As such, it seems clear that there are no hard and fast membership rules for the adoption of a Scouse identity. Ultimately, Boland argues that the Scouse identity can be conferred "based on accent, geography and sense of place/belonging" by those who already hold it (Boland 2010, 3). Thus, to be perceived as a member of the Scouse identity group, it is not enough to simply self-identify as Scouse — other members of the Scouse 'in-group' must also recognise you as a 'true' Scouser.

However, this can become more complicated by broadening the Scouse label. For example, those from outside Merseyside may consider people from the Wirral as Scouse, when those people themselves do not identify as Scouse. Similarly, those from areas such as Kirkby and Huyton in Knowsley may see themselves as Scouse but would not be classified as 'true' Scousers by those from within geographic Liverpool (Boland 2010, 17). Without wishing to go further down the rabbit hole of who counts as Scouse or not, it is enough to recognise that the membership rules are fuzzy; geography, accent, and self-identification all play a part, as does recognition from other members of the identity group. Furthermore, the extent to which these are applied depends on who is doing the defining — internal judges may have higher thresholds than external.

Although slightly woolly, this is an important point to note when considering the ingredients of Scouse, because it is important to realise that the identity is not simply a geographical or sonic phenomenon. Boland ultimately concludes that "a more inclusive and meaningful conceptualization of Scouser must have a vocal frame of reference, rather than narrowly geographical, because the accent/dialect is the primary social and cultural identifier of a Scouser". This cultural identifier, along with geography, "both affect the construction of Scouse identity and differentially determine the legitimacy of being a true Scouser" (Boland 2010, 17).

This is a view shared by Crowley, for whom the role of the Scouse accent was itself very important in developing the idea of a local identity:

> with regard to Liverpool speech in the early to mid twentieth century... there is clear evidence that words and sounds were postulated (often incorrectly) as belonging uniquely to Liverpool... the point was to establish a link between the city and a form of language. (Crowley 2012, 107)

A prime example of this is the word 'butty' — buttered bread with a sprinkle of sugar, which nowadays simply means 'sandwich'. In 1931 butty was described in the *Liverpool Post and Mercury* as an 'age-old' Liverpool term, but Crowley shows it was commonly used in Yorkshire, Lancashire, Cheshire, and Staffordshire too (Crowley 2012, 41).

Once the city had started to regard words and sounds as uniquely Scouse, this began to be seen by those outside the city as a defining feature of a Liverpool or Scouse identity. Within Liverpool, Scouse also had class connotations; "Scouse became the index not simply of Liverpool identity, but of Liverpool working-class identity... and of the 'real' Liverpudlian" (Crowley 2012, 107–8). This is interesting, because it suggests that there was a clear path from a Scouse identity which contains strong working-class elements, to one that harbours strong anti-Conservative elements, especially during a period of supposed class dealignment.

8.2.2 Cultural

The emergence of a Scouse identity cannot be understood without reference to Merseybeat, which itself cannot be understood without reference to the Beatles. As Roberts notes, the

> Merseybeat phenomenon helped make the city internationally renowned in an arena separate from trade and shipbuilding, with the added effect of taking emphasis away from religion. The advent of The Beatles had a profound impact on the global music scene and other local acts such as The Searchers and Gerry and the Pacemakers added to the enthrallment. (K.D. Roberts 2015, 339)

For Atkinson, "it was in 1963–64 that Scouse entered into a modern mythology, as the result of the rise to fame of The Beatles" — their 'banter' with hosts is held up in contrast with "the (middle-class) Received Pronunciation accents of BBC presenters". Ultimately, "Liverpool provided a means through which England's post-empire crisis, a crisis that had considerable effect on the national identity, could be positively addressed" (Atkinson 2009). As Roberts notes, "The Beatles became internationally recognised and their popularity brought renewed interest in their home city. For Liverpool, The Beatles, in turn, became a contributory ingredient in the city's newly emerging identity" (K.D. Roberts 2015, 339).

Steve Rotheram, the former Labour MP for Liverpool Walton (2010–2017) and currently Mayor of the Liverpool City Region, argued that

> [t]hrough the Beatles and the Merseybeat era... with the accent being an easy identifier, when you went abroad you became a 'Scouser'. It didn't matter whether you were Catholic, Protestant, or anything else; because people just wanted a piece of you. It was a badge of honour! It opened lots and lots of doors for people, certainly for a Scouse lad with ladies who weren't from the area. They loved the Scouse accent, because of what is supposedly identified. It was a cultural identity. (K.D. Roberts 2015, 341)

Another key element of the importance of Merseybeat was in providing an alternative to religious activities, as

> Liverpool's youth found expression through making or enjoying music rather than subscribing to seemingly dated sectarian tunes. Merseybeat formed part of a broader cultural expression... Previously the 'Twelfth' and St Patrick's Day were welcome distractions from the tedium of slum living. (K.D. Roberts 2015, 340)

Thus, a 'positive self-concept' could be built around the success of people from Liverpool, especially the Beatles but also those within the Merseybeat orbit. The link between the average Scouser and these global stars was based upon a common accent, not just a common area of origin, which would allow outsiders to quickly make the connection as well. Hence, the identity was validated or supported by those outside the in-group, thereby serving to reinforce and legitimise it. As noted by the BBC,

> Liverpool became known for its comics, such as Jimmy Tarbuck and Ken Dodd (who also doubled up as a singer, covering the song 'Tears' which was the best-selling single in 1965, the UK's third best-selling single of the 1960s, and the only one of the top-five best-selling singles of the

> 1960s which was not by The Beatles), as well as its entertainers, like Ricky Tomlinson, playwrights, poets and artists. (BBC News 2010)

As Belchem argues, "a succession of Liverpool-born comedians... acquired national celebrity for their humour... as a defining moment for Scouse, an early instance of economic decline and cultural assertion" (Belchem 2000, 50). Similarly, the Everyman Theatre, symbolically situated on Hope Street, which runs from the Anglican Cathedral to the Catholic Metropolitan Cathedral, became a hub for home-grown talent and an avenue for the exploration of Scouse voices.

8.2.3 *Sporting*

The second main element of a Scouse identity in the 1960s stemmed from Liverpool's sporting success, specifically in the realm of football. Football played a similar role to the arts, in giving people an alternative to religious events. However, much more than that, it gave people a new 'tribe' or sense of identity. Boyle argues that support for football teams "help[s] to give specific identities symbolic form" and, unlike in Glasgow where support for Rangers is linked to a Protestant identity and Celtic to a Catholic identity, in Liverpool support for both major teams avoided sectarian divides and instead manifested "itself in a strong sense of a city identity", working to strengthen the idea of a Scouse identity (Boyle 1995, 175–76).

By providing yet another way to spend one's time and to feel a sense of belonging, away from religion, football showed younger generations in Liverpool that conflict did not have to be between Green and Orange, but instead could be between Blue and Red, that is whether one supported Everton or Liverpool. Helpfully for the development of a Scouse identity, which team you supported was not based on geographical or religious lines (unlike in Belfast or Glasgow), but was rather 'inherited' from one's parents often with little or no rhyme or reason (Boland 2010, 11–12). This can be traced back to both Liverpool clubs being closely associated with the same Conservative councillor, John Houlding, who was the first president of Everton Football Club before founding Liverpool Football Club in 1892 (Boyle 1995, 135).

For Reverend John Williams

> football, music, and the arts helped bring us out of the valley of darkness. They created unity. All these wonderful things happened in the Sixties. It was a great time of liberation. People said, 'So what if I go into a Catholic

> church! What is the point in maintaining this façade?' (K.D. Roberts 2015, 342)

Frost agrees, arguing that the "notion of 'Scouse' is strongly articulated and celebrated through football, the two are bound together very tightly", but also notes that "historically the exclusion of black people from football, and from many other pastimes, serves to underpin the boundaries of Scouse identity as something that attempts to marginalize blacks". This can also be applied to the cultural and musical realms. This racist element of Scouse identity will be explored in more detail later in this chapter, but it ties in with Crowley's analysis of Scouse as a specifically white working-class identity (Frost 2000, 213).

8.2.4 Economic

Another element in the creation of a Scouse identity was economic prosperity. As we have seen, in the 1960s economic growth proved to be fleeting, but it was a powerful driver for the creation of a positive Scouse identity. As Kilfoyle argues, in the 1960s "Liverpool was a great place to be. Economically I could go from a job to a job to a job" (K.D. Roberts 2015, 344). For Liverpool-born Andy Burnham, Labour MP for Leigh in Manchester (2001–2017) and now Mayor of the Greater Manchester City Region,

> Liverpool was a fairly prosperous city. It was giving everybody a job and with The Beatles and everything it was slightly ahead with a new way of thinking. Everyone was doing alright so nobody had a reason to be scapegoating anybody. Everybody was having a good time and forgetting it. Liverpool saw itself as different. (K.D. Roberts 2015, 346)

Not only did economic growth help to erode sectarian prejudice, it also provided a feeling that Liverpool was a place of economic and cultural dynamism, later another reason for pride in one's hometown. Similarly, it would also make the pain of economic decline more pronounced, as people had seen and felt the benefits of city-wide economic success relatively recently.

8.2.5 Political

Finally, Liverpool underwent a political change in the 1960s, which shaped the nascent Scouse identity. Historically, poverty had long created a sense of collective solidarity between people in Liverpool, which created a similarity of outlook increasingly able to cross sectarian lines (K.D. Roberts 2015, 338). This fed into the collective understanding of Liverpool, and the solidarity within Protestant communities and within Catholic communities morphed into solidarity within the Scouse community. Whether this level of solidarity was actually the case 'on the ground', or rather another example of a shared myth, is less important than it being a perception of Scouse identity shared by those who identify as Scouse.

Alongside the increasing shift towards Labour, on a constituency level at least, the 1960s were a time of flux which, for Kilfoyle, "affected every type of attitude; religious attitudes, sexual attitudes, moral attitudes, everything" (K.D. Roberts 2015, 344). Roberts argues that, again, the Beatles were an important factor in shifting political beliefs:

> many in the city began to take on a more socialist perspective, many were also embracing a Lennonist (as well as a Leninist) ideology. Lyrics like, 'All you need is love' and 'Imagine there's no heaven', usurped longstanding sectarian dogmatism. (K.D. Roberts 2015, 344–45)

In consequence, throughout the 1960s "[p]oetry, comedy, music, television, left wing politics, and football were all contingents shaping the character of Liverpool" (K.D. Roberts 2015, 346). For Crowley, "Scouse indexed Liverpool as a physical place, a site of cultural production and the location of a particular form of identity... an expansive cultural repository for the generation of images of a specific type of contemporary urban working-class life" (Crowley 2012, 110). For Frost, Scouse as a 'micro-culture' has been "'belligerence', with militant trade unions and class struggle... of defiance and struggle, of hardship", rooted in the experiences of the working class (Frost 2000, 197). This has also been shown by Holdsworth, who finds that for students, who come to the city to study, "the identification of scousers [*sic*] is associated with urban, white, working-class, male youths... and, moreover, [they learn] that this group [is] best avoided" — but she also recognises that this was based on "anecdotal and second-hand accounts of problems" rather than first-hand experiences (Holdsworth 2008, 232).

Employing the theoretical framework of social identity theory, it is clear that in the 1960s the Scouse identity provided ample scope for individuals to maintain or enhance their self-esteem, or develop a positive self-concept. Whether that was through supporting one of Liverpool's two footballing giants, taking pride in Liverpool's cultural contributions, claiming to be from the same geographic area as global superstars like the Beatles (or Ken Dodd), or simply speaking like them, the Scouse label provided a way to enhance positive self-esteem. Interestingly, there was something for both the working and the middle class in this concept. Football has cross-class appeal, whilst the non-Merseybeat cultural element tended to be out of reach for many in the working class. Roberts argues that "the Scouse identity played an important role in uniting Liverpool residents... the Scouse identity was coming to fruition with a certain arrogance. The city had reason to feel proud and this pride was important" (K.D. Roberts 2015, 348).

8.3 Scouse: Bring to the boil

If the 1960s saw the crystallisation of the Scouse identity, rooted in the positive experience of the city and its achievements, the 1970s and 1980s saw it evolve from a symbol of good times to a way of coping with bad ones. As Reicher notes,

> the mere salience of group divisions is sufficient to instigate a psychological dynamic toward intergroup differentiation. This may be a general process, but the way in which it translates into action is a function of a series of contextual factors. (Reicher 2004, 929)

Similarly, for Crowley, "identity isn't a natural or ahistorical thing, but a social process from which emerge certain (precarious) modes of cultural stability and fixity that are posited over and against changing historical, political and ideological realities" (Crowley 2012, 135).

This can be taken to mean, rightly, that context matters. There was nothing inevitable about the Conservatives' irrelevance in Liverpool, but it is in the battle between the Militant-led Labour council and the Thatcher-led Conservative government that the root of Conservative irrelevance can be found. Section 8.3 will trace the process by which this occurred.

8.3.1 The rise of Militant

Militant played a key role in cementing anti-Thatcherism into the Scouse identity. This is only hinted at in the literature but will be developed in greater detail in subsequent sections of this chapter. Before that, it is worth considering the rise of Militant in Liverpool.

There have been numerous works on Militant, ranging from writings by those who were involved with or sympathetic towards the Tendency (e.g. Heffer (1991) and Taaffe and Mulhearn (1988)); via those who were opposed, such as Kilfoyle (2000); and those who purport to put forward an unbiased history, for example Parkinson (1985) and Frost and North (2013); to those such as Ridley (1986), who wrote specifically for an academic audience.

Kilfoyle paints a grim picture of Liverpool at the start of the 1970s:

> ignorant of its plight, devoid of the political nous necessary to cope with its predicament (even if it had been aware of it), geographically misplaced, and living largely in a cultural time warp, as the part-illusory perception of the city at the centre of the swinging sixties proved ever more outdated. The reality was far more prosaic: second-generation, long-term unemployment was growing and job opportunities were becoming fewer as business after business closed down and companies fled a port bedevilled by lack of investment and atrocious industrial relations. The city's population was falling dramatically, not least due to the housing policy of successive councils, and the Scouse diaspora grew as some of its finest talents were forced to look elsewhere to realise their potential. In short, Liverpool faced a gloomy prognosis. (Kilfoyle 2000, 4)

The voters turned to the Liberals to solve the city's problems in 1973. However, unable to gain a majority on the council, the Liberals had to govern in informal coalition with the Conservatives, whilst Labour more often than not refused to rule as a minority administration.

Militant had its base in the Liverpool Walton constituency, which by the 1950s had "become a hub of far left politics within the Labour Party, with the selection of Militant founder Ted Grant as parliamentary candidate in 1955" (Frost and North 2013, 33). Militant began to flex its muscles in the union movement, working hard during the city's Indian summer of the 1960s, when, according to Kilfoyle, the city fathers were oblivious to the real living conditions of a large number of Liverpudlians (Kilfoyle 2000, xix–xx). The rise of the Liberals and their policy of keeping the rates low resulted in the need to raise council housing rents more than elsewhere,[1] giving the "small group of energetic young people, most engaged almost full-time in politics" a wedge issue with which they could win local popular support (Ridley 1986, 131). This policy also allowed Labour to paint the Liberals as "jumped-up Tories" (Kilfoyle 2000, 103).

Militant's ideology was broadly undiluted workerism, and the Tendency was followed by very few intellectuals and middle-class professionals, who would have been looked down on. Instead, the faction was dominated by a

1 Before the Thatcher government replaced them with the Community Charge (known as the poll tax), property owners paid 'rates' to their local council based on the estimated value of their property, multiplied by a 'rate poundage' set by the local authority. Like today, property values were rarely reviewed due to political considerations and, under Thatcher, a cap was set on potential rate increases.

macho and sexist culture well suited to Liverpool's political climate (Ridley 1986, 131–33). The task of the Militant entryists was made easier with the rise of the Social Democratic Party (SDP), which "cleared many right wingers out of Labour" (Frost and North 2013, 48).

Labour's hollowed-out constituency and ward parties were easy targets for Militant. Kilfoyle describes the faction as having "an ideological framework, articulate spokespersons, a well-oiled organisation, high morale and an almost incestuous network of trusted individuals. What remained of the older Liverpool Labour Party was very simply no match for this, on any level" (Kilfoyle 2000, 135). Davies disputes the idea of a weak party organisation as an explanation for the rise of Militant in Liverpool, because "organisation was poor in many other parts of the country at this time, but only in Liverpool did Militant become so significant" (Davies 1999, 21).

However, in light of discussions earlier in this chapter, it is not hard to see how Liverpool Labour's political heritage could lead to a situation where a determined far-left group could manoeuvre their way through the Liverpool Labour Party, using practices already established within the city: weak party structures, a lack of clear internal democracy, and a history of boss politics created a political context in which the Trotskyite Militant Tendency could effectively pursue an entryist strategy and 'take over' the Liverpool Labour Party, even when just a minority of Labour councillors were Militant members.

Parallels can be drawn between the Liberal rise in the early 1970s and Militant's campaigning strategy in the early 1980s: Militant's campaigning "spearheaded an enormous revitalisation of the labour movement in the area" and saw "a complete break with the pedestrian, low-key approach of the right and sometimes of the left wing in organising and preparing election campaigns" (Taaffe and Mulhearn 1988, 65). Liverpool Labour went into the 1983 election with their own local newsletters, inspired by the Liberals' *Focus*, called *Liverpool Labour News* and *Not the Liverpool Echo*, which were distributed to every household in the city (Taaffe and Mulhearn 1988, 54). In 1983, Liverpool bucked national trends and saw a swing towards Labour, although this had more to do with the local party's pledge to face down Thatcher than any great warmth felt for Michael Foot's party. In the 1984 local elections, on a turnout of 50 per cent (up by 8 percentage points on 1983), Labour won 46 per cent of the vote (Frost and North 2013, 80).

Militant's rise occurred against the backdrop of the 1980s, which saw economic hardship hit Liverpool. Frost and North state that the unemployment rate rose from just 5 per cent in the mid-1960s to 20 per cent by 1981, with 40,000 jobs lost between 1979 and 1984 — half of Liverpool's manufacturing base (Frost and North 2013, 8–17). In 1985 the *Liverpool Echo* reported that "[a]lmost 32,000 Merseyside youngsters were chasing just 112 careers" (K.D. Roberts 2015, 354). The government laid the blame for this economic downturn firmly at the feet of the people of Liverpool: Thatcher told Robert Kilroy-Silk, the MP for Knowsley (the constituency next door to Liverpool), that "[t]he problem with your constituents is that they don't start up their own businesses. They've got no entrepreneurial spirit. They've got no get-up-and-go" (K.D. Roberts 2015, 354).

Another example of the Conservative government's view of Liverpool can be seen in Secretary of State for the Environment Patrick Jenkin's appearance on Radio City in 1985, where he is reported to have said

> you always want special privileges on Merseyside... always clamouring, always clamouring for special treatment... I can tell you the rest of the country is getting sick of the raucous clamour from Liverpool always asking for special concessions.

Frost and North state that "Liverpool Council responded by stating the city was not seeking special favours, but justice" (Frost and North 2013, 99).

As a result of the conflict between the Labour-led council — which rhetorically presented themselves as Liverpool — and the Thatcher government, local voters became "unwilling to sanction the local face of Margaret Thatcher" (Kilfoyle 2000, 106). Importantly, this was not just an issue with a leader, or a set of politicians — it was seen as the whole Conservative ideology having turned its back on Liverpool. In the battle between Militant's socialism and Conservative Thatcherism, there was no space for Salvidge-era Tory democracy. Even if Thatcher did seem to care about the plight of Liverpool, as Heffer argues she did, her desire to crush Militant triumphed (Heffer 1991, 191–92).

This raises the question, however, of why in previous eras of high unemployment in Liverpool the Conservatives had not been rendered electorally impotent. As Parkinson notes, "Merseyside has had the highest rate of unemployment of any English conurbation in every decade since the 1950s". This suggests that the Conservatives had the ability to do well despite the relatively higher levels of unemployment. However, during the 1970s "the rate of unemployment in Liverpool quadrupled from 5 per cent to 20 per cent" and by "1985 it was 27 per cent, double the national average" (Parkinson 1985, 13). Until the Thatcher era,

> the city's economic misfortunes did not have a major direct impact upon the health of the municipal economy itself, because high levels of public expenditure and a relatively generous government grant system protected the local authority from the most severe financial effects of structural decline. (Parkinson 1985, 9–10)

As such, Liverpool had previously been insulated from the effects of its poorly performing economy and once this support was taken away economic concerns really came to the fore, to the Conservatives' detriment. Or, as former Labour councillor Jimmy Rutledge claims,

> [t]he old Tories might have wrung their hands and said, 'well we'll see if we can come up with some form of scheme to alleviate the suffering'. But the hard face of Thatcherism and this sort of new injection or revival of *laissez-faire* capitalism and economic liberalism; it was just so bleak. In a sense that filtered through to people who weren't overtly political; probably your average Labour voter who voted because of a class instinct or because of family tradition and who thought, this is really, really serious. (Frost and North 2013, 27)

Over time, this economic and, for some, moral decline seeped into the public consciousness via the media, with Jones and Wilks-Heeg outlining how "Liverpool became virtually synonymous with urban social problems in the news media, feature films and television drama" and a "destination for those seeking out urban blight" (Jones and Wilks-Heeg 2004, 344). Boland states that, following the Toxteth riots in 1981, which involved the first use of CS gas by police on the UK mainland,

> [t]he then-Chief Constable of Merseyside connected the riots to pathological flaws in local people. He argued the 'true Liverpudlian' possessed a 'turbulent character' that was 'proportionately tougher, more violent'; this was carelessly linked to large scale in-migration from Africa, Ireland, China and the Caribbean (Boland 2008, 359)

Although important for the history of Liverpool, the Toxteth riots did not play a significant role in the story of Conservative decline. In the local election before the riots, in 1980, the Conservatives won 29.4 per cent of the vote; this had fallen to 25.1 per cent in 1982. This drop of four percentage points is largely in line with the Conservative Party's national polling performance: the party polled an average of 39 per cent in April 1980 compared to an average of 35.7 per cent in April 1982 (Pack 2022).

The consequent appointment of Michael Heseltine as 'Minister for Merseyside' was not enough to stem the flow of Conservative voters. The regeneration efforts he led, while welcome, did not make a material difference to the daily lives of many Liverpudlians, especially when set against the reduction in funding to the council by the Thatcher government (Frost and North 2013, 71). The National Audit Office recommended that the Merseyside Development Corporation, which was set up by Heseltine, should be wound down because it achieved so little (BBC News 2006). In a rare display of unity, both Militant and Maggie agreed that Heseltine's approach had failed, with Thatcher stating "for the most part his efforts had only ephemeral results, I would not blame him for that: Liverpool has defeated better men than Michael Heseltine" (Thatcher 2013). Given this lack of success, it is not surprising the Conservatives' regeneration programme did not produce electoral benefits.

Even Liverpool's sporting prowess was not immune from the shame of the 1980s. Although English football as a whole had a problem with hooliganism in the 1970s and 1980s, the spotlight once again fell on Liverpool. The European Cup final between Liverpool FC and Juventus, held at Heysel Stadium in May 1985, ended in tragedy before the match had even begun. Before the match, "39 Juventus supporters died as a wall collapsed after a charge by Liverpool fans" which was "viewed by millions of people across Europe and beyond". For Boland, whilst "the behaviour of sections of the Liverpool fans was inexcusable", even before the match concerns had been expressed about "the suitability of the stadium, ticketing arrangements and inadequate policing for such a high profile event". The overall effect of the Toxteth riots and Heysel was to associate the city with "mob violence and hooligan behaviour" (Boland 2008, 359–60).

This reputation was compounded in April 1989 by the Hillsborough disaster, when a crush at the Hillsborough stadium in Sheffield killed 96 people and injured 766. This was the worst disaster in British sporting history. More than two decades later, the Hillsborough Independent Panel found widespread evidence of a police cover-up and no evidence that Liverpool fans had played a role in the disaster (BBC News 2012). However, immediately following the disaster the media reported on the incident in ways which traduced those fans. This was epitomised by *The Sun*'s infamous 'Truth' article — although less sensationalist versions featured in other newspapers — which "inaccurately informed that LFC 'yobs' had caused the Hillsborough disaster, stolen money from the pockets of dead bodies and urinated over them, and beaten up police officers giving the kiss of life to the most severely injured" (Boland 2008, 363). Even though these allegations were later proved to be utterly false, at the time it further tarnished the image of Liverpool's football fans, as well as people from Liverpool more generally. This was especially important given the key role that football played in the original construction of the Scouse identity, and the allegations fed into an existing discourse around the perceived moral failings of Scousers.

As a result, the cultural, sporting, economic, and — with the rise of Militant and the negative coverage that garnered — political decline of Liverpool in the 1980s "brought significant negative media coverage of the city" (Boland 2008, 360). This even led to critiques of the morality of Scousers, and their status as human beings. Reflecting on the turbulent 1980s and the city's reputation, Madsen commented "[t]he conventional wisdom of Liverpool is that it is strike-bound, bankrupt, run-down, wasted, hopeless and run by loony left-wingers" (Madsen 1992, 634). For Boland, this "social stereotyping and stigmatisation" represents "a different form of 'cultural knowledge' that has dogged the city for many years and proved very difficult to shift" (Boland 2008, 360).

8.4 Scouse and the theory

Before linking the Scouse identity to the theoretical framework of identity change, it is worth revising Tajfel and Turner's work on social identity theory. Their argument is that an individual's identity is a key element of their self-worth, as individuals strive to "achieve or to maintain positive social identity", which is "based to a large extent on favourable comparisons that can be made between the in-group and some relevant out-groups". Hence, when their "social identity is unsatisfactory, individuals will strive either to leave their existing group and join some more positively distinct group and/or to make their existing group more positively distinct" (Tajfel and Turner 1979, 40).

We can see that Liverpool's social, economic, and reputational context would not allow individuals to maintain or enhance their self-esteem based on membership of the Scouse in-group. Burnham argues that by the 1980s Liverpool was increasingly comparing itself to the rest of England, and that "Scouse identity almost became asserted as anti-English... people were defining themselves against the rest of England and not against each other internally" (K.D. Roberts 2015, 348). Sykes argues that people in Liverpool saw themselves as victims not of unfortunate circumstance, but of a "negatively oriented discursive image within national space" — a popular refrain in the pubs of Liverpool — which served to create stereotypes resented by Scousers but widely accepted across the country (Boland 2008, 364).

Evidence of this can be found in an article in the *Daily Mirror* from 1982, which stated: "They should build a fence around it [Liverpool] and charge an admission fee. For sadly, it has become a 'showcase' for everything that has gone wrong in Britain's major cities" (Lane 1997, xiii). Marriner argues that Liverpool became "synonymous with vandalism, with high crime rates, with social deprivation in the form of bad housing, with obsolete schools, polluted air and a polluted river, with chronic unemployment, run-down dock systems and large areas of industrial dereliction", unable to diversify its economy (Marriner in Wildman 2012, 119–23). This is not fertile ground in which to grow a positive self-identity.

As previously mentioned, those holding an unsatisfactory social identity — i.e. one that is perceived negatively and does not enhance self-esteem, like the Scouse identity during the 1980s — have three potential routes for change:

1. *Individual mobility* — an individual moves from one group to another.
2. *Social creativity* — the group redefines or changes the basis for intergroup comparison.
3. *Social competition* — the group competes directly with the out-group (Tajfel and Turner 1979, 43–44).

As individual mobility is a personal solution, its suitability is limited when the unsatisfactory identity is shared by thousands of people. Social competition was also unlikely to bear fruit, given the asymmetries of power between Liverpool and the government, and the inability of the city to compete with more economically dynamic cities owing to the range of significant social, economic, and political problems that Liverpool faced in that period. Hence, only the 'social creativity' route was viable.

Change via social creativity can be achieved in three ways. Firstly, the parameters of comparison can be changed by adopting a new criterion (moving the goalposts). Secondly, the value assigned to the attributes of the group can be changed, so formerly negative aspects would now be positive (changing the rules). Thirdly, changing the out-group against which the comparison is based (changing the rival team), which does not require a change in the identity of either group (Tajfel and Turner 1979, 43–44). As I will explain, to change its identity via social creativity the Scouse in-group decided to follow the second path, and changed the basis of comparison

— rejecting Thatcherite values and embracing other metrics against which the group's worth could be measured.

There is clear evidence that this strategy was followed, and particularly that the values of certain characteristics could be changed. Roberts argues that "for the city's adverse economic conditions, responsibility [was] directed squarely at Thatcher's neo-liberal capitalist strategies" (K.D. Roberts 2015, 354). Regardless of the fact that any government spending over 40 per cent of GDP can hardly be described as 'neo-liberal', this reflects the strategy adopted by Scousers to develop "positively discrepant comparisons between in-group and out-group" — in this case Scousers and Conservative government, respectively — to "produce high prestige" and thus enhance self-esteem. An economically rational actor, upon a cost–benefit analysis of the situation, would probably have found that cooperating with the government or compromising would have done less economic damage to the city than attempting to resist and fight. However, Tajfel and Turner point to evidence which suggests that the "social-competitive pattern of intergroup behaviour holds even when it conflicts with obvious self-interest", and can actually reinforce these identity groups, making conflict harder to resolve (Tajfel and Turner 1979, 42).

As such, the social creativity route was taken and a change in the values associated with each group was attempted through rejecting Thatcherism, specifically competition, the free market, and the private sector, to replace these with an emphasis on 'solidarity'. For example, Boland argues that "[t]he reaction to Ken Bigley's death, Hillsborough, James Bulger, Anthony Walker and Rhys Jones are actually examples of community spirit rather than communal self-pity"[2] and quotes Liverpool FC footballer Jamie Carragher, who said, following the nationally reported murder of 11-year-old Rhys Jones, who was shot in the back by gang member Sean Mercer, "[o]ne of the best things about this city is that people pull together when it matters most and this is one of those times" (Boland 2008, 364). However, this image of solidarity may be closer to myth than reality. Boland also highlights how

> the identity of Rhys' killer was well known in the city, amongst police, residents and even schoolchildren, and yet no-one came forward with

2 Ken Bigley was a Liverpudlian engineer abducted, tortured, and murdered by Islamic extremists in Iraq in 2004; James Bulger was a 3-year-old boy from Kirkby who was abducted, tortured, and murdered by two 10-year-old boys in Liverpool in 1993; Anthony Walker was an 18-year-old black British man from Huyton who was murdered in Liverpool in an unprovoked, racially motivated attack in 2005; Rhys Jones was murdered by a 16-year-old gang member from Croxteth in 2007.

> firm evidence to arrest the gunman, due to fear of gangland retribution. For outsiders, this undermines the traditional sense of community that has historically characterised Liverpool. (Boland 2008, 364)

Further, Roberts reports that the former Chair of the Merseyside Police Authority stated that "the magic of Liverpool is that it isn't England. We are global and we have learned to tolerate and respect each other's traditions" (K.D. Roberts 2015, 338). At the same time, however, scholarly work on the Scouse identity and Liverpool's history points to the long legacy of racism and ghetto-building within the city. The 'race riots' in Toxteth are often attributed to institutional racism perceived within the local police force, and the increased socio-economic disadvantages ethnic minorities in the city faced, and indeed still do face (Murden 2006, 440–45).

This ghetto-building had policy implications. In a debate following the Toxteth riots, Anthony Steen, Conservative MP for Wavertree (1974–1983), argued that the twelve community centres on Upper Parliament Street encourage "growth of rival gangs. They are fiercely independent and, far from helping racial integration of the area, they have caused racial separation" (HC Deb 1981, vol. 8, cc1397–503, col. 1428). As such, Steen highlights the effects that local government action and funding had on fuelling of racial divisions, which undermines claims to define Scouse identity by geography or accent. Race is clearly an element in Scouse identity, with the Scouse label more open to whites than others.

Evidence from the Liverpool Black Caucus to a House of Commons Select Committee on Employment in 1986 argued that "a clear situation of racial inequality in the allocation of council housing in Liverpool" existed, notably:

> Black households are disadvantaged compared to White households... a lower quality dwelling overall; they have been excluded from sheltered accommodation... and virtually excluded from the better quality environment of the suburban areas. Though Liverpool's Black population is relatively small it is concentrated in 5 contiguous inner city wards: Abercromby, Arundel, Granby, Picton and Smithdown. (Liverpool Black Caucus 1986, 34–36)

Roberts argues that this is still the case; the "idea of there being 'White' and 'Black' areas in Liverpool is widely accepted" (K.D. Roberts 2015, 281).

Similarly, some scholars have argued that the Scouse identity itself is racially exclusive. Frost argues that Scouse is rooted in a white working-class culture which excludes ethnic minorities, specifically the black community (Frost 1995; 2000). Elements of this can be seen in Militant's lack of concern with 'black issues', focusing on a class-based reading of Liverpool's problems (K.D. Roberts 2015, 282; Frost and North 2013, 127). Frost argues that historic — and indeed current — racism in Liverpool has led to a splintering of identities in Liverpool, with many black people developing their own identity that is "positive, embracing and inclusive" (Frost 2000, 204–5). This suggests that, for some people at least, the Scouse identity did not reflect the idea presented in section 8.2 and that the idea of solidarity should be refined to 'solidarity with white Scousers'.

Finally, both of the city's football teams have had issues with racism. Everton topped one newspaper's racist 'league of shame' in 2000 and was one of the last teams in British football to sign a black player (Brown and Chaudhary 2000), whilst still having "racist elements within the club's fan-base" (K.D. Roberts 2015, 290). Similarly, Luis Suarez's racial abuse of Manchester United's Patrice Evra caused embarrassment for Liverpool FC, as did the fact that Suarez received support from a significant number of Liverpool fans (K.D. Roberts 2015, 290).

Hence it is fair to claim that Scouse 'solidarity' is a myth, or at least an exaggeration, developed as a response to Liverpool's inability to be the economic equal of other cities, such as its neighbour and rival Manchester. The idea of solidarity is also undermined by the racism apparent during the development of the Scouse identity, which continues today, as well as the role of racism in the city's footballing scene. Crowley argues that "Liverpool's racial history has been and remains one of segregation and discrimination, despite all the consoling references to 'mixed-race' marriages" (Crowley 2012, 136). Despite the questionable real-world appropriateness of the Scouse claim of solidarity, the fact remains that it was a core part of the *socially-constructed* Scouse identity, which stood in direct contrast to the Thatcherite concept of self-help, characterised by her key ally Norman Tebbit's immortal — and often paraphrased — advice to 'get on your bike' and look for work. An emphasis on the myth of solidarity was a clear attempt at social creativity, to devise a positive self-identity *vis-à-vis* the Thatcherite/Conservative out-group.

The Militant-led Labour council was also vital in developing an emphasis on anti-Conservatism and public sector employment within the Scouse identity, especially during their confrontation with central government over council funding. This was not an especially difficult achievement, as Liverpool had already undergone a leftwards shift, as outlined in section 8.3, and because the Scouse identity was rooted in the (white) working class, which provided fertile ground for anti-Thatcherism (Frost 2000, 198). Further, there were very few Conservative voices capable of presenting a pro-government argument to the people of the city. Both Kilfoyle and Parkinson highlight how, as the confrontation with Militant continued, a deep, pro-Liverpool, anti-Government feeling ran through supporters of all political parties in 1984, based on a widespread belief that the city was being victimised (Kilfoyle 2000, 115), even among the Liverpool's Conservatives (Parkinson 1985, 66). Similarly, Frost and North report how

> [f]ifty-five per cent of those polled blamed the Tories for the crisis and 86 per cent said the government did not care about the city, including half the Tory supporters. Eighty-eight per cent said the government should talk to the city. (Frost and North 2013, 116)

The strength of this new anti-Thatcher and anti-Conservative element of the Scouse identity can be seen in the fact that people who disliked both the Conservatives and Militant would rather back Militant. Parkinson reports that a "voter canvassed by a Liberal candidate expressed the mood precisely in saying 'I can't stand the Militant. But at least someone is standing up to the Bitch in London'" (Parkinson 1985, 67).

As such, the Scouse identity was reconstructed to include a heavily anti-Thatcher and anti-Conservative strain, in order to adapt to the fact that Liverpool was economically flagging in the supposed boom era of the 1980s. As Frost notes, "[i]n any analysis of identity formation and subsequent notions of 'belonging', awareness of one's own existence only becomes significant in relation to the 'other'... identity is something that is negotiated through the prism of social and political relations". Unsurprisingly, the Conservatives were an important element of the 'other' (Frost 2000, 195).

This point is supported by Murden, who states that "economic decay, unemployment, poverty, riots, strikes and radical politics all made Liverpool bad news, representative of the dark side of Thatcher's Britain" (Murden 2006, 469). Here he blames Thatcher's Britain, rather than the action of Liverpool's politicians (hardly blameless), union figures, rioters, football fans, or, indeed, voters. That Liverpool's problems are of Thatcher's making is a popular strain of thinking within Liverpool, despite the fact more than three decades have passed since her resignation.

The Hillsborough disaster undoubtedly played a part in the formation of an anti-establishment identity. For Fusdahl, this disaster, and the "government's failure to bring justice to the families is one of, if not the most explicit reason for Scousers' hatred towards Margaret Thatcher" (Fusdahl 2015, 43). The importance of this disaster for the Liverpool psyche can be seen in the fact that, as a result of *The Sun*'s infamous headline four days after the disaster (mentioned in section 8.3.1), Fusdahl argues that there is now a popular feeling in the city that "you cannot call yourself a proper Liverpool FC fan or Scouser if you read *The Sun*" (Fusdahl 2015, 46).

The fact that many people in Liverpool felt victimised by an establishment that demonised Liverpool fans did not help the Conservatives since, after ten years of government, they were the establishment. As Frost and North argue:

> The long awaited inquiry into the Hillsborough disaster finally reported that the police and media had conspired to denigrate Scousers as drunken thugs who stole from the dead, to cover up their own failings. A nation saw that a city and its residents had been systematically maligned as, at best, over emotional and romantic, at worst, work shy scroungers that claim 'it's never our fault' and who have become residents of a 'self-pity city'. (Frost and North 2013, 3)

Similarly, Burnham argues that the supposed anti-English strain of the Scouse identity

> happened somewhere in the Eighties and possibly events like Hillsborough massively contributed to that. The feeling [was] that the whole city was being done down by a London establishment: a political establishment, a media establishment, a police and legal establishment. (K.D. Roberts 2015, 348)

Finally, this new identity was reinforced and perpetuated in Liverpool through socialisation. However, unlike the socialisation that maintained the Conservative vote share until 1973, this socialisation faced fewer sources of restraint. Both Labour and the Liberal Party could thrive within the confines of the new anti-Conservative Scouse identity, whilst the Conservatives were electorally irrelevant and unable to offer political resistance. Culturally, the city has embraced its anti-Conservatism with pride. Hence, this hostility has continued unabated, with little scope for that to change.

8.5 Comparative identity

It is clear from the analysis in this chapter that the Scouse identity acquired a heavily political, anti-Conservative hue in the 1980s as a result of the Thatcher–Militant clash, and this explanation is central to ongoing Conservative irrelevance in the city. What is also interesting is that this does not seem to have been the case in other, similar, northern cities — or indeed, if it was the case, this is not identified in the literature on local identities. The following section will look at the literature on local identities in Manchester, Sheffield, Leeds (and the broader Yorkshire area), Newcastle, and the north of England as a whole, to explore whether Liverpool is generally unique in northern England in having a politicised identity.

The political influence of local identities has long been muted. Marshall argues that

> the 1890s were indeed the years in which, as conventionally asserted, the nationalisation of culture began fully to exert itself... especially as this was the also the period in which the British Empire, and with it a sense of British race patriotism, reached its apogee. (Marshall 2011, 204)

This does not mean that regional or local identities became irrelevant, but rather that their political salience was simply dampened. However, as the case of Liverpool shows, local identities could still re-emerge in response to external events or new out-groups. Indeed, Marshall argues that "it is still possible to identify late-nineteenth and early-twentieth century movements and impulses that sought to preserve and project regional, usually county-based English identities" (Marshall 2011, 204).

In many northern areas, the 1980s acted as a catalyst for the rise of cultural identities, especially those based on sport and, as argued by Milestone, music:

> cities such as Sheffield, Liverpool and Manchester began to develop their own pop infrastructures. Bands and performers also increasingly foreground their local identities. Bands began to play with their northernness. The bleak, solemn, decaying industrial landscape suited the mood and atmosphere of much of the music of this period. (Milestone 2008, 1172)

For Monaghan, "the most active sites of ideological resistance" to Thatcherism were not the Labour Party, the media, nor the 'intellectual left' of *Marxism Today* and the *New Left Review* but rather "the creative arts, particularly in the realm of literature and film" (Monaghan 2001, 2).

The question to be explored below is: did these identities, whether they be northern, regional, or local, contain a strong politicised element which could explain party performance?

8.5.1 Manchester

A significant portion of the literature on the Mancunian identity since the Second World War focuses on the role of football teams and how locals — particularly men — constructed their own identities *vis-à-vis* the teams they support. There is not much of a discussion of a Manchester-wide/Mancunian identity, however, nor is there much in the way of a discussion of the political aspects of these footballing identities.

For example, in the rivalry between Manchester's two largest football teams, Manchester United and Manchester City, the construction of identity is hugely important. Manchester United may have had greater sporting success, but the increasing commercialisation of the team, via rising costs of being a supporter in ticket and kit prices, has led to claims from both rival Manchester City and significant elements of the United fan community that Manchester United lacks 'authenticity'. King argues that, as a result of this, United fans have

> re-emphasized their Mancunian identity... these fans now emphasize the importance of being Mancunian, which was never a particularly important issue while United were unsuccessful in the 1970s and 1980s and before commercialism had increased the number of out-of-town supporters encouraging other fans to question the authenticity of United. (King 2000, 428)

Interestingly, the United-based Mancunian identity is not necessarily a geographically bound identity, unlike Scouse. King goes on to argue that

> the notion of the locale of Manchester, to which the masculine Manchester United fans now appeal, has emerged in the special context of the 1990s and refers not primarily to birth or residence in Manchester, though they are certainly are not irrelevant, but rather to the adoption of the central forms of practice of this group such as the wearing of designer clothing which are seen as properly Mancunian. (King 2000, 422)

The fanzine *United We Stand* emphasises the "theme of Manchester's diversity":

> Manchester has never been about boundaries, never been about lines on the map or about local authority bureaucracy. Manchester is not so much a city, as a state of mind. The whole history is one of progress and one of change but more importantly one of people. People who refuse to accept the boundaries of the mind. The least English city in the country, a city that drew influence from all over the world. To deny that is to deny your

> history, to deny the essence of Manchester. That's the Manchester that City fans seek to deny as they increasingly resemble small-town hicks, little-Englander mancs, insular, backward and decidedly non-mancunian. (King 2000, 434)[3]

King argues that this rejection of English identity, via a rejection of the England national team, is because Englishness is

> no longer see[n] as a universal identity which encompasses all English people but rather only an expression of the particular interests of regionally located groups. For these United fans, English nationalism is the appropriate identity of the South (which has benefited from the free market policies of national governments, particularly under Thatcher) or of those small clubs (also often in the South) whose fans' only hope of foreign travel (and status) is with the England team. (King 2000, 429)

This claim to diversity, and rejection of Englishness, are also common in the Liverpool identity. The theme of glorifying and romanticising local identities is common to both Liverpool and Manchester, with both identities embracing an anti-English component in order to elevate themselves above that against which their identity cannot compete. This is noted by Porter, who reflects how anti-English identity is reflected in the banners displayed at home matches, which read "you can stick your fucking England up your arse" and "Argentina", similar to the "we're not English we are Scousers" banners seen at Liverpool matches (Porter 2011, 154).

There are, however, three key questions which arise out of this evidence. Firstly, is this simply a way to annoy more patriotic supporters from other clubs, such as West Ham or Leicester City, under the guise of football 'banter'? Secondly, if not, then to what extent is this anti-English identity directly related to the national football team, rather than an English national identity more broadly? Thirdly, if this is a rejection of an English national identity, to what extent does it have a political, or electoral, hue to it?

This anti-England identity is coupled, it is argued, with a pro-European one. For King, travel across Europe to watch matches, as a result of Manchester United's sporting success, is important. "This familiarity with Europe is significant because it could potentially play a part in the development of a supranational European identity, where these United fans genuinely begin to see themselves as primarily Europeans rather than as British" (King 2000,

3 You do not have to look far to find virtually identical claims made by Scousers.

425). However, whilst the development of a pro-European hue to the United identity, compared to an English or British identity, is evidenced, the claim that this has developed into a pro-European Union/supranational identity is rejected by the fans (King 2000, 426). Instead, a pro-Europe identity comes from a desire for their team to compete, and win, on a European level, in order to provide the fans with positive self-esteem:

> this notion of Europeanhood has nothing to do with any putatively common cultures and histories shared with the other nations of Europe. Rather these United fans want Manchester United to be recognized as the equal of the biggest European clubs and they want themselves to be seen as the equals of the fans in these clubs. (King 2000, 427–32)

Similarly, Manchester City is an important site for identity formation, and draws upon the

> premise that 'real' Mancunians support City, which is 'Manchester's team', implicitly suggesting that the supporters of Manchester United, City's more illustrious local rival, are outsiders... City is portrayed as 'cool' and 'authentic' whereas United is constructed as crass and exploitative. (Edensor and Millington 2008, 172)

This notion of 'authenticity' is linked to working-class identity; Manchester City is portrayed and perceived as a community "in possession of values entrenched in local tradition, rather than empty corporate pledges and consumerism" and "traditional working-class community values and pride in supporting a local team", which the club, and fans, use to differentiate themselves from the middle-class, geographically mobile United supporters (Edensor and Millington 2008, 184–85).

Despite the importance of football as a site of identity formation, Porter argues that "[f]ootball culture in England however has remained largely free of overtly political affiliation, save for the highly performative displays of patriotism that surround international competition", but support for local teams can provide a "passionate yet often temporary resurfacing of local pride" (Porter 2011, 153). As such, football in Manchester does not seem to provide much of a basis for an explicitly — or even implicitly — politicised local identity. This is unsurprising, as this was also the case in Liverpool. There is, however, a dearth of relevant literature examining the Mancunian identity beyond football.

8.5.2 *Sheffield and Leeds: A Yorkshire identity?*

If the literature on the composition of a Mancunian identity is sparse, then the literature that sets out what may comprise a Sheffield or Leeds local identity is virtually non-existent. Instead, there is a discussion of a regional Yorkshire identity (in the same way that a Geordie identity is often subsumed into a north-eastern identity — see section 8.5.3) which will be explored in this section, followed by an alternative explanation for varying Conservative support in Sheffield and Leeds.

Gore and Jones outline a very broad conception of a Yorkshire identity:

> native Yorkshire folk are colloquially known as 'Tykes', speaking with a strong, broad accent that features many dialect words that hark back to their Nordic forebears. They have a reputation for speaking their mind, for not suffering fools gladly but at the same time calling complete strangers 'love', for showing resourcefulness and determination in the face of adversity ('Yorkshire grit'), and for not squandering their hard-earned money on trifles or baubles. It should also be noted that the region's primary contribution to British cooking, the Yorkshire pudding, is in its home patch traditionally eaten as a first course, with gravy, rather than as an accompaniment to the Sunday roast... All this might suggest that there is a strongly delineated and entrenched regional identity in Yorkshire and the Humber. However, while this has some validity at one level, in many senses it is only skin-deep. (Gore and Jones 2006, 142)

As with Manchester, it is unclear how this would — or in the case of Yorkshire pudding, could — translate into individual political behaviour. Indeed, Gore and Jones later note that "[w]hile there may be a 'Yorkshire' identity, its currency and role within the region is a relatively minor one, as a factor either influencing political decision-making or driving economic development" but instead it is "fairly powerful in terms of external image, both in terms of how many residents portray themselves and how the region is perceived by outsiders. However, as with all stereotypes, the image is in many respects backward-looking" (Gore and Jones 2006, 153). This point is shared by Marshall, who argues that between 1850 and 1918, "[a]lthough it had no political basis, Yorkshireness remained a powerful sub-identity within England" (Marshall 2011, 2).

Thus, in the existing literature a Yorkshire identity seems a dead end in terms of explaining Conservative decline or irrelevance. In any case, if identity were important, we would expect it to play out on a more local, rather than regional, level, due to the contrasting success of the Conservatives in Sheffield and Leeds.

There is, however, one interesting comparison with Liverpool to be made. During the nineteenth century there were strong migratory flows to the Yorkshire region from Ireland. However, these Irish immigrants arrived "without recreating... sectarian tensions" which, in Liverpool, were so important in driving Conservative support (Gore and Jones 2006, 144).

Instead of an identity-based explanation, it is worthwhile to revert to a more basic argument: Sheffield is less likely to vote Conservative than Leeds, not because of a local identity but rather because of contrasting economic performance since the 1980s. As Gore and Jones outline, in Yorkshire,

> even until fairly recently, the economies of different parts of the region have been strongly shaped by their natural resources. This in turn has tended to give a differentiated slant to people's outlooks and attitudes in the constituent parts of the region, frequently to the point of parochialism. (Gore and Jones 2006, 141)

From the late 1970s, "South Yorkshire County Council and Sheffield City Council became known informally as the 'Socialist Republic of South Yorkshire'", used mockingly by local Conservative councillors but "adopted willingly and with a sense of pride by those in the Labour Party and trade unions" (Payling 2014, 602). Payling outlines how

> [t]he 'Socialist Republic of South Yorkshire' was just that; socialist policies tuned to the needs of South Yorkshire and Sheffield residents. It integrated radical policies aimed at building new constituencies of voters, but did so in such a way as to avoid alienating its core working class voters and, indeed, to win some of them back. (Payling 2014, 605)

This concern with class politics, at the expense of new social movements or identity politics (Payling 2014, 625), stemmed from the significant economic problems faced by Sheffield, was similar to the 'workerism' or 'labourism' of Militant in Liverpool, and stood in contrast to the 'new left' movements taking hold elsewhere. By 1987 unemployment was at 16.3 per cent, with nearly 20 per cent of men searching for a job, owing mainly to the decline of the mines and steel industry (Payling 2014, 611).

Further, Sheffield was faced with huge disparities of wealth within the city, generally across an east–west divide. Writing in 2006, Gore and Jones outlined how Sheffield Hallam was "the most affluent parliamentary constituency outside London and the South East", and seventeenth overall. Additionally, "school-children in Sheffield Brightside are eight times less likely to go to university than their Hallam counterparts". For Gore and Jones this means that "people in east and west Sheffield... essentially live parallel lives — disconnected spatially, socially and economically — in a 'two-speed' city" (Gore and Jones 2006, 149).

Contrastingly, Leeds has enjoyed strong economic growth. Whilst "Yorkshire and [the] Humber has seen a much slower rise of the service economy and consequently has struggled to generate new jobs on a scale sufficient to replace those lost", Leeds has been the exception. Leeds has "traditionally acted as the mercantile and financial centre for the West Riding woollen textile industry, and as such was well placed to redirect its focus towards the growing financial, legal and business services sectors". Unsurprisingly, however, "some of its communities were badly affected by loss of blue-collar jobs in engineering, and are still struggling to readjust", again leading to worries about a 'two-speed' city (Gore and Jones 2006, 147).

This imbalance also extends to the regional level, where

> 37 per cent of neighbourhoods in South Yorkshire are classed as being in the most deprived quintile, compared to 5 per cent for North Yorkshire... 7 per cent of neighbourhoods in South Yorkshire are within the least deprived quintile, compared to 31 per cent in North Yorkshire... Gains in the 'Golden Triangle' of Leeds, Harrogate and York are matched by market failure in poorer parts of the region (Gore and Jones 2006, 148–49)

In consequence, the strong Conservative performance in Leeds compared to Sheffield can perhaps be explained by economics, rather than through identity. Conservative decline in Sheffield occurred because of high unemployment and general economic decline, which are known drivers for Labour Party support, whilst increasing affluence or relative economic success in Leeds would preserve some Conservative support.

8.5.3 *Newcastle*

Edensor and Millington argue that Newcastle's football team, like Manchester's, utilised a "particularly coherent regional identity" which played on "immediate local support" in brand terms (Edensor and Millington 2008, 184). This is supported by Byrne and Benneworth, who claim that "the North East's three big football clubs all draw on an essentially local and highly specific fan base... Newcastle, Sunderland and Middlesbrough, are all seen as

North Eastern, in a sense which excludes Yorkshire" (Byrne and Benneworth 2006, 115).

In describing Newcastle specifically, Beal argues that "whilst other cities of England and Scotland (Liverpool, Manchester, Glasgow) are divided by football, Newcastle is United. There is only one 'Toon' (Newcastle) and there is only one 'Toon' (Newcastle United)" (Beal 2004, 35). She claims that the geographical element of the broader Geordie identity — "a Geordie is supposed to be born within spitting distance of the Tyne" — is very loosely defined:

> although the heart of the "Geordie Nation" and the capital of "Geordieland" is most certainly Newcastle, or "the Toon" as it is called locally, those who would consider themselves as Geordies can be found throughout Northumberland and even in the northern part of the old County Durham, at least in Gateshead and South Shields. (Beal 2004, 34)

There is also the sense of a (relatively) local 'other', in this case the 'Mackems' of the city of Sunderland to the south, "distinguished in language by their tendency to drop aitches and to use words such as matey, and in custom by their adherence to Sunderland FC" (Beal 2004, 34).

Beal claims that this strong sense of local identity arises because of Newcastle's geographic isolation. Similarly, Pearson argues that

> [i]n the North East, England, or rather the notion of England, seems a long way off. The North East is at the far corner of the country but it is separated by more than just miles. There is the wilderness of the Pennines to the west, the emptiness of the North Yorkshire moors to the South and to the north, the Scottish border. The nearest major city to Newcastle is Edinburgh, and that is in another country. (Pearson, in Beal 2004, 35)

As a result of this, there is "no other region of England in which a single centre has so great an influence over such a wide area, and it is the presence of this 'capital' which gives a focus to the 'Geordie Nation'" (Beal 2004, 35).

However, whilst there is evidence that this regional identity trumps class, insofar as "[m]iddle-class Geordies consider themselves Geordies, and have their own network which reinforce local solidarity… Middle-class Geordies do not speak, or aspire to speak, RP, but have a 'posh Geordie' accent all their own", there is again no evidence that this coherent regional identity has a strong political flavour, let alone a strong anti-Conservative flavour (Beal 2004, 35).

Green and Pollard argue that whilst "[t]he area known today as North East England is ultimately defined by its location in the north and east of England", the north-east sees itself as northern much more than it does eastern. Ultimately, they conclude that the region has "a very fragile history of an incoherent and barely self-conscious region" (A. Green and Pollard 2007, 209–25). This is perhaps best shown in the 'no' vote in the North-East England devolution referendum in 2004, which rejected the establishment of a North-East Assembly by 78 per cent to 22 per cent.

As such, there is very limited evidence of a politically salient local or regional identity in Newcastle or the wider north-east, let alone a politically charged identity. Byrne and Benneworth outline how historically north-eastern identity was supported by both Labourite manual and public service workers, and Conservative industrial white-collar grades, with both main parties at this time having had "a strong regional orientation" (Byrne and Benneworth 2006, 112). Since both parties bought into the regional identity, the scope to politicise it one way or the other was reduced.

One final interesting point of comparison is, again, the issue of Irish migration. Like Yorkshire, and unlike Liverpool, the Irish and Welsh immigrants who moved to Newcastle throughout the nineteenth century "retained distinct identities in the region... but they seem to have made little difference to the identity of the region". Further, "there seems to have been little evidence that assimilated Irishness or Welshness contributed significantly to the development of what one might call northeasternness" (A. Green and Pollard 2007, 220). Moreover, neither did it result in sectarian tensions nor the creation of any identity that defined itself against Irish Catholic immigration (Byrne and Benneworth 2006, 118).

Overall, then, the literature shows that a Geordie or north-eastern identity are primarily descriptive labels rather than identities that drive behaviour in a meaningful way, especially when it comes to political behaviour.

8.5.4 *Northern-ness*

Finally, it is worth considering whether there may be a pan-northern identity that served to depress Conservative voting across the region. Numerous authors have identified a common cultural base for a northern identity, specifically from the late 1950s to the mid-1960s when a new relationship "between place and culture" emerged: the "use of the decaying industrial landscape... regional accents and distinctly northern landscapes... centred on young, working-class protagonists — generally portrayed as witty, cool and anti-establishment" who found their specifically northern environment "both stifling and depressing but also friendly with a strong sense of community and tradition" (Milestone 2008, 1169–70).

Despite this cultural turn in the post-war era, Sandford argues that "[a]ny pan-Northern identity, however, has not translated itself into political consciousness in England". He attributes this to the overcentralised nature of the British state, the relative lack of pan-northern economic integration, and the importance of working-class identity relative to regional identity (which is why northern-ness is associated, for Sandford, with "working-class solidarity"), especially since the working-class had representation via the Labour Party while the north lacked regional political institutions (Sandford 2006, 81–83).

Taylor argues that English identity is actually rather a southern English identity, and summarises Colls and Dodd's argument that

> [t]he Home Counties are a product of the second phase in the construction of modern Englishness at the turn of the 19th and 20th centuries. At this time the London metropolitan area reasserted its traditional dominance of English society and a new view of Englishness was constructed around it. (Taylor 1993, 140)

Further, industry, a generally northern phenomenon in the national consensus even if not in reality, was "excised from what came to be viewed as English culture". Accordingly, Taylor supports Horne's view that Manchester, as an industrial power and a "great English world city of the 19th century" is better understood as "the first modern American city", because its industrial nature "was defined out of Englishness and its region, the heartland of the industrial revolution, [and] condemned to a tatty 20th century provincialism" (Taylor 1993, 140).

Despite this, Taylor claims that "the North continues to refuse to be a self-conscious political entity" (Taylor 1993, 137). The anti-Conservative Thatcherite turn, in this reading, is inherently linked to the lack of economic growth experienced by the north, and therefore Conservative decline was simply a prosperity issue, rather than an identity-based phenomenon (Bailoni 2014).

8.6 Discussion

The influence of local and regional identities on voting behaviour is understudied. This is reflected in the fact that there is very little consensus even on what is actually meant, for example, by a Manc or Geordie identity.

This is a significant gap which is in urgent need of being filled. One issue with such a dearth of literature on the topic is that it becomes easier to fall into the trap of describing certain correlating political outcomes — such as a lack of Conservative support and a strong local identity — as being causally related.

In the case of Liverpool, it was argued that a conception of Scouseness/a Scouse identity acquired a strong anti-Thatcher and anti-Conservative element in order to boost collective self-worth, in direct response to the conflict with the Thatcher government. However, there is no evidence of this being the case in the other four northern English urban areas studied. Whenever a localised identity is mentioned an explicitly political element is conspicuous by its absence, doubly so in contrast to the literature on Liverpool. This argument does not claim there is no political element in other local identities. Certainly, further research is needed, especially on the explicit components of a regional identity, on what gives it political salience (a common political 'other', perhaps?), and on whether this is present in all urban areas or just a few.

Without this knowledge, we are left with traditional economic or class-based arguments for voting behaviour. The Conservatives in Leeds have outperformed the other urban areas because the city suffered less economically under Conservative governments, whilst Manchester, Sheffield, and Newcastle suffered more. However, in Liverpool Conservative decline and irrelevance were much stronger than in the other urban areas, and stronger than we would expect in terms of demographics because of the role of identity change. This is supported by the regression output shown in Figure 5.24, which shows the Conservatives significantly underperforming in local elections *vis-à-vis* other northern cities, even when controlling for electoral and demographic factors.

Finally, there are two brief points to make regarding the role of socialisation. Firstly, whilst in Liverpool we saw Conservative voting fuelled by socialisation based on a historic Protestant identity, imbued with strong political saliency by the presence of a large Irish, Catholic 'other', this was not the case elsewhere. In fact, where in the literature this Irish diaspora is mentioned, it is argued that they had very little effect on identity formation at all.

Secondly, the lack of evidence of an explicit political identity, or indeed an explicitly political component to local identities, suggests that a continued socialisation of identity is not the cause of Conservative success or later decline in these other northern areas. Whilst in Liverpool there is a strong element of anti-Conservatism or anti-Thatcherism embedded in the Scouse identity, which perpetuates Conservative irrelevance, this does not appear to be the case in other cities.

However, it is impossible to draw any firm conclusions about the role of identity in local areas owing to the dearth of literature on the subject. Unlike the (limited) literature on the Scouse identity, existing literature for these other urban areas has focused on identity labels — Manchester United/City supporter, Tyke, north-easterner — without any critical consideration of the components that make up these identities, let alone any consideration of a political element to them.

8.6.1 Scouse in the city

The elements of Scouse identity outlined in this chapter are not simply abstract features, but can be seen and experienced in the day-to-day lives of people in Liverpool. An example of this can be seen in the furore surrounding the unveiling of a statue of Cilla Black, paid for by her sons, in the Cavern Quarter in Liverpool in January 2017.

The *Liverpool Echo* posted a video of the unveiling on Facebook, which within three weeks had received 427,210 views, 14,000 reactions, 1,935 shares, and nearly 700 comments (*Liverpool Echo News* 2017). Such was the range of emotion shown towards the news story, that the next day the *Liverpool Echo* ran a subsequent article titled "The Cilla Black statue has REALLY divided opinions in Liverpool" (Davis 2017).

The article noted that "its unveiling has left many ECHO [*sic*] readers wondering whether the statue should exist at all — stating that her Conservative Party leanings and the fact that she left Liverpool as her music career kicked off should exclude her from the honour". In line with the idea of a vehement anti-Conservatism being co-opted into the Scouse identity, a range of comments argued that her open support for the Conservatives — and specifically Thatcher — was an "absolute disgrace" (Davis 2017).

However, there were people who disagreed with this argument, and made themselves known in the comment section on the article. One reader said that "Liverpool was a Tory city in the 1960s. Hence her, Doddy [Ken Dodd], Tarby [Jimmy Tarbuck], Kenny Everett etc. Some people on here seem to think you're only a true Scouser if you're Catholic and vote Labour" (Davis 2017).

This anecdote is by no means meant to be exhaustive or representative of Liverpool identity as a whole — that requires much more research. However, it does go to show that, for many people, feelings of anti-Conservatism are inherently linked to their own identity as a Scouser, or at least as being from Liverpool, and are based on a view that the Thatcher government was against Liverpool. One commenter sums this up perfectly with the line "[s]hould Tory lovers like Cilla be having statues in the city that party tried to destroy?" (Davis 2017).

This throws up an interesting question: to what extent is this element of the identity anti-Conservative or specifically anti-Thatcher? This is an important question, as it ties into strategies for resurgence. It will be easier for the Conservatives to get a hearing in Liverpool if anti-Thatcherism is the key element in the Scouse identity, whereas if anti-Conservatism is the key driver then the party faces a longer struggle.

8.7 Conclusion

This chapter has outlined how Conservative irrelevance was cemented via the politicisation of the Scouse identity. Although we can talk of a Scouse identity that began long before the 1960s — albeit under various terms, such as Dicky Sam and later Whacker, with their origins in a 'unique' pattern of speech dating back to the eighteenth century (Crowley 2012, 107, 143–61) — the identity only took on political salience following the decline of the hegemonic cleavage between Irish Catholicism and Lancastrian Protestantism that previously divided the city, and the rise of economic and social hardship that undermined the self-worth of people in the city.

For Roberts, the Scouse identity is held as passionately as these historic sectarian identities, but instead of creating rivalries within the city, it unites Liverpool against other groups: "Hostility to the Conservatives (especially Margaret Thatcher), Westminster, and even other cities (notably Manchester) compounded the sense of unified 'Scouse' identity as internal religious rivalries passed largely into memory" (K.D. Roberts 2015, 348). This has seeped into 'popular' histories covering the Militant era (see, for example, Lees' (2011) 'social history' of Liverpool). What is interesting, however, is that there is scant evidence that other northern English local identities have taken on such a politicised hue.

This shift represented a change in the zeitgeist of the city. Social and political change had led to a re-evaluation of the idea of Scouse identity, which was "buttressed through the pressure of significant reference groups", in this case the Thatcher government, making the 'habit' of anti-Conservatism stronger (Himmelweit, Humphreys, and Jaeger 1985, 205). This is essentially an argument based on socialisation, but instead of leading to Conservative success it reinforced the party's irrelevance to Liverpool. Butler and Stokes have found evidence that "once a partisan tendency becomes dominant in a local area processes of opinion formation will draw additional support to the party that is dominant" — essentially reflecting the socialising effects of local neighbourhoods (Butler and Stokes 1974, 129).

Can this be changed? It is foolish to discount change — who would have foreseen the rise of the Liberals in 1969? Yet it is equally foolish to think that all types of change are equally likely. As has been argued in this chapter, identities are contextual, and thus changes in context can shift identities. The anti-Conservative hegemony in the city may seem "monological and unchangeable, but then that is part of the trick of hegemony, and such an effect only lasts as long as the dialogism of social reality is suppressed" (Crowley 2012, 135). Quite.

9 Conclusion

This book has sought to explain the causes of Conservative decline in Liverpool since 1945. Chapter 1 established that the common folk-tale of Thatcher as the main cause of Conservative decline is implausible, as it does not fit with the electoral performance of the Liverpool Conservatives. Instead, this book provides a tripartite framework for understanding Conservative fortunes in Liverpool, focusing on local election results rather than general election results. The first period is one of electoral success (1945–1972), the second of electoral decline (1973–1986), and the third a period of continued irrelevance or lack of resurgence (1987 onwards). As is clear from the timings of these periods, Conservative electoral decline began before Thatcher became party leader, let alone prime minister, and hence cannot be attributed wholly or even primarily to her actions in government.

This book set out to explore a range of potential causes of decline, drawing upon the limited literature on the Conservative Party in Liverpool. These were:

1. Local party structures and organisation.
2. Biases within the electoral system.
3. Changes in the city's demographics.
4. Migratory patterns.
5. The breakdown of the link between Protestantism and Conservatism.
6. A specifically anti-Conservative identity widely held in Liverpool.

As argued in Chapter 3, neither the success nor the decline of the Conservatives could realistically be explained by organisational issues. The local party organisation was beset with problems, including personalities unsuited to leadership positions, a focus on the ward rather than the constituency as the basis of organisation, and poor campaign strategies. Whilst there were occasions when poor party organisation was given as a reason for defeat at the polls, there were also years when the Conservatives did well in municipal elections despite poor organisation. Hence, there is no real correlation between the party's electoral results and the state of its organisation.

Instead, organisational issues only became important for the Conservatives when they were faced with the Liberal Party's motivated, young, innovative party machine pursuing their pavement politics strategy. Moreover, the Labour Party's local structures were also weak and moribund after the Second World War, yet they did not face electoral decline. As such, whilst organisation may have played a role, it was by no means the only, or even the main, cause of Conservative decline in Liverpool.

A study of biases within the ward structure in Liverpool shows that the Conservatives did indeed face a consistent bias against them that hampered the translation of votes into seats. Generally, the Conservatives needed a higher share of the total vote to achieve a set percentage of seats than did Labour or the Liberals. However, a deeper examination shows the sources of this bias to be mainly attributable to the distribution of the Conservative vote and to differential turnout. These are not inherent biases in the electoral system per se, and it is perfectly valid to argue that the Conservatives could have addressed these issues via more effective campaigning. Similarly, demographic change was ruled out as a cause of Conservative decline because generally, over time, the demographic makeup of Liverpool actually became more favourable to the Conservatives.

This study also presents evidence to support the claim that outward migration was harmful to the Conservatives, using the 1981 census migration data. However, Liverpool had been experiencing net outward migration since 1931, and the Conservatives still achieved electoral success until the 1970s. Although those who left the city were more likely to be from Liverpool's wealthier wards, and those who came to the city were more likely to come from poorer wards across Merseyside, this obviously does not guarantee that Liverpool lost Conservative voters and gained Labour voters. More evidence is needed to be able to say whether this was the case. However, the decline in the Conservative vote share is too sudden to be due to a long-term structural factor like migration.

In terms of explaining Conservative success and decline, the first key argument of this book builds upon the breakdown of the link between

Protestantism and Conservatism. It is argued that post-war Conservative support was driven by the historical cause of Protestantism, even though sectarianism was no longer a directly relevant social cleavage in Liverpool. Instead, historically, Protestantism 'created' Conservative voters, and this voting behaviour was transmitted through the generations by a process of socialisation. This provided a voter base for the Conservative Party in Liverpool beyond what a class-based perspective might suggest.

Decline began with the Conservative victory in the 1970 general election, which boosted Labour's vote share in subsequent local elections as the electorate began to express dissatisfaction with the Heath government. Significantly, this general election was the one in which the Liberals began their innovative and successful use of pavement politics as a campaign catalyst, which served to undermine the Conservatives on the local level in Liverpool. The all-out local election in 1973 saw the Conservatives pushed to third place, which allowed the Liberals to place themselves as the main opposition to Labour and slowly squeeze the Conservative vote. This was assisted by the significant disadvantage the Conservative suffered in being required to achieve significantly higher vote share to win seats. Thus, the stage was set for the decade-long decline of the Conservatives in Liverpool and this occurred long before Thatcher came to power. This analysis thus challenges the traditional understanding of Conservative decline in Liverpool.

The factors behind the party's decline cannot explain why the Conservatives have failed to mount a resurgence akin to that which they managed in the early 1960s. For this, we must examine the role of the Scouse identity. The second key argument of this book is that as Liverpool faced economic and societal decline in the 1980s those who held the Scouse identity sought to boost their collective self-esteem. They did this through a process of 'social creativity', which rejected those traits deemed positive by Thatcherism and embraced rival concepts such as 'solidarity'. As a result, the Conservatives became 'the other' in Liverpool, bar a few exceptions such as Michael Heseltine, who was celebrated largely because he went against the grain of Thatcherite economic orthodoxy. The lack of Conservative figures in the city to present an alternative view only served to reinforce the idea of Liverpool as an anti-Conservative city. This was voiced politically by the Militant-led council, and supported by the Liberals, who could place themselves as the main anti-Labour party without having to worry about being outflanked on their right. Hence, anti-Conservatism, and especially anti-Thatcherism, became a key element of the Scouse identity. This linking of the Scouse identity to Conservative decline is a further original contribution to our knowledge of local voting behaviour, especially in the context of Liverpool.

Ultimately, as the causes of Conservative success, decline, and irrelevance differ, there is no single, all-encompassing cause of Conservative decline in Liverpool.

This book also speaks to a broader literature on local party politics. It provides a case study of party system change in a specific local context, and the drivers of local party success and failure. It shows that local politics can be influenced by local identities, and that these local identities can be shaped and perpetuated through local socialisation processes. However, a brief examination of local identities in other northern English cities shows that not all local identities are politically salient, and that the relationship between local identities and local party politics needs to be explored in greater depth.

9.1 Conservative Party responses to decline

For their part, the Conservative Party has largely accepted its fate in Liverpool, although there have been some minor attempts at boosting the party's fortunes in the city and the wider Merseyside area. For example, influenced by the perceived success of Michael Heseltine's time as Minister for Merseyside, David Cameron decided to create the position of Shadow Minister for Merseyside in 2007. His good intentions were somewhat undermined by choosing Chris Grayling, the Conservative MP for Epsom and Ewell in Surrey, for the role.

This unofficial position aimed to jump-start the process of rehabilitating Cameron's Conservatives in Merseyside, and specifically Liverpool, as part of his broader detoxification process. Although a worthwhile endeavour, Grayling was certainly not the right man for the job. Kilfoyle jokes that he was chosen "[b]ecause his mother once met someone who knew someone from the Wirral" (quoted in Yates 2009).

Grayling found himself in trouble with the local press for opposing the opening of a new tram system in Liverpool (*Liverpool Echo* 2009a), for saying that "Manchester United's Gary Neville, quite open in his dislike of Liverpudlians, would be a 'good role model' for local youths" (Yates 2009) — Grayling later claimed to have meant to name the then Liverpool FC defender Jamie Carragher — and for comparing Speke, a deprived area that has problems with crime, with Baltimore, as portrayed in the American crime drama *The Wire* (*Liverpool Echo* 2009b). An opinion piece, by Joe Riley in the *Liverpool Echo,* described Grayling as "ham-fisted" (Riley 2012).

Broader political trends also make Liverpool an unlikely site for Conservative resurgence, even if we completely discount the heavily anti-Conservative Scouse identity outlined in this book. Across England, Jennings and Stoker note how cities are becoming Labour strongholds while the Conservatives do well in less urban areas, a trend which is likely to continue (Jennings and Stoker 2017). Although this pre-dated the vote to leave the European Union, the Brexit referendum certainly accelerated this trend. In Liverpool, although more people voted to leave the European Union in 2016 than voted for the Labour mayoral candidate in that year, Liverpool as a city voted to remain. However, constituency-level estimates of the leave vote show support for leaving the EU varied across Liverpool (Hanretty 2017). These estimates are shown in Table 9.1.

Table 9.1: Estimated leave vote for each constituency in Liverpool

Constituency	*Estimated leave vote (%)*
Walton	52.2
West Derby	49.8
Garston and Halewood[1]	48.0
Wavertree	35.3
Riverside	27.3
Liverpool average	41.8

[1] Three of the constituency's eight wards are actually situated in Knowsley: Halewood North, Halewood South, and Halewood West.

Given the relative lack of support for leaving the EU across the city as a whole, and also given the socio-demographic makeup of the constituencies that most strongly supported leave (the two constituencies with the highest vote to leave — Liverpool Walton and Liverpool West Derby — are the most and ninth-most deprived constituencies in England (House of Commons Library 2020)), it is unsurprising that the Conservatives were unable to capitalise on a potential realignment around Brexit. To further support the claim that the Scouse identity is rooted in anti-Conservative sentiment — rather than pro-Labour sentiment — the 2014 local elections saw the UK Independence Party (UKIP) come third, after Labour and the Greens, polling over 15 per cent in 11 of the city's 30 wards, and over 10 per cent in a handful more. These were mainly working-class northern wards. Unlike other parts of the country, in which UKIP acted as a stepping stone or 'gateway drug' for Labour voters to eventually switch to the Conservatives, this has not occurred in Liverpool (Curtis 2017).

Similarly, the 'red wall' — seats in which the Conservative Party underperformed given the constituencies' demographic profile, and which gave Boris Johnson such a commanding majority following the 2019 general election — did not crumble in Liverpool. A study by Kanagasooriam (who coined the phrase) and Simon, which sought to provide a definitive definition of the concept, even had to include a dummy variable for Merseyside in their model (Kanagasooriam and Simon 2021, Table 1). It will come as no surprise that the present author has argued that this is attributable to the spread of the Scouse identity across Merseyside, rather than any unique geographic features Merseyside may have.

It is ironic that the party opposes the one thing that could give them representation on the council overnight: proportional representation (PR) for local elections. Scotland introduced the single transferable vote (STV) for local elections in 2007. In that year, the Conservative Party in Liverpool won 6 per cent of the vote, and in 2008 it won 8.5 per cent of the vote. In both cases the party won no seats. In Glasgow, however, after the introduction of STV the Conservative Party won 7.7 per cent of first-preference votes and won a single seat. In 2012 the party won just 5.9 per cent of the first-preference vote in Glasgow and still won a seat. It is obvious that under STV the Conservative Party would at least have a toehold on Liverpool City Council, but it is equally obvious that the national party is opposed to any form of PR, even if Conservative voters are not (Redfield & Wilton 2020).

9.2 Conclusion

This book has challenged traditional theories about the decline of the Conservative Party in Liverpool. Although, to some extent, the Liverpool Conservatives were historically supported by sectarian tendencies, the erosion of sectarianism and its replacement with class antagonism was not the harbinger of electoral decline. The Conservatives continued to be a significant player in Liverpool's politics until the early 1970s, when they were relegated to a supporting role in a three-party system. This decline, however, began too early to be solely attributable to Thatcher. Thus, the two most common theories for Conservative decline — sectarianism and Thatcher — can only be partial explanations. Instead, we must separate the causes of success, decline, and irrelevance, as each era was driven by different phenomena.

Furthermore, this study has generated questions around how local identities influence political behaviour, an area ripe for future research. Three potential research strands stand out:

1. Do meaningful local/urban identities exist? If so, where?
2. Can these identities be unpacked to reveal discrete, identifiable sub-elements, or are they simply descriptive labels? Is there a consensus surrounding these sub-elements?
3. Are these identities politically salient?

These questions can be illuminated by a comparison with the Scouse identity. In examining the first question, the Scouse identity clearly exists and the literature suggests it is important in framing identity within Liverpool. Is this the case in Sheffield, for example, or is a (south?) Yorkshire identity more important there? Alternatively, is local identity politically irrelevant and instead traditional class- or Brexit-based identities that have become politically salient?

In Liverpool, the second and third questions can be answered by anti-Conservatism, especially anti-Thatcherism, opposition to *The Sun* newspaper, a sense of city-wide solidarity, a claim to support the underdog, and pride in the city's cultural past, among other sub-elements. Also, there is often talk of being a multi-cultural city like London, but a welcoming one, unlike London. Can we say the same about a Geordie or Manc identity?

A more challenging question is whether we can actually say this about Liverpool; the literature itself has not supported this beyond reasonable doubt, but rather relies on anecdote and personal experience, cultural output, and responses to specific events that are meant to be extrapolated to represent everyday life. There has been no attempt in the current literature to quantify how widely held the Scouse identity is, for instance.

A future research project into this question ought to make use of a multi-method analysis, going beyond hearsay and anecdote, and combine quantitative polling and focus groups to explore what it actually means to be Scouse, Manc, northern, and possibly other identities. It would explore questions of whether these identities are primarily location-based descriptors or instead meaningfully shape behaviours, especially political ones.

Today, the Conservatives are an electoral irrelevance in Liverpool. Their failure to win a single seat in the 2019 general election, followed by their poor performance in the city's mayoral, local, and city-region elections in 2021, marks over a quarter of a century of electoral failure in Liverpool.

However, in the 2016 local election the Conservatives won 4 per cent of the vote and no seats, the same outcome achieved by the Liberals in 1967. Seven years on from 1967, however, the Liberals took control of the council. Could the Conservatives manage a similar feat? Stranger things have happened in Liverpool's political history.

Appendix 1 Regression tables

Table 10.1: Regression analysis output for 1953–1970

	Conservative	*Labour*	*Liberal*
Intercept	1845.427***	590.165*	−3601.948***
	(307.183)	(277.395)	(734.487)
Election year	−0.886***	−0.321*	1.842***
	(0.156)	(0.141)	(0.373)
Turnout (%)	−0.141*	−0.170**	0.390*
	(0.065)	(0.059)	(0.153)
Con. government	−15.442***	14.176***	3.051
	(1.721)	(1.575)	(3.067)
Liberal candidate	−0.050	−2.807***	
	(0.899)	(0.811)	
Green candidate	–	–	–
% male	−1.113**	1.814***	−0.940
	(0.349)	(0.312)	(1.018)
% aged over 45	0.209*	−0.076	0.433*
	(0.087)	(0.078)	(0.174)
% overcrowded	−0.186*	−0.077	0.626*
	(0.090)	(0.079)	(0.286)
% unemployed	0.084	−0.157	−0.363
	(0.122)	(0.112)	(0.297)
% working class	−0.162***	0.257***	0.019
	(0.046)	(0.041)	(0.099)
% homeowner	0.442***	−0.495***	0.209**
	(0.036)	(0.033)	(0.073)
Catholic area	−8.076***	8.152***	−2.003
	(1.835)	(1.655)	(5.770)
N observations	661	705	125
Adj. R^2	0.667	0.772	0.438
R^2	0.673	0.776	0.483
AIC	4948.494	5192.989	925.461
P value	0.000	0.000	0.000

*** $p < 0.001$; ** $p < 0.01$; * $p < 0.05$.

Table 10.2: Regression analysis output for 1971–1986

	Conservative	*Labour*	*Liberal*
Intercept	1747.077***	–702.635	1199.140
	(328.342)	(380.346)	(630.456)
Election year	−0.937***	0.357	−0.476
	(0.166)	(0.192)	(0.319)
Turnout (%)	−0.183***	0.069	0.161*
	(0.045)	(0.052)	(0.079)
Con. government	−8.905***	10.298***	1.855
	(1.215)	(1.396)	(2.236)
Liberal candidate	–3.789*	–16.018***	
	(1.860)	(2.134)	
Green candidate	2.840	–3.195	−0.383
	(1.695)	(1.963)	(2.968)
% male	3.058***	0.334	−4.660***
	(0.710)	(0.802)	(1.295)
% aged over 45	0.960***	0.218	−0.955**
	(0.177)	(0.202)	(0.330)
% overcrowded	−0.495**	0.773***	−0.643
	(0.167)	(0.192)	(0.411)
% unemployed	−0.134	0.419***	−0.029
	(0.103)	(0.119)	(0.211)
% working class	−0.623***	0.367***	0.361***
	(0.057)	(0.065)	(0.107)
% homeowner	0.064	−0.391***	0.395***
	(0.041)	(0.047)	(0.078)
Catholic area	–10.297***	4.147	8.092
	(2.238)	(2.562)	(5.013)
N observations	392	399	342
Adj. R^2	0.713	0.803	0.307
R^2	0.722	0.809	0.329
AIC	2776.172	2947.116	2793.717
P value	0.000	0.000	0.000

***$p < 0.001$; **$p < 0.01$; *$p < 0.05$.

Table 10.3: Regression analysis output for 1987–2003

	Conservative	*Labour*	*Liberal*
Intercept	1705.285***	320.550	–595.475
	(205.312)	(636.233)	(710.478)
Election year	–0.864***	–0.166	0.425
	(0.102)	(0.316)	(0.353)
Turnout (%)	–0.231***	0.117	0.301*
	(0.038)	(0.118)	(0.133)
Con. government	6.602***	10.704**	–18.191***
	(1.118)	(3.599)	(4.030)
Liberal candidate	–	–	
Green candidate	–0.135	–7.676***	–1.227
	(0.512)	(1.592)	(1.772)
% male	0.710**	1.359	–4.922***
	(0.255)	(0.765)	(0.855)
% aged over 45	0.580***	0.007	–0.526**
	(0.050)	(0.159)	(0.178)
% overcrowded	0.388	1.787	8.142***
	(0.598)	(1.903)	(2.129)
% unemployed	–0.525***	–0.064	0.180
	(0.094)	(0.287)	(0.322)
% working class	–0.180***	0.214*	–0.104
	(0.030)	(0.094)	(0.104)
% homeowner	–0.161***	–0.555***	0.811***
	(0.040)	(0.125)	(0.140)
Catholic area	–2.969*	0.201	–1.302
	(1.165)	(3.532)	(3.942)
N observations	395	429	432
Adj. R^2	0.629	0.631	0.577
R^2	0.639	0.640	0.587
AIC	2186.566	3399.423	3520.535
P value	0.000	0.000	0.000

*** $p < 0.001$; ** $p < 0.01$; * $p < 0.05$.